Ian Marchant is Reader in the History of Technology and Culture at the Imaginary Free University of Radnorshire. His previous publications include *In Southern Waters*, *The Battle For Dole Acre*, *Parallel Lines*, *The Longest Crawl*, *Something of the Night* and *A Hero for High Times*. He is an intermittent presenter on Radio 4's *Open Country*, and a regular diarist for the *Church Times*. He lives in Presteigne with his family. *Sola fides sufficit.*

PRAISE FOR *ONE FINE DAY*

'A unique and exhilarating exploration of time and love; Ian Marchant conspires with his diarist ancestor to bring to life the eccentricities and the importance of the early eighteenth century. Elegiac, consistently funny, deeply moving.'

Richard Beard, author of *Sad Little Men* and
The Day That Went Missing

'This book is too engaging, in both senses of the world, to be anything but loved ... [Marchant] throws a rope to the past and lets it teach us things we would do well to remember. Neighbourliness; civic virtue; decency in the form of honesty. This book is wonderful.'

The Oldie

ONE FINE DAY

A Journey through English Time.

Being an Account of the
Discoverie, Discernment and Disposal
of the Diary of Mr. Thomas Marchant
of Hurstpierpoint in the County of Sussex
written in the time of confinement

by

his seven-times-great great-grandson

MR. IAN MARCHANT

Together with a number of illustrations by

MR. JULIAN DICKEN

september

1 3 5 7 9 10 8 6 4 2

This paperback edition published in 2024 by September Publishing
First published in 2023 by September Publishing

Typeset by RefineCatch Limited, www.refinecatch.com
Printed in the UK by CPI Books Ltd

MIX
Paper | Supporting
responsible forestry
FSC® C171272

ISBN 9781914613555
Ebook ISBN 9781912836963

September Publishing
www.septemberpublishing.org

For my daughters, Esme, Eleanor, Victoria and Stephanie.
For my brother, Trapper 'Christopher' Blastock.
For my dad, and ascendant second cousin once removed, Ralph Foxwell.

Blood is thicker than water, but love is thicker than blood.

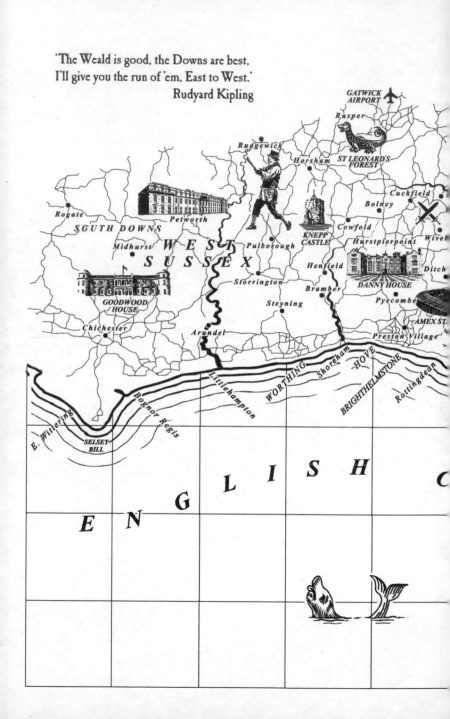

'The Weald is good, the Downs are best,
I'll give you the run of 'em, East to West.'
Rudyard Kipling

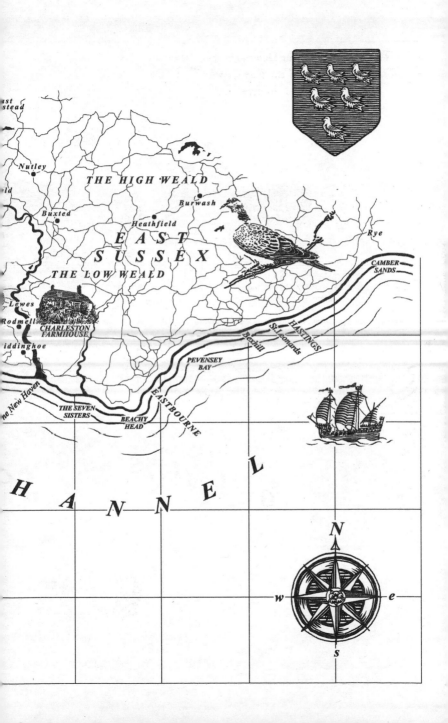

CONTENTS

Antiquity is not always a mark of verity.

PROLEGOMENON

in which the Author wishes himself on the Slow Road
through Ideal England, travelling from where he is to
where he is from.

I.

GOOD AND QUICKLY
SELDOM MEET

The Old Grammarye, Broad Street, Presteigne,
Radnorshire. Sunday, the 29th March, 2020.
A cold day.

One fine day, when all this is over, I will take again the slow road,
and drive across England to visit my long-ago family in Sussex.
There is a fast way to drive from here to there. It's 220 miles and,
apart from the first fifty and the last thirty miles, it's all motorway. I
use it only in dire need. It takes me around six hours; four-and-a-half
hours driving, plus an hour or so sulking about in service stations
drinking insipid coffee, whilst disliking people just for being there.

The slow road is shorter by about ten miles, but it involves no
motorways at all, and will take more like nine hours. This time is
made up of six hours of actual driving, and three hours of footling
around – a stop for lunch, a poke about in a charity shop or an
interesting church, a stop for tea, possibly a nap. I've evolved this
slow way over the last thirty-five years. You could put Presteigne to
Newhaven into your sat-nav until forever, and you'd still not find
the way, not all of it. I cross the Lugg Bridge from Radnorshire into
Herefordshire, skirt Leominster and Ledbury, and bridge the Severn
at Maisemore. I go round Gloucester, up Birdlip Hill, and onto the
fast road to Cirencester. But then, as I come into subtopian Swindon,
rather than heading down to the M4 by where the Honda factory
used to be, I turn left, and take the road to Fairford.

I always look forward to stopping by the old town. It has easy parking, good coffee, efficient public conveniences, and the only full set of medieval stained glass to be found in any English parish church. Dating from about 1500, when the church was new, the windows depict the life of Christ, from the Old Testament prophecies of His coming, to His sitting in final Judgement. The Fairford windows are a great and glorious expression of Christendom's high noon. They were imported from Burgundian Flanders for the opening of the new church, one of the last 'medieval' churches built in England before the Reformation.

When travelling through northern France and the Low Countries, it's almost commonplace to see glass of this quality, but in England, there is just Fairford. The odd window has survived in other churches, here and there, and the cathedrals have hung on to a fair bit of their medieval glass, but most of the stained glass you see in English parish churches is Victorian or later. The survival of a complete set of late medieval stained-glass windows is a kind of miracle, because 1500 was not a great moment to be depicting the life of Christ in stained glass in England. Before the Reformation, churches were polychromatic with dazzling colour, but by the 1540s the stripping of the altars, the whitewashing of the wall paintings, and the smashing of the glass had begun. It was as if colour were a sin that had to be purged from the body of the Church. Protestant Reformers would condemn depictions of Christ as idolatrous, sacrilegious, and, above all, popish. The only way to learn about God was by reading the Bible in black and white, not by gawping at technicolour windows.

A century later, during the English Civil War,[1] iconoclasm became Parliamentary policy. 'The Committee for the Demolition of Monuments of Superstition and Idolatry' gave an air of respectability

---

1 The series of civil wars in Britain and Ireland which included the First English Civil War (1642–46) are known to historians as 'the Wars of the Three Kingdoms'. They ran, on and off, from about 1639 until about 1690, followed by a brief revival in 1715, with a final curtain call in 1745.

to the thugs who were kicking your church in. No one is quite sure how the Fairford windows survived the Civil War, but the best bet is that the churchwarden had the foresight to take them down, and to bury them in a field until the hostilities were through. Every other church got its windows smashed up. Imagine your local church – the windows, the statues, the pictures – kicked in, desecrated, in just the same way, and for just the same reasons, that the Taliban dynamited the Buddhas of Bamiyan.

The Civil Wars were between fathers and sons, friends and neighbours, between this town and the next. Death hid behind every hedge, was waiting down every street. In 1650, the Puritan divine Richard Baxter wrote, 'if you had seen the general dissolution of the world, and all the pomp and glory of it reduced to ashes, if you saw all on a fire about you, sumptuous buildings, cities, kingdoms, land, water, earth, heaven, all flaming about your ears, if you had seen all that men laboured for, and sold their souls for, gone … what would such a sight as this persuade you to do?'

It's a good question. We shall find out, I fear, in our own age of pestilence, famine, and war.

My paternal grandfather, Charles Jesse Marchant, was a carpenter by trade, and he helped to build RAF Fairford during Hitler's War. It was planned as a base from which gliders could be flung into Normandy on D-Day, and it still has a role today. The runway at Fairford is the only one in the UK long and strong enough to host heavy US bombers (or to land the Space Shuttle), so it was used to launch B-52s during both Iraq wars, and also in the illegal 1999 NATO bombings of Belgrade. In July every year, RAF Fairford is home to the Royal International Air Tattoo, where war fans can see their favourite weapons of mass destruction close up, and take selfies with them.

As the warplanes climb into the sky, the Cotswolds open up beneath their wings. There below, like a collage made from antiquated greeting cards, is a vision of Ideal England, a rural idyll of farriers and coachmen and jangling horse brasses and stamping shire horses pulling the plough through the honest English soil; of goodwives in shawls spinning by their open thatched cottage doors, hollyhocks reaching for the never-ending sun; of ruddy-faced yeomen supping nut-brown ale before an open fire in a welcoming inn.

Ideal England has several regions in addition to the Arcadian Cotswolds. There's Grim Oop North, divided into Bluff Yorkshire, moors and mountains and vets and if tha' ever does owt for nowt, do it for thissen; and Breezy Lancashire, donkey rides on the beach for a tanner, Elsie Tanner with a ladder in her stockings, and Fred Dibnah up a ladder on the chimney of a dark satanic mill. There's the Coast, tanned fishermen with wise lined faces sitting on lobster pots mending nets or pointing out to sea with their pipes; and the West Country, which is a cross between Arcadia and the Coast, but with smocks and cider.[2]

And then there is Sussex, good old Sussex, home to some of England's most potent myths about itself. When people think of the white cliffs, they are not really thinking about the Dover cliffs, which are a bit grubby, and overlook a lorry park, but the brilliant white cliffs of the Seven Sisters, a chalk sine wave rising in pitch towards Beachy Head, with the meanders of the Cuckmere River in the foreground. This is probably the best-known 'view' in England, as the dozens of tourists gathered in the car park at Exceat Bridge to take photos against the backdrop of the cliffs attest.

If anyone knows just one date and one place in Sussex history, it's 1066 and All That, the Battle of Hastings, where the last English king, Harold II, died trying to save England from the Conqueror. The story of the English defeat was made into the Bayeux Tapestry, so that, later, Nigel Farage could wear a Bayeux Tapestry tie with his checked shirt and raspberry-coloured corduroy pantaloons.

Dad's Army was set in Ideal Sussex. Walmington-on-Sea is supposed to be in Sussex (though much of it was filmed in Thetford, in Norfolk), and Captain Mainwaring is the best-known (albeit fictional) alumnus of Eastbourne Grammar School. That final V sign,

---

2　For Americans, one of the most important regions of Ideal England is Scotland. Luckily, the Americans haven't noticed Wales, which has its own fictions to cope with.

bouncing up and down in the TV show's credits; that's Sussex telling Hitler to fuck off. My stepfather Ralph Foxwell, born in Pevensey in 1926, was in the Home Guard, and he stood sentry duty over the Seven Sisters. He was in an 'Auxiliary Unit' – the platoons of young men who were trained to operate as guerrillas behind the German lines, should the invasion come. He is a trained killer; aged ninety-five at the time of writing, I still wouldn't like to take him on.

I have heard his war stories all my life, and they are all set in the Sussex Downs. One thing that has always struck me about them is the immediacy of the Battle of Britain for people living in Kent and Sussex. The fighting was overhead, sometimes only a few hundred feet overhead, day after day, watched by children in their holidays from school. My stepdad and his brother were (somewhat feebly) strafed by a JU-88 bomber, whilst they were haymaking on the Glyndebourne estate. They watched the dead bodies of Canadian soldiers being unloaded from barges at Newhaven bridge after the Dieppe raid. A week after D-Day, they fished hundreds of life jackets from the Sussex Ouse, carried almost to Lewes by the incoming tide. Doodlebugs grumbled over the Downs and across the Weald, looking like they were on fire, on their way to do one last round of damage to London.

Like most of the few remaining old people who actually took part in Hitler's War, my stepfather is anti-jingoistic and pro-European, but it can be hard sometimes to hear his peaceable Sussex burr above the baying voices of those for whom Ideal England is Alone Then, Spitfires over the White Cliffs of Dover, Two World Wars, One World Cup, giant poppies hung from street lights Oi Oi In-ger-land. This version of Ideal England is the revenant Empire, risen from the grave to possess men in their sixties and seventies who learned history and politics from old copies of *Commando* comic, and who have come to believe that they fought in the war themselves.

Land of our Birth, our faith, our pride,
For whose dear sake our fathers died;

> *O Motherland, we pledge to thee*
> *Head, heart and hand through the years to be!*

That's Rudyard Kipling, from *Puck of Pook's Hill*, published in 1906. Kipling's patriotic fervour for the land of England was, in particular, for the Sussex countryside around Burwash where he lived out his days. Pook's Hill is in Sussex, and Sussex, for Kipling and many of his readers, represented the Motherland.

> *I'm just in love with all these three,*
> *The Weald an' the Marsh an' the Down countrie;*
> *Nor I don't know which I love the most,*
> *The Weald or the Marsh or the white chalk coast!*

Also Kipling, also from *Puck of Pook's Hill*. The marsh is hard to spot these days. Much of it has been built on. The Brighton/Worthing/Littlehampton conurbation is the fifteenth largest in the UK – population 474,485, according to the 2011 census. The M23 divides Sussex in half top to bottom, and the A27 quarters it. Gatwick fills the sky. Red lights pulse from the windfarms out at sea, and on the horizon container ships like floating islands pass up channel on their way from Shanghai to Felixstowe or Rotterdam.

The 'Down countrie' and large parts of the Weald have been institutionalised, and are now part of the South Downs National Park. Folded within its breast is another Ideal Sussex, not just different from, but opposed to Kipling's, which I call Bloomsbury Country. Rodmell village second homeowner, Mrs. Virginia Woolf, despised those she saw as members of the jingoistic and vulgarian hoi polloi. And not just generally, but also in particular. She loathed the people of the Ouse Valley, such as my family, calling them 'white slugs'.[3] Whatever the area around Lewes and Glynde once meant to the Bloomsbury Set (something to do with authenticity, as it

---

3 Mrs. Woolf called Newhaven the City of the Dead, so it is immune from inclusion in Bloomsbury Country.

usually does with people who want to get their head together in the country), what is left, if you are not careful, is a pale impression of a place, a Charleston Farmhouse tote bag, distressed pastel-painted creative hub in a converted stable block sort of place. A boutique festival sort of place, an artisanal gin Michelin-starred pub, Airbnb *Country Living* place, a defanged, disenchanted landscape where there's a Range Rover Evoque round every nook and corner, and where whimsy is queen.

And lest you suspect that I'm against whimsy, I live as far away from the real world as I can manage, in a chocolate-box town on the border of Wales and England, in a 500-year-old cottage, where I sit in my book-lined study, smoking my old pipe, writing on an antediluvian word processor. Whimsical psycho-topography is my genre, after all.

There is still a long way to go from Fairford to Newhaven, in every possible sense. I bridge the headwaters of the Thames at Lechlade, then follow the Vale of the White Horse to Wantage, before crossing the high Berkshire Downs to the Newbury suburb of Speenhamland. On past Greenham Common and Watership Down, past Jane Austen's Chawton and Gilbert White's Selborne, I enter West Sussex in a wood somewhere between the villages of Liss and Rogate.

Sussex is where I grew up.[4] It's where my mum and Ralph Foxwell were born and where he still lives. When I was twenty-one, I moved to Hove, and lived there for eight eventful years. My mother died in Brighton, my daughter Esme was born in Brighton and my daughter Eleanor grew up there. Brighton, Lewes, Hastings, and even Peacehaven are full of family and friends, people I like and love and have loved. But Newhaven is my town. I went to school in Newhaven, Meeching County Primary and Tideway School and Sixth Form. I took my class identity from Newhaven and the Lower Ouse Valley; long on proud working class, but with a twist

4　It was Sussex until 1974, when it was divided into two counties, East and West.

of embittered landless peasant. I had my first kiss and my greatest heartbreak in Newhaven. I played in the best band from Newhaven, ever, and lost the tapes. In the autumn of 1985, in a downland combe running parallel to the A259 between Newhaven and Seaford, I spent a rewarding few days as the Buddha, due to the ingestion of large quantities of Nepalese temple balls. I stopped being the Buddha when I found God in Bishopstone churchyard, manifest in a sea fret that sparkled like Lurex. I have told these stories since I started writing, stories about how I am from Newhaven, and proud. But ...

I never really felt I belonged to Sussex. I was born in Shalford, in Surrey, and lived there till I was five. My birth father, Alan Raymond Marchant, was from Surrey, and so was my grandpop, Charles Jesse. As far as I knew, so were all the Marchants, ever. And my mum might have been born in Sussex, but she lived in the Surrey village of Ewhurst from the age of two until she married my father, aged twenty-three. Even though we moved when I was five to a village in Northamptonshire, I still spent much of my school holidays at my respective grandparents' houses in Surrey, in Ewhurst and Shalford, which became, for me, enchanted places, my own Ideal England.

Ewhurst is tucked under the southern lee of Pitch Hill, and in my memory is surrounded by greenwoods veined by streams and studded in spring with countless primroses, basketfuls of which I would pick with my grandmother, before walking back to her almshouse cottage to make posies tied with wool for me to take round the village to her friends and neighbours. My parents and Ralph's parents were married in Ewhurst church; Ralph's brother was born in the village, and he has an aunt in the graveyard. My grandmother, two aunts and an uncle, and now my mum, are all buried there too.

Shalford was my first home; its places were my first places, the first things of which I was aware. The church with its copper spire, out on the Guildford Road, is the church where I was christened. The Parrot, next to the River Wey, was where my father and my uncle went to after cricket on the green, and so it became the first local, outside which I would be left sleeping in my pram while my dad drank Guinness and my mum had a Babycham. Grandpop Charlie's always mysterious and wonderful builders' yard, smelling of Douglas fir and putty, was the first workplace, and on the first walks, up to St. Martha's, or along the Pilgrims' Way, or on the riverside path into Guildford, I heard my first histories, and my first myths. Surrey was home, my childhood Eden, from which I was plucked.

When I was ten, my parents split up, and my mum took us from Northants to stay with her family in Newhaven, where she married her second cousin, Ralph Foxwell, who ran a small farm with his brother. But Surrey was where I identified with, not Sussex. Really, in Newhaven, my home town, I'm an incomer. In Sussex, I'm from off, from away, just as much as I am here in the largely imaginary Welsh county of Radnorshire, where I first moved aged twenty-eight, because I could no longer hack living in Brighton. Ever since I was a lad, I've had an issue with Sussex, or, at least, with Ideal Sussex, with myths like Kipling's Motherland and Mrs. Woolf's 'Bloomsbury Country'. Neither seemed to match the hard-scrabble existence of Newhaven, or the reality of Ralph's life on the land. Sussex, I felt, was just not for me. I wasn't even from there.

And yet, tonight, I long to drive once more on the slow road through Midhurst and Petworth, Pulborough and Storrington, Steyning and Bramber, through Preston Village and Falmer, and down the Kingston road, through Rodmell and Piddinghoe, and come home at last to Newhaven, where my mum and old Ralph Foxwell will be waiting at the door, anxious for my arrival.

DISCOVERIE

in which the Author discovers both his family tree and
the parlous state of his health, makes himself a cup of
instant coffee, undertakes a perilous sea journey, travels
to the Dawn of Time in Wallonia, uncovers his family's
part in bringing the arms trade to England, and arrives in
Sussex at last to relate how the Fortunes of War enabled
his ancestors to acquire a Gentleman's Estate.

II.

IT IS A POOR FAMILY THAT
HATH NEITHER A THIEF NOR A
WHORE IN IT

My mum was anxious for as long as I knew her, and with good reason, I guess. Her father abandoned his home in 1940, leaving my grandmother, my nine-year-old uncle and my seven-year-old mother destitute; destitute, but very much cheered by his going. My mother's life up to that point had been one of grinding poverty and horrifying physical abuse. When her father left, their lives became just the grinding poverty, and therefore much more bearable. But she lived in fear that someday he would come back and savage her with his belt and fists, as he had every day of her hard childhood until the day he left. She bore the mark of him on her back and her arms to the end of her life.

This fear morphed into a recurrent nightmare. She told me about these night horrors a few months before her eightieth birthday, in 2013. She said it was because she still wasn't utterly sure that her father was dead, though he would have been about 110 years old. She wanted to know for certain that he was. Dead and buried.

All my mother knew was his name, which was Albert Edward Bulbeck, and that he was born in Cuckfield, Sussex, in 1901. It would not be easy. My mother's people are from the deepest countryside, landless peasants who went into service as housekeepers and coachmen, or who worked as platelayers and brickmakers and private soldiers, dirt-poor Anglo-Saxons who hid themselves away in the vast forest of the Weald for a thousand years. They have left little trace, except in the shape of the fields, the lay of the hedges, the turn of the lane.

My wife Hilary took it on. After months of research in record offices, in the old newspaper library in Colindale, and online, she established that my grandfather Albert, the terror of my mum's life, had died in 1980, and was buried in Ipswich. What's more, Hilary established that after abandoning his first family, Albert Bulbeck went on to have a second in Suffolk.

Unknown until a few weeks before her eightieth birthday party, my mother now had two half-brothers and a half-sister. We contacted this other family, and one of the half-brothers, Alby, was more than happy to be in touch. He visited my parents in Newhaven a few times, and always called at Christmas and on my mum's birthday. After he had married my mother, Ralph Foxwell came off the land, where he had worked his whole life, and got a job as a fork-lift driver on Newhaven's North Quay. Uncle Alby was a master mariner, captaining small coasting vessels in and out of the ports on the east and south-east coasts. We are as sure as we can be that they met, back in the 1970s and 1980s, when Alby regularly unloaded stone setts and beech boles from Rouen at the North Quay under Ralph's supervision, without knowing that they were half-brothers-in-law.

On finding out that her father was dead, my mother's nightmares stopped, and never came back. Her anxiety turned into a scar, rather than fear of a present danger. Genealogy was therapeutic, and helped my mum to sleep free from terror, or the terror of her father's return, at least. It gave us a bunch of new relatives, too. As an episode of *Who Do You Think You Are?* it would have it all.

An important part of Hilary's research involved using one of the well-known online genealogy sites. As a prudent Ulsterwoman, she had only bought a three-month subscription. In early 2019, the site offered one extra free day, as an inducement to return. What to do with it? Her family is hard to trace, because most Irish birth records were destroyed in the 1920s.

'Shall I have a look at the Marchant side?'

'Sure. Thank you. Not much to find, I suspect.'

I told her what I knew.

I was born and christened in Shalford, just to the south of Guildford. My father grew up in Shalford, though he was born in Farncombe, three miles away. My grandfather, Grandpop Charlie Marchant, was a carpenter and builder who had his own small firm, Marchant and Cheale, based in an old-fashioned builder's yard just outside Shalford. His father, Thomas David Marchant, had been the baker in Bramley, the next village south through the heathy woods towards Cranleigh. His nickname, like a few old-fashioned baker boys, was 'Lardy', and he'd passed it on to my grandpop, my birth dad Alan, and even me, after I'd been dumb enough to tell some pals at school about the hereditary nickname.

Grandpop Charlie Marchant's sister was called Marjorie, our beloved Great-Aunt Madge. She told us cousins that her father, Thomas Marchant the baker, never revealed to anyone where he was from, except to say that he'd run away from home. Aunty Madge said that she thought he was from further south, from the seaside maybe, but that he'd never said any more about it. Charlie and Madge and their brothers and sisters never knew where their father was from, or anything about his family.

That was all I had to give Hilary to go on. I expected little. I made a lovely cup of tea, smoked a pipe, and watched some Argentinian narrow-gauge railway videos on YouTube.

An hour later, she emailed me this:

> Jean-Jacques de Marchant. Born 1435 in Namur,
> Belgium, died 1518. 14 x great great-grandfather
> Jean-Baptiste de Marchant. Born 1466 in Namur,
> Belgium, died 03/02/1540, buried in Couvin. 13 x
> great great-grandfather
> William Marchant. Born 1520 in Preston,
> Sussex, died 18/12/1558 in Preston. 12 x great
> great-grandfather
> Miles Marchant. Born 1545 in Preston, died

13/12/1605 in Edburton, Sussex. 11 x great great-grandfather

Richard Marchant. Born 1584 in Edburton, buried Horsham, Sussex, 14/11/1625. 10 x great great-grandfather

Thomas Marchant. Born 1615 in Albourne, Sussex, buried Albourne, 4/08/1686. 9 x great great-grandfather

William Marchant. Born 1648, buried Hurstpierpoint, Sussex, 17/08/1706. 8 x great great-grandfather

Thomas Marchant. Diarist. Born 23/03/1676, died Hurst, 14/09/1728. 7 x great great-grandfather

William Marchant. Born in Hurst, 26/10/1701, died Hurst, 16/12/1776. 6 x great great-grandfather

Thomas Marchant. Surgeon Born 1731, died Hurst, 17/08/1802. 5 x great great-grandfather

William Marchant. Surgeon to His Majesty's Powder Mills. Born in Hurst, 1759, killed 13/12/1790 in Waltham Cross, Essex. 4 x great great-grandfather

John Marchant. Born in Hurst, 1786, died, 22/04/1848 in Brighton Workhouse. Buried in Hurst. 3 x great great-grandfather

Thomas Marchant. Born in Hurst 01/01/1807, died 02/09/1872 at Bridge Farm, Cuckfield, Sussex. 2 x great great-grandfather

Elkanah Marchant. Born in Hurst, 09/02/1841, died December 1931 in Burgess Hill, Sussex. Great-great-grandfather

Thomas David Marchant, born in Hurst, 1871, died 1928 in Bramley, Surrey. Great-grandfather

Charles Jesse Marchant, born Bramley, 29/03/1904, died 20/09/1984 in Witley, Surrey. Grandfather

Alan Raymond Marchant. Born in Farncombe, Surrey,

13/11/1931, died 06/05/2010 in Waterford, Ireland.
Father

I stood over Hilary's shoulder while she showed me her workings.

'How sure are you?' I asked.

'I'm as sure as I can be after a first look.'

'But why did it take twelve weeks or so to find out that my mum's dad is dead, but in an hour you've got back almost 600 years?'

The answer is that tracking down the Bulbeck line, and then tracing Albert Bulbeck's other family, had involved proper hard research, because no one else had done the necessary graft in the records to link his two families up. Hilary had done the work, and entered the data, so now it was available through the Ancestry website. For the Marchants, however, a lot of other genealogists had already sifted through birth, marriage and death certificates, census returns, parish registers, denizen rolls and other proofs of existence in time. She, we, were the fortunate beneficiaries of this work. In the space of an hour I had acquired a pedigree. I am still not sure how I feel about this. This is not who I am; or, perhaps in light of this discovery, not who I thought I was. I had a working-class upbringing, in a working-class town, and I had a working-class education. I do not quite pass, even now, as a middle-class person; and certainly not as someone with a pedigree of any kind. In fact, lack of a pedigree has always been a source of pride. Look where I've got, from where I started, that sort of thing.

One ancestor in particular made me do that thing in cartoons where a character's eyes come out on stalks.

Thomas Marchant. Diarist. Born 23/03/1676, died
Hurst, 14/09/1728. 7 x great great-grandfather

Diarist? What diarist? Why did no one tell me I had a diarist for an ancestor? Is writing somehow hard-wired in my DNA, a recessive gene, maybe, that lay dormant until the day I submitted a short story to *Doctor Who Monthly* and came runner-up in the over-fifteen story writing contest, aged twenty-eight?

And what diary?

This diary:

It was easy to find, a short Google search away, a click on Amazon. My great-grandfather Thomas the Baker's attempt to cover up his origins had come to naught, in a couple of hours one Tuesday evening, a hundred years after his death.

Thomas Marchant kept his diary, with a few breaks, between 29 September 1714 and 7 September 1728 (Old Style). It was passed down through the family, until in the mid-nineteenth century some 5 per cent was transcribed by a distant relative, the Reverend Edward Turner, and published in the Sussex Archaeological Society journal of 1873. E.V. Lucas used extracts from these transcriptions in *Highways and Byways in Sussex*, published in 1904, as have various social historians over the years. The diary itself was thought lost, but in the mid-1990s one of the members of the Hurst History Study Group, another descendant of Thomas called Anthony Bower, tracked down the current owner, who allowed copies to be made for the West Sussex Record Office in Chichester. It is from one of these copies that the volunteers and friends of the Hurst History Study Group made their transcription of the whole text, which they published in 2006.

And so I am in the extraordinary position of knowing what my great-great-great-great-great-great-great-great-grandfather Thomas Marchant was doing on pretty much any given day 300 years ago.

As an example I've chosen the 16th of March.

Three hundred years ago, with a quill pen, by the light of a candle lantern at Little Park Farm in Hurstpierpoint, old Thomas wrote this in his diary:

> The 16th March 1720 Thursday. A wet day. The boys
> win'd barly. 8 quarters. I were at William Nicholas's in the

*A fine day in Hurstpierpoint -
the diary of Thomas Marchant
1714 - 1728*

morning teaching him to make ox harness. Dick Wood shooed the carthorses. Thomas Hamper's man hew'd a tree. Paid old Dick Banks 1s for his son for mending 2 augers.

Three hundred years later, with my Lamy fountain pen, by the light from two daylight spectrum bulbs at the Old Grammarye in Presteigne, this is what I wrote in mine:

16/03/2020. A beautiful day, cold and clear.
Coronavirus is here. Drove into Leominster for usual
weekly shop at Morrisons. It was like Christmas, but
much less jolly. The lass on the checkout said it had
been mad for days. No loo roll, pasta, flour, beans,
tinned toms, long-life milk, etc. Staff frantically
filling shelves as fast as they could. Picked up a book
on order at Rossiter's – Chesterton's 'Orthodoxy'.
Lass there said that they too had been as busy as
Christmas, as people stocked up on reading material.
In the eve, HM Govt ordered new restrictions. All
pubs, bars, theatres to close. Increase social distancing.
All large gatherings stopped. Self-isolate for 14 days
if you have it, or come into contact with it. Over 70s
avoid going out, only essential journeys to be taken,
etc., etc. It's clearly heading for lockdown like in Italy.
I checked our store cupboard – if they locked us
in tonight, I reckon we could last a month. Thank
goodness for Brexit stockpiling.
It falls on us to live in hard times. We thought that
everything was going to be fine tomorrow, because
it was fine yesterday. Now we can only hope that
everything will be fine again, one fine day.

Lockdown became, for me, a chance to meet Old Thom Marchant and his family and friends, to inhabit their world, to share their concerns. Thom and I had to stay at home, and learn to live with one another, like millions of other families across the Earth. We had no choice but to sit by the woodburner and tell tales.

The social historian Lawrence Stone wrote: 'If the historian of pre-nineteenth-century society seriously wants to pluck at the skirts of truth, she is obliged to use common sense and arguments of probability to apply correctives and supply lacunae.'[5] If I wanted to know something of the world of Thom, the diary was not enough, not by itself. I wanted to explore what might be regarded as circumstantial evidence; and, of course, the historical imagination, without which the past can never truly be brought to life.

We have much in common, Old Thom and I. We are husbands and fathers who are trying to support our family and our communities. We both like to stroll about the town, see a bit of street theatre, hang out backstage, meet our chums and go for a drink, especially on Saturdays. We are both susceptible to inexplicable headaches on Sunday morning. We are both communicant members of the Church of England. The words I hear in church on a Sunday are very often the same that he would have heard in 1714, as we share the *Book of Common Prayer*. We both whistle at least one common tune. We both like cricket, a bit, though we are neither of us fanatics. We both seem to enjoy the company of women, a lot. He paid people to shave his head – so do I. We are both political animals, we are both interested in new ideas and we both have some understanding of science.

There are differences too, of course. His body temperature was, on average, higher than mine, because I have access to anti-inflammatory drugs and antibiotics. His world, however, was colder than ours, because he kept his diary in 'the little ice age' when global temperatures were on average 2 degrees colder than they are now, and Frost Fairs were held on the frozen Thames. His calendar was different from ours – his was the so-called Julian calendar, whilst

5   'The Educational Revolution in England, 1560–1640', *Past and Present*, no. 28, July 1964.

ours is the more accurate Gregorian. He was eleven days ahead of us, and his years started later.[6] Until 1752, when England adopted the Gregorian system, New Year's Day was 25 March, Lady Day, the Feast of the Annunciation, nine months till Christmas. This is why some of the diary dates I use might seem out of kilter; the year starts in March, so an entry for February 1720 comes after September 1720.

There's a sense too in which actual time moved differently. The writer Jay Griffiths argues that just as each place has a *genius loci*, a spirit of specific place, there was once also a *genius temporis*, a spirit of specific time. This spirit seems to have died as time began to be standardised with the arrival of the railway timetable in the 1840s, but there would once have been Hurstpierpoint time. Thom had a clock, but it would have been set by the sun, or perhaps with reference to a more advanced clock at Danny House, the big house just outside Hurstpierpoint where he spent much of his leisure. There would have been no use for what we would regard as 'accurate' time, just a need for neighbours and communities to broadly agree what was when.

His days do seem to move differently from mine in March 2020. He packs a lot in. He is busy running his farm, conducting business, dining out with friends, helping to administer the parish, watching cricket, setting up a school &c, while I was in the house with my wife and step-daughter, looking out on silent streets, wondering what was to come, with little to do except to try and find a way to listen to Thom, to remember and reimagine the world we have lost.

6   And so, strictly speaking, 'this very day' is not 16 March 1720, but 27 March 1721, a 'Munday'. More on this – and the weather – in chapter VI.

Early on in the process of reading and understanding the diary, when I was reflecting late one January 2020 evening on the differences between Thom and me, I realised the unbridgeable thing that comes between us is industrialisation. He lived right at its beginning, while I am living somewhere towards its end. Old Thom Marchant was one of the last people before industrialisation to understand how his world worked – and how to be largely self-sufficient in it. He knew where his food came from, his fuel, his water, his clothes. He knew how the welfare system worked, and was part of its administration; he knew who looked after the roads, too. He collected taxes. He was not separate from the system, but part of it. He was a Sussex yeoman farmer who worked with horsetraders, dung carriers, hedgers and ditchers &c, but who was also a well-to-do, notable, voting member of Sussex society, who knew and worked with dukes, MPs, cabinet ministers, members of the Royal Society, political exiles and people who were prepared to suffer for their religious beliefs.

Three hundred years ago industrialisation was just at its birth. I remember from the writing of my book about Britain's railways, *Parallel Lines*, that the world's first railway viaduct, the Causey Arch near Newcastle, built for horse-drawn wagons running on wooden tracks, opened in 1725, a hundred years before the Stockton to Darlington Railway. I scoured my memory for other early dates in the Industrial Revolution. Newcomen's steam engine – 1712. Its function was to pump water from Cornish tin mines, but a hundred years later, when the steam engine moved onto the rails, then Britain would be changed beyond all recognition. Thom's moment is the moment when that change started to be noticeable, at least to historians.

What else? I remembered O level history, where we studied the Industrial and Agricultural revolutions. Abraham Darby's blast furnace in Coalbrookdale, Shropshire – when was that? 1710, something like that. But did Darby invent it, or was it just the use of coke that he perfected, rather than charcoal? Were there blast furnaces before those in Coalbrookdale?[7] There had to be. It was one in the morning, and I'm afraid I resorted to Google.

Of course, Darby didn't invent the blast furnace. They had been in use in England for 200 years by the time he worked out how to use coked coal to make iron. Before that they used charcoal. The first English charcoal burning blast furnace was in Buxted, in Sussex, in 1493. And where did they come from before that? My jaw dropped open. Blast furnaces came from Namur. Namur. That's the place where the first Marchants on Hilary's list came from.

I got off Google and did proper research.[8] I now knew why they came. And far from Thom being a bystander at the dawn of industrialisation – he, we, were complicit in it. The Marchants were one of some 300 families who, between about 1490 and 1600, moved from Namur (now in Belgium) and the Pays de Bray (which is between Dieppe and Rouen) to Sussex. These families brought the technology necessary to mass-produce iron. And thus to produce cannons.

Ernest Straker in *Wealden Iron*, published in 1931, realised the import of what had happened in Sussex:

> In Tudor times, about the close of the 15th century, a
> new process was introduced from the Continent, and
> soon after the casting of iron cannon, at first by the
> help of foreign experts, was commenced in Sussex.
> This manufacture rapidly grew in importance, and
> soon led to a considerable export trade, frequently
> illicit. In our island this was the first step of the

---

7 A three-legged cooking pot to hang over a fire would have been the most used pot in the kitchen at Little Park Farm. Thom would have known who made his cooking pots, and where they came from, which was from somewhere nearby. He knew where the iron came from to make it – again, almost certainly from Sussex. This was about to change, as these three-legged cooking pots, in use for centuries, were to become the world's first mass-market product, as they were the earliest things that the Coalbrookdale works made and sold.

8 You can find a list of all sources on my website www.ianmarchant.com.

> change from a practically self-supporting and mainly
> agricultural community, exporting their surplus
> produce in an unmanufactured state, to a nation
> depending for the greater part of its sustenance on
> manufactured exports, and was intimately connected
> with the rise of overseas trade and colonisation.

The Marchants carried a foreign virus that would mutate into the industrial system, and then we forgot that we had done so.

Think of what this change has brought us to. We post-moderns are so much the things of the Industrial Process that most of us have no idea how we would survive without it. In 2020, the Process was shown to be fragile, splintering perhaps beyond repair. Everything depends on everything else. A bottleneck in supply lines could mean life or death. China coughs, and the world stockpiles loo roll. Italy locks down, and there are no tinned tomatoes or pasta. Spain and the Netherlands lock down, and there are no fresh tomatoes, either. No one is coming to pick the harvest when it ripens. The grape rots on the vine, and there is nothing to be done.

Consider the all but infinite complexities of the Process upon which we all depend, and which might take nothing more than a nanoscopic speck of DNA and protein to bring it shuddering to a halt.

Consider, if you will, a morning cup of instant coffee, taken in a mug, with milk.

Let's walk it through.

First, you fill the kettle with water. How comes there to be water in the tap? How does it get into our homes? How is it clean? How do we know? Who looks after the cleaning process? How are pipes maintained and mains flow regulated? How do taps even work?

Let's allow the water, of which we know so little, into our electric kettle. How does that work? We all know that water and electricity don't mix, so why isn't an electric kettle dangerous? Dunno. What I do know is that the bimetallic thermostat which stops your kettle boiling dry and setting fire to your lovely home was invented and developed by a British engineer called John C. Taylor, whose company has sold somewhere in the order of 200 million units. How they work, keeping us safe from the potentially lethal consequences of kettles boiling dry, most of us have no clue. I don't know what metals are used, or how they are mined and refined, or what the components might be, or how they are wired together. Nothing. I also understand almost nothing of the fantastic fruit of human endeavour that is the electrical generation industry, which brings together the sinister humming nuclear stations, the immensity of biomass stations like Drax, the susurrating windmills standing in the sea, and the system whereby the power is distributed and regulated so that it is safe to be let into our homes and kettles.

Now the water is hot, let's find a mug. Let's assume that it's an earthenware one. The Brighton and Hove Albion League One Champions 2010–2011 mug I'm drinking from tonight is an inexpensive one, but it is still the result of vast industrial effort. The extraction and preparation of clay is a wildly complex business, which has been developed and refined over the last 20,000 years, and now involves high-tech geological expertise, gigantic earth-moving machines, globe-spanning shipping processes and complex world trade treaties (the UK is one of the world's largest exporters of china and ball clay). All this before one mug has been moulded, fired or decorated. I know nothing about how this particular mug was moulded, fired and decorated, except that it clearly was. I could call the club shop, and ask them where they get their mugs from, but mine is a knock-off, produced by some fly-by-night pirate mug operation to take advantage of the Albion's triumphant promotion. So I know even less than I might about who the designer was, how the transfers were made, where the mugs were decorated, how they were distributed and sold.

At home, we use Cafe Direct's 'Machu Picchu' freeze-dried Fairtrade coffee. We buy it via a website, EthicalSuperstore.com. We see a thing, we have a line of credit, we click Buy and Hey Presto! The genie delivers all our wishes, even though we know that it's not actually a genie who grants our every wish, but some poor bastard in a 'fulfilment centre'. An ethical fulfilment centre sounds especially Orwellian, as I doubt there is much fulfilment, ethical or otherwise, to be had for those who work there.

We have transferred credit from us to Ethical Superstore. In my case, via the Hongkong and Shanghai Banking Corporation, but how? Unthinkable amounts of capital: financial, human and technological, have gone into creating the system of dream fulfilment that is shopping for wishes via the interweb. Our postlady is called Sue, and our delivery guy is called Karl, that much I do know, but how our stuff gets to them to deliver, and how their vans work, are maintained, fuelled &c, I have but the vaguest possible notion. Nonetheless, coffee arrives, in packs of a dozen.

It comes in a stylish oval glass jar, with a coffee-coloured plastic screw top. How are jars like this made? How is glass made? Dunno – boiling up sand or something, isn't it? Where are the stylish oval lids extruded? Dunno. Someone does, of course. A multitude of people could answer this multitude of questions. Here's the thing – each of us, as industrialised units with industrial functions to fulfil in the Process can understand one tiny part of that Process, but never the whole thing.

For example, I am the sort of person who could have written the guff on the back of the jar about passion, ethical considerations, aroma &c. It says, 'Grown at high altitudes within the Inca heartland of the PERUVIAN ANDES, this coffee is RICH and FULL-BODIED with dark chocolate overtones.' I don't understand how the label was printed, or how it came to be attached to the jar, (presumably through the operation of hugely sophisticated machine tools), but I do know what it's like to be a penniless hack knocking out nonsensical copy for a pittance. And therefore what it is to need a mug of instant coffee.

We pick up a spoon, preparing to burst the foil lid with a satisfying pop, a pop that a great number of people have gone to a great deal of trouble for us to enjoy. Before we get in, look at the teaspoon. Is it one of the silver-plated ones we got from Aunty? One of the 1990s IKEA ones we got as part of our divorce settlement?

One of the ones that we seem to have nicked from De Grays Cafe in Ludlow? All of these spoons are the product of heavy industries of Byzantine complexity, that we have never once given a moment's thought to.

As to the coffee, which purports to be from the 'Inca heartland of the PERUVIAN ANDES' – how in the holy name of Viracocha does it come to be here? Who grows it, how it is grown, or processed, packed, exported, we don't know. Are the beans processed near to the coffee farms, and are they freeze dried rather than spray dried? How's that done? What are the various advantages and disadvantages? (Of course, I realise there are hipster readers going, 'Mate, I know' – as I say, everyone knows a fragment of the process.)

How can we begin to even imagine how the milk has got as far as our kitchen? It comes from a dairy farm somewhere, but we don't really know why and how it is safe to drink. We have no clue about how this splash of semi-skimmed in our coffee came to be here, or what happened to the other bit of fat.[9] And why hasn't the milk turned overnight? Dire Straits complained about having to move the refrigerators that we need to keep our milk fresh, and who can blame them, but that's the least of it.

So much human endeavour, expressed in unthinkably complex industrial processes, carried out by countless millions of workers, has come together at this moment, the moment of you waking up, making coffee and getting ready to go to work, almost certainly as a servant in some way of the Process that has brought this coffee-bean-derived drink to your lips.

Will this system hold? Should it? Who can say? Future readers will know better than I. They will have the benefit of hindsight, while I am stuck in this particular instance of immediacy. But in his diary, Mr. Thomas Marchant, of Hurstpierpoint in the County of

---

9   As an example of how complicated it is to get you your pinta, think of this – most likely the cows that yielded it were inseminated by frozen bull sperm, much of it flown in from the US and Canada. Someone, somewhere, has wanked a bull, so that you can have a latte.

Sussex, gives a taste of what everyday life was like before this Great Machine that we live in came to be.

I knew that night in January 2020, when I realised that blast furnaces came from Namur, that I would need to go to see for myself ye olde ancestral home in Belgium. It is so rare for non-aristocratic families to be able to trace their ancestry this far back that it would be remiss of me not to. The Sambre–Meuse valley, the Sillon industriel, with Namur at its midpoint, was the first place in mainland Europe to industrialise. How could this not be a big part of the 'before' story? After all, it looked as though my fate, and that of my family, had to some extent been determined by the history of iron working. We were shaped by geology. I decided I would make the trip at Easter.

But later in January, I had a change of fortune. I was diagnosed with prostate cancer, and not the good kind that you die with, but the bad kind that you probably die of. They told me it was incurable; 'Manageable, but incurable.' A diagnosis like this makes you get a move on. I changed my plans, and booked ferries and hotels for the last week of February.

'No matter what,' I said to Hilary, 'we are going to Belgium.'

III.

THERE NEEDS A LONG TIME TO KNOW THE WORLD'S PULSE

The 22nd February 1720. A dry day. Willy and Dick King plough'd in the forenoon. Fetcht the ladder pole from Saddlescomb. My Brother Will here in the evning. My Brother John Courtness here afternoon.

On 20 February 2020 I had an appointment for a biopsy on my prostate, which is much worse than it sounds. A day to recuperate, and then we would be off.

What we didn't know, as we set out for the Dover ferry on the morning of 22 February, was that the world was about to close its doors, and that we would be the last tourists for we didn't know how long. We also didn't know for sure, as we drove through driving sleet and rain from Presteigne to the port of Dover, whether we should be doing this at all. Two days before, the consultant who performed my biopsy had warned us not to go.

'You could get sepsis,' he said.

I explained that I was writing a book about my family, and how they were present at the opening moments of industrialisation, and that I quite clearly needed to go to Belgium.

'Your health is more important than your work.'

My work is high risk, involving as it does sitting about all day squinting at a computer, drinking sugary tea and eating hot buttered toast, smoking the odd pipe, and walking up to Elda's Colombian Coffee House for a crispy bacon sandwich and a double espresso at one-ish. Little did he know, I sacrificed my health for my work many years ago. A trip to Belgium was the least of it.

I was on heavy-duty antibiotics after the biopsy and had started taking a testosterone blocker, which, I had been assured, would give me the symptoms of a menopausal woman; top of the list, extreme fatigue. I had been told that at some point I would need chemotherapy, sooner rather than later. To listen to his advice would have meant that the trip to Namur could not be possible until chemo was done, and I wasn't prepared to wait that long. To cancel the trip would cost the £400 or so we had spent on ferries and hotels. I asked my Macmillan nurse (for I suddenly had such a person in my life) what she thought. She argued the case with the consultant and obtained his reluctant consent. But his warning words were on my mind, as you might imagine.

Storms had cut Presteigne off from the rest of the world for much of late January and most of February. It was difficult to find a way out that was not closed due to flooding, and impossible to find a road that was not scarred by potholes. We took the fast road, but it was dark and dreich. We were escaping the consultant and the diagnosis, but we also felt we were somehow escaping Blighted Blighty to travel in the EU without restriction, maybe for the last time. At Clacket Lane services on the M25 we bought the kit you need to drive legally in France and Belgium – the red triangle, the breathalyser, the first aid kit, the spare bulbs, the gilets jaunes and a magnetic GB badge, which we declined to use as we have a Welsh number plate. CYM is much more to our taste. We arrived at our hotel in Dover, ready to catch the 8 a.m. boat to Dunkerque in the morning, and sat miserably in the adjacent Harvester, trying to eat while a bunch of loutish Faragistas at the next table shouted with their mouths full about the human vermin who were crossing the Channel every day in their tens of thousands, apparently.

> The 23rd February 1720. A fine day, small frost. I were
> at Brighton market afternoon. Lost a ewe this afternoon.
> Smith set beans. My wife was at Danny afternoon.

On 23 February 2020, the still powerful aftermath of the last of a succession of bitter winter storms was blowing up the Channel, but a break in the weather meant that we could cross, as the wind dropped to Force 7. It was an unattractive prospect. The man at check-in asked if we were 'going home', because of what he saw as our French name. No one had asked this before, and it seemed like a good omen; he advised us to take the Calais boat as the Dunkerque boat wasn't in yet.

The DFDS announcer told us when we boarded that due to bad weather the outside decks would be closed. Hilary is not a great sailor, despite, or because of, a lifetime of Stranraer–Larne crossings in winter. She's learned to face where she's going, so we found a table for two next to the forward cafe-bar. I bought us a coffee each, which we clung to as the ship left the harbour and lurched into the weather.

About halfway across that rough crossing, the boat plunged into a huge wave, and Hilary was thrown off her chair, almost hitting her head on the corner of a low table. A young man sprawled with his phone across the adjacent banquette leapt up and held her. I struggled to stand while he helped her over to an armchair. The ship's bursar came to find us, to make sure Hilary wasn't hurt, and to give her a small bottle of tepid water by way of compensation. We talked a little with the young man who had helped us. He was a Romanian bus driver, Bucharest to London one week, London to Bucharest the next. He said his English wasn't great. I pointed out it was much better than our Romanian. He said that he was worried what would happen to his work after Brexit.

We felt triumphant to be landing in France again, against the odds. It seemed so liberating. If I had sepsis, I also had my EHIC card. If Britain was to cut itself off from Europe – well, at least we were here now. We took the coast road north, and stopped for breakfast at a Flunch concession in the Auchan superstore on the outskirts of Dunkerque, which is like a Morrisons cafe if it were run by Heston Blumenthal.

Twenty minutes' drive later, we crossed into Belgium. I had achieved my ambition. I had come back, after 500 years, to listen for the whisper of the past. Anxious, smelling of piss, seriously unwell and exhausted from the hormones, I didn't feel like much of a representative of the future. Yet, here I was, back at the beginning of what I am.

Stories should start at the beginning. And in the beginning, as hippies will tell you if you're not very careful, we were stardust. All that we are, from one point of view, are highly organised systems of various elements formed by nuclear fusion in giant stars, and spewed out into the universe as the collapsing stars violently transitioned into supernovas. Iron is the last element produced by runaway fusion just before the stars go supernova. That's why there is so much of it in the world. About 35 per cent of the Earth's mass is a molten liquid iron–nickel alloy, which makes up the planetary core.

Roughly 2,400 million years ago, the oceans were full of dissolved iron, and very little dissolved oxygen. Then, cyanobacteria emerged, the first life capable of photosynthesis, which meant that oxygen levels started to rise. This is known as the 'Great Oxygenation Event'. The newly abundant oxygen combined with the dissolved iron to make iron ores, either haematite or magnetite, which sank to the bottom of the sea. About 1,800 million years ago, this process stopped, or slowed right down, because most of the dissolved iron had oxidised, so the iron ore deposits we have now mostly date from this vast period of time.

Let's skip forward a mere 1,400-ish million years to what geologists call the Devonian period, which was between 420 and 360 million years ago.[10] Geological periods being on the long side, it is divided into subdivisions, early, middle and late, and then further divided into stages. Three of these stages, the Givetian, the

10   Geologists say of the dates, 'Well, roughly that, give or take 2.5 million years either way.'

Frasnian and the Famennian are named after present day towns in the Ardennes: Givet in France, and Frasnes-lez-Couvin and Marche-en-Fammenne in Belgium, because those were the places where geologists found the 'type-site' samples which enable them to identify geological strata.

One of the most notable markers of the Devonian period was high tectonic activity, as landmasses collided and made new continental formations. Somewhere in one of those stages, most likely the Frasnian (between 382 and 372 million years ago, about the time the first forests appeared), two massive tectonic plates came together with a bump, causing mountains to rise, big ones, and lots of them. This event, or series of roughly contemporaneous events, is called 'the Variscan orogeny', and as orogenies go, it was a mother. Its remains run in a band across the northern hemisphere, from the Tian Shan mountains in China, through the Urals, the mountains of the Balkans and Greece, Montblanc, the Harz mountains in Germany, the Pembrokeshire Coast and, in the US, the Appalachians.

The Ardennes Mountain was formed too, bringing with it huge banded layers of the iron which had precipitated into the oceans. Wait another 350 million years or so for the soft bits of the old Ardennes Mountain to get largely worn away (and for humans to evolve), and then you can mine the iron, which is now close to the surface.

About 0.006 per cent of a human is iron, but we each, in the industrialised north, account for somewhere between 7,000 and 14,000 kilograms of processed iron per person, across a lifetime. Think how much iron it must have taken to make that cup of coffee. In this sense, the Iron Age has never ended. But for archaeologists and historians, the term has a precise meaning. It marks a period of time between the moment when producing iron became so cheap and easy that it overtook bronze in usefulness and the date when history starts. It annoys people when I talk about this.

The first part is easy to understand. In the Bronze Age, as you might expect, bronze was easier and cheaper to produce; but there were bits of iron about. Iron collected from meteorites had been known for thousands of years, but it was rare and valued more than gold. One of Tutankhamen's greatest treasures was a cold-worked knife made from meteoric iron. An Iron Age starts when archaeologists start finding large quantities of iron objects, and bronze seemed to have lost utility and value. This happens in different places at different times.

It's the second part that drives people mad. How can history have a start date? But of course history has a start. History deals in dates. If something can't be dated, it's prehistory. When was the first date? Not, when did the world start, but, what is the first event that humankind can put a date to, and say, Oh so and so happened in the year whenevs? This also happens at different times in different places. In China an Iron Age never really happened, because the written history of China starts well before iron displaces bronze in the archaeological record as the most commonly used metal. In Ancient Greece, the Iron Age ends in 500BCE, with the writings of Herodotus, the 'father of history'. In Ireland, it didn't end until about 400CE, and in Scandinavia not until about 800CE.

In what is now Belgium (and also in Britain), the Iron Age ended in about 50BCE, with the appearance in Rome of Julius Caesar's account of the Gallic Wars. Not having the Latin myself, due to my education in a fearsome 1970s comprehensive, I have been spared having to read the thing. For generations of public school children, however, Caesar's *Gallic Wars* was the first Latin text that they would be required to attempt to translate, due to Caesar's direct and easily understood prose. Its first sentence is so well known amongst prep school kids, that 'the three parts' get a mention in Sellar and Yeatman's historical parody of mis-remembered school history, *1066 and All That*. Here it is, the moment of the ending of the Iron Age in north-west Europe, and the cause of much misery for young Latin learners:

> All Gaul is divided into three parts, in one dwell the
> Belgae, in another the Aquitans, and in the third,
> those that call themselves Kelts, known to us as Gauls

> ... Of all these the most powerful are the Belgae
> because, for long they have been far-removed from
> civilised human pursuits, least frequented by merchant
> imports that effeminate their rational soul ...

If I am descended in some way from the Belgae, I'm afraid both Caesar and my ancestors would find my rational soul irredeemably effeminated. Caesar clearly admired the Belgae, and they fought him and his legions long and hard. I would have been standing at the back, making snarky comments to amuse girls, and preparing to run.

The Belgae were a confederation of Celtic tribes who arrived in the area of the Ardennes about 200BCE, one of the last Celtic groups to arrive in northwest Europe, probably because they'd dawdled about and merged with various Germanic tribes on the way. The Celts, who had been entering and crossing Europe from about 800BCE, most likely came from over the Caucasus mountains, probably bringing with them the skills for iron working on a scale sufficient to declare an Iron Age. They practised agriculture, stock breeding, mining and metallurgy. Although they were unlettered (which is why they had to wait for Caesar to write them up before they could enter history) they had developed an advanced system of river and sea transport. Shortly before Caesar arrived, some of the Belgae had crossed the Channel to settle in south-east England.

The Celtic 'migrations' are currently viewed as a cultural shift as much as a movement of people. The Celts are still good at this. Think Irish pubs. No matter where you are on earth, there is a fecking Irish pub, though this doesn't necessarily mean that any actual Irish people are involved in any way. Two distinct cultures crossed into Europe from the Caucasus, the first, from about 800BCE onwards, was the Hallstatt. Then, from 300BC, the La Tène culture spread, which was Celtic but influenced by contact with Greek and Etruscan civilisation. The art of the La Tène culture utilised the swirling curved botanical motifs and animal figures that we would now call 'Celtic' art. Much of what has survived of their ornate metalwork is in bronze, such as the Witham and Battersea shields, because bronze doesn't rust. But what made them rich and successful were iron swords, iron axes and iron-clad ploughshares. In the Ardennes, and subsequently in Sussex and Kent, the Romans would employ these skilled people and their understanding of their landscapes to make the iron that would hold the Empire together.

There are those who consider Belgium featureless and, although I am not one of them, at first glance you would have to say they have a point. The drive through Belgium to Namur on dank motorways didn't give many clues to its extraordinary richness, except for the exit signs: Antwerp, Bruges, Ghent. But even in a grey procession of trans-European wagons and German-registered Beamers going much faster than us, kicking up the kind of spray that you'd expect to encounter if you were a round-the-world yachtsperson, it started to become clear that Belgium's character was able to assert itself through the mizzle. For example, Belgium outside of Brussels isn't bilingual. One half speak Flemish, one half speak French, and that's it. If you are from one half of Belgium, you can't read the motorway billboards in the other. We crossed the border from France into Flanders, and managed to work out that the billboards in Dutch were urging us to have a coffee and a power nap. But when we crossed into French-speaking Wallonia, the signs told us that we needed to get to bed earlier. Easy for them to say, given the difficulties of finding your hotel in a new city whilst remembering how to drive on the right. When we finally got there, the hotel was comfortable and warm. We ate mussels and frites in the next-door restaurant, and followed the French billboard's advice.

The 24th February 1720. A fine day, frosty. Dick King sick. Terry thrasht with Banks, mov'd dung at Kester's afternoon. Thomas Hamper fetcht a large press from

> my Father's. John Gun begun serve Smith's beasts this
> evning.

In the morning of 24 February, we walked around Namur. Belgium has a highly developed sense of humour. In the city's main square, there's a statue of two men with tethered snails, one in a cage. They are based on two cartoon characters, the inseparable friends Djoseph èt Françwès, serialised in the local newspaper *Vers l'Avenir* by the painter and caricaturist Jean Legrand. Françwès and Djoseph apparently symbolise the 'shit postponed is the same as no shit at all' attitude of the Namurians, which is very much how I've managed to get this far. The snails in the sculpture are respectively caged and tethered in case they try to make a break for it.

On the roundabout by the confluence of the Meuse and the Sambre was a statue of stilt walkers egging one another on to have a go. Namur has had a tradition of fighting on stilts since 1411. Perhaps old Jean-Baptiste de Marchant fought — lots of people in Namur still seem to. The Combat de l'échasse d'Or takes place in Namur the third Sunday of September. The people of the old town, on

yellow and black stilts, fight against the people of the suburbs, on red and white stilts. At the sound of the drums, they start moving and fighting, the aim being to make the opponent fall off their stilts. The last man standing wins the Golden Stilts. Until I saw the statue, I didn't know that fighting on stilts was a thing, but once you've come across the idea, it can only strike you as fun to watch, if not to do.

Looming over the confluence of the rivers is the castle on the rock, known as the Citadel. It is a natural site for any powerful force to build fortifications. The Romans, the Merovingian kings and the Carolingian Empire all wanted to hold this rock, and thus control both the navigation of the upper waters of the two rivers and the burgeoning regional iron industry. After Charlemagne's death in 813CE, his Empire splintered into the jumble of statelets that became known as the Holy Roman Empire, and Namur became an autonomous county under the Empire's loose control. The Count of

Namur's residence, built in 900CE, still stands on the Citadel, open to the public.

The Citadel is Namur's principal tourist destination. From the rivers' confluence, we found several signposted ways up and around the Citadel. It's a series of fortified terraces, like a ziggurat, or Maiden Castle, rising in concentric steps to the inevitable restaurant and giftshop on the top. We climbed the steps and steep paths. Lest we forget that we were in Belgium, natural home of surrealism, on one of the terraces there was a newly erected, very large gilded bronze statue of a man riding a giant turtle. The sign told us that it's called *Searching for Utopia*.

It's a self-portrait of artist Jan Fabre (the rider, not the turtle). The city, together with some private donors, and with fundraising by the inhabitants of Namur, paid 500,000 euros for it. It's big – it weighs 6,500 kilograms, is seven metres long and five metres wide. The locals call it 'The Turtle', and who can blame them? Locals hardly ever read artist statements, wherever you are in the world.

From the top of the Citadel you can see the history of Namur laid out before you. The original settlement, a small walled town, was on the spit of land just below. Namur proper spread along the opposite side of the Sambre, and also up the *rive gauche* of the

Meuse. Across the Meuse is another part of the city, called Jambes, which was once a separate town, owned by the bishops of Liège, who, rather awkwardly, were long-time enemies and rivals of the counts of Namur.

Namur is not just a city, but a county of Belgium. It was once an autonomous County of the Holy Roman Empire, until it was sold to the Dukes of Burgundy in 1421. The Duchy of Burgundy was another loose confederation of not always contiguous territories, rather than something we would recognise as a nation state. In the fifteenth century, Burgundy was pretty much the most enlightened, the richest, the freest place in Western Europe. The Renaissance came from Burgundy as much as it did Florence.

I felt thrilled to be in Namur, and could feel a visceral connection to my ancestors. They knew this view from the Citadel, they must have done. This was their landscape. They must have known Liège, too, and probably the imperial 'capital' at Aachen. I thrilled with what I can only describe as a kind of historical enchantment. I had come to realise that I live in the past as much as I do the present.

So why did the de Marchants leave?

> The 25th February 1720. A fine day, frosty. I din'd at my Father's. We went thence to the Swan. There was Mr Burry, John Snashall jr, John Smith, John Box sr.

There are lots of museums, worldwide, dedicated to the history of the production of iron, as no one knows better than my wife and children. There's one in the Ardennes, called, so far as I could make out from their bilingual website (French and Dutch), the Domaine du Fourneau Saint-Michel. It seemed to be an outdoor museum of reconstructed buildings from all over the south of Wallonia, one of which was a preserved blast furnace from the eighteenth century. The furnace appeared to be part of the larger site, but a separate museum.

Sitting at home before the trip, squinting at my laptop, it had been impossible to work out if the iron museum would be open at the end of February, which would mean that we could see it, or if it didn't open till the first of March, which meant that my poor wife would have to forgo the pleasure. At tourist information on top of the Citadel in Namur, no one could help us. The lady behind the desk admitted that there was such a museum, but she didn't have any information about it as it was too far away (about 65 kilometres). She too looked at the website, and also couldn't quite make sense of it. We would have to see for ourselves.

On 25 February 2020, we drove south from Namur into the wild vastness of the Ardennes proper. Coppiced woods marched away over the hills on the horizon. All along the roads were hides, and men with hunting rifles peering into the forest. A little north of the town of Saint-Hubert, whose huge and somewhat crumbling basilica is dedicated to the eponymous patron saint of huntsmen, we found the Domaine du Fourneau Saint-Michel, and looked to see if it was open.

There was no one at the entrance gate, and no way of paying. The museum was deserted, but seemed nonetheless open, so we went in. It was a collection of rebuilt and restored agricultural houses and workshops, much like the Weald and Downland Living Museum in Sussex where the BBC's *Repair Shop* is filmed.

The exhibits were unlocked, and we were free to wander. There was a school, a church, a bakery, a cider press, a cobbler's workshop, a smithy – all collected from across Wallonia, and lovingly re-erected in this museum. An iron-rich stream ran through the site, and snow-drops sparkled on its banks. All of these buildings were open for us to wander through. All of them were empty of visitors and staff.

There were facilities, too. The modern lavatories were open and warm and clean, at least before I got there. Signs pointed to a cafe, and we followed the path through the deserted site. When we found the cafe, it was empty of anything save a few stacked chairs, yet the automatic doors swished open at our approach and closed behind us as we backed out. I was reminded of Chihiro's family at the start of *Spirited Away*, wandering through a deserted theme park.

It wasn't until we left that we finally noticed the sign at the entrance to the car park – 'opens 1 March', i.e. three days hence. It had seemed open to us, open and trusting. We hadn't seen the site of the blast furnace, but that, as we very quickly discovered, was because it was a mile down the road at the Musée du Fer et de la Métallurgie ancienne, which was very much open. So I got to see a proper preserved Walloon method ironworks after all, albeit one from the eighteenth century.

And what, you may ask, was the Walloon method, and why did it matter? It was this method that the de Marchants and 300 or so other families brought to England, and you're going to have to brace yourself for a little *métallurgie ancienne* because I've come a long way to bring you here.

When iron was first produced in useful quantities in Europe, smelters used what is known as 'the direct method', in small furnaces called 'bloomeries'. They built a four- or five-feet-high shell from clay, that looks very like a large, badly made pot, such as the 'snake' ones you used to make at school. This shell is open at the top, and has a small tube coming out of the side, called a tuyere, attached to some kind of bellows. You fill the bloomery with charcoal, set it on fire, and get the fire hot by blowing in air through the tuyere. Then you start dropping in iron ore from the top – then more charcoal – then more iron and so on. Meanwhile, someone pumps away at the bellows, for twenty-four hours or more, until the founder decides that the process has gone on long enough. Because one workman pumping away has not got the thing hot enough, the iron does not run molten. Rather, when the process is deemed over, the forgemaster breaks open the clay bloomery, and fishes out a hot ball of mixed iron and slag, called a 'bloom'.

Next, the iron workers biff at the bloom with big wooden mallets; but not too hard because you don't want the bloom to disintegrate into bits. The biffing chases out the impurities. After hours of this, you should be left with a bar of malleable wrought iron. If the iron contains a very small amount of carbon, then you have accidentally made steel. If it contains more than 2 per cent, it's too brittle to use. So the biffing is very important. Smelting at these low temperatures means the wrought iron is largely free from carbon contamination. In order for the direct process to work, it needs high grade ores; so although iron was vital for cultures across Europe from 800BC onwards, it could only be produced in relatively small amounts.

So devoted am I to the cause of being a late-middle-aged geezer, I belong to a Facebook group called 'Iron Smelters of the World', where people post video clips of their attempts to make iron in a bloomery. Although most of them cheat by using a powered airblower rather than sitting beside a blazing furnace pumping away at a pair of bellows day and night, they rarely manage to produce anything more than a few grams of malleable iron.[11] Yet this was how iron was made for centuries.

It was the Chinese who first used blast furnaces, which used water power to operate the large pair of bellows, which pumped air into the furnace to get it so hot that the iron would run molten out of the bottom. There is some archaeological evidence that Vikings trading down the Volga may have encountered the idea via the Silk Road to China. Certainly, evidence of large-scale operations in Sweden suggest it was the first place in Europe to utilise blast furnace technology. Sweden had high grade ore, trees for charcoal, fast-running water and refractory rock for building furnaces that could operate at high temperatures; so high that the iron ran liquid. Higher temperatures brought more iron, but much of it was brittle cast iron, useless unless purified (or fined) using foundries. This is the 'indirect method', because it takes two stages – the melting of the iron, using water-powered bellows, and then fining using huge, water-powered

---

11 This negligible amount of wrought iron is the only new wrought iron being produced anywhere in the world. We have forgotten how to make it. The eighteenth-century method of producing it in large quantities was called 'puddling', and the last factory that made it closed in 1973. Any wrought iron used by smiths today is made from old iron melted down.

hammers to knock out the higher levels of carbon impurity from the cast iron. In the fourteenth century, iron was Sweden's largest export, mostly to Lübeck, from where the Hanseatic League sold it into the Holy Roman Empire, France or England.

The Count of Namur, Willem I, granted the first charter to iron workers in 1345. Willem's sister Blanche married King Magnus IV of Sweden, and it's probable that Magnus had encouraged Willem to import the technology into Namur. Namur was ideally situated because of its fortifications (in 1388, the first in Europe to be built to accommodate cannons), its place on the confluence of the Meuse and Sambre (both navigable to some extent), and its mineral and forest resources.

For the Walloon method to be perfected, it needed one more tweak. Water-powered blast furnaces were good, but they could only run for eighteen hours a day, because of the need to run off slag. Slag is the stuff that is left after the iron has been melted, and is a bad thing. So the furnacemen of Namur built a hole in the side of their furnace, a so-called forehearth, which made possible a revolutionary increase in output. The furnaces could now run non-stop. Higher temperatures and forehearths meant that slag could be cleared quicker, which meant lower-grade ores could be used.

The first furnace and forge was built at Marche-les-Dames, a few miles downriver from Namur, under the auspices of the count. The Hundred Years' War between England and France had started in 1337, and it's almost certain that the establishment of the furnace and forge at Marche was to supply ordnance for sale to the warring armies. In Europe, cast iron was not anciently used at all. It only became useful with the advent of firearms – at first for shot and later for cast cannon. 'Pots and pans, firebacks, tombstones, iron railings and ultimately the use of iron in structural engineering lay well in the future.'[12]

Cannon and bombards were used in continental warfare throughout the fifteenth century. John the Fearless, the second Duke

---

12   From *Adventure in Iron* by Brian G. Awty, Wealden Iron Research Group, 2019.

of Burgundy, used artillery in 1408 at the Battle of Othée, and in 1411 Burgundian artillery was used in the siege of Coucy. These cannons, bombards and ribaults were not capable of firing accurately, or over anything than a short range. They were scary, I'm sure, but they also blew up. The mechanical siege engines which slung rocks at the walls of besieged cities and had been in use for centuries, were more deadly and more accurate than the gunpowder fired cannon, which were there to cause noise, sow confusion, and to make the enemy quake with fear. But the Dukes of Burgundy could see their potential, and if the Duchy of Burgundy was to step into the bright sunlight of history, as the wealthiest, most advanced 'state' in Europe, they would need to continue to develop artillery. And, for that, they needed Namur.

The counts of Namur owed fealty to the Holy Roman Empire, which in turn offered some protection. As fortunes changed in the Hundred Years' War, the count made sure his ironworks were situated in the territory of the Empire, and out of the reach of the English and French. But links were strong between Namur and the Duchy of Burgundy, and the dukes were well aware of the extraordinary production levels of the Namur ironworks, and of the potentialities of the cast-iron cannons. In 1421, Philip the Good, 3rd Duke of Burgundy, bought Namur, lock, stock and gun barrel. Namur was still recovering from the Black Death, and land values had dropped by up to a half, so Philip got it on the cheap.

My ancestors, without so much as a by-your-leave, had just become Burgundians.

The 26th February 1720. A fine day. Mr Jeremiah Dodson preacht. I were at Mrs Catherine Beard's in the evning.

On 26 February 2020 we caught the train from Namur to Aachen, from Belgium to Germany, changed at Liège-Guillemins and Verviers. Wet snow was falling on the hills. It was easy in that landscape to think of yesterday's huntsmen coming home empty-handed, like Bruegel's *Hunters in the Snow*.

Aachen was Charlemagne's capital, the heart of the Holy Roman Empire for 700 years. Although the city has suffered from time, the cathedral, Charlemagne's palace chapel, has survived and evolved over 1,200 years. It is a glory, a wonder, a testament to the power of faith. And, like all such, it needs income. In order to see Charlemagne's throne, and to get up close to the *Marienschrein*, you had to take the guided tour. We were just in time to take the last one of the day. There was only one other tourist, a man as tall as me, with a camera round his neck. Cornelia the guide spoke to him in German, and then said to us, 'This gentleman is happy for me to conduct the tour in English,' which she did, for fifty astounding minutes, and to our new friend's evident delight. 'I'm an Anglophile,' he said. 'I must be the only person in Germany who has listened to all thirty-eight hours of David Cameron's autobiography. It is all so sad.' As we stood in front of the Charlemagne shrine, Cornelia told us that he got his name in part because of his height. 'As tall as us,' said our new friend. I asked his name. 'Klaus.'

'Klaus the Great,' I said.

> The 27th February 1720. A fine day. Moll Terry's father lay here. Mr Orlton etc din'd here. My wife and I supt at Thomas Norton's North End.

Our last night in Belgium, we stayed in Ghent. On the motorway back from Namur, visibility was still poor, German-registered Beamers still whooshed past at the speed of rapidly declining middle-aged testosterone levels, and wagons with exotic number plates still kicked up all but impenetrable vapour trails, just like on the way in. This time, though, it was sleet rather than mizzle that the windscreen wipers couldn't quite work hard enough to clear.

Ghent is a wonderful city, full of lovely hotels, none of which we could comfortably afford, even at the end of February. So we booked to stay in an Ibis Budget hotel. Ibis Budget hotels are clean, modern, comfortable, affordable, and always located in a bleak *banlieue* or industrial park on the remote outskirts of wherever it is you're staying. The Ghent example backed on to a commercial waterway overlooked by an abandoned power station. In front of the hotel, the Islamic Faculty of Europe was sandwiched between a plumbers' merchants and a Toyota dealership. Freezing sleet continued to fall outside as we queued at reception. Behind us were a group of perhaps fifteen cheerful Italian men, none of whom spoke French, Dutch or English. In order to make themselves understood, they spoke Italian, but slowly and loudly, just like the British abroad speak English, with equal success. Usually, in Ibis Budget hotels, our fellow guests are people who are working, so we assumed they were construction workers, or some such.

It was 27 February. A dozen or so municipalities in northern Italy had been in lockdown for a week, the first in Europe. I don't think we gave it a moment's thought. We certainly didn't practise social distancing in the lift we shared with several of the Italians, because no one even knew what it was. We asked reception to book us a taxi to take us into the city centre. The driver spoke excellent English. He told us that the police would be out in numbers, because KAA Gent were playing host to AS Roma in the Europa League. That's why the hotel was full of Italians. We shrugged. Rome wasn't in lockdown, after all.

Ghent was bitter cold, the cold that gets in your bones. We were heading for St. Bavo's Cathedral, because we had come to see a picture, specifically an altarpiece, Hubert and Jan van Eyck's *Mystic Lamb*, which had been newly restored. It's kept in a side chapel, and there was a queue, but if ever a queue was worthwhile, this was it. We got to the front, and stood in silence before the *Mystic Lamb*. Although I know lots about art, I don't always know what I like. I certainly don't know how to describe the picture. Look it up. The World made right again by the loving self-sacrifice of an innocent.

According to the first art historian, Giorgio Vasari, in his *Lives of the Painters &c* of 1550, Jan van Eyck invented oil painting. Vasari was based in Florence, and his book makes little mention of the 'Northern Renaissance', but even he had to admit the power of Van Eyck's work. There are only about twenty Van Eycks still in existence; the best known to British art lovers is probably *The Arnolfini Marriage*, which hangs in the National Gallery. Like many people, I've stood in front of the picture, amazed at its wit and technical proficiency, without knowing that Van Eyck was the first, the daddy, the fountainhead. Van Eyck was Elvis in Sun Studio, the Beatles in Hamburg. He invented it.

Jan van Eyck was the court painter to Philip the Good. In a letter of 1435 Philip 'sternly chided' his financial experts for failing to pay the annual instalment of the life pension that he had granted Van Eyck. Worried about losing his services, the duke stated that, 'we would not find his like more to our taste, one so excellent in his art and science'.

Philip the Good was the wealthiest noble in Europe. This was the golden age of Burgundy, the apogee of Christendom. With the Great Council and the Estates General, Burgundian Flanders was beginning to evolve modern democratic civic organisation. Erasmus, the great humanist scholar, one of the doorkeepers of both the Protestant and scientific revolutions, was Burgundian. Caxton set up his first printing press, not in London, but in Burgundian Bruges. 'Burgundian' was a byword for lavish dress, conspicuous consumption and making merry. People in France and Belgium still talk of the 'Burgundian character' – cheerful, easy-going, enjoys a good time.[13]

Namur wasn't just useful in terms of the technology it offered,

---

13 Uncannily, this does sound like the vast majority of my family.

but because its territory divided that of rival city Liège into two. The dukes wanted to make their territory contiguous, and Namur was another piece in their puzzle. In the north, they held some of the most urbanised areas north of the Alps – Bruges, Ghent, Brussels, Amsterdam. In the south, as you might guess, they controlled what we might think of as 'Burgundy' – the place where the wines come from. The dukes' capital was in Dijon, where they over-wintered in the Ducal Palace, but, in the spring, they set off on a progress. For most of the year, therefore, the court was itinerant between the northern and southern holdings. The last of the Valois dukes, Charles the Bold, wanted to finally link the two territories.

Unlike his old dad, Charles the Bold was not good. He was bold, you have to give him that, especially if 'bold' is a synonym of stark-staring bonkers. He was a savage who lived and died by the sword. He attacked Dinant, a short way up the Meuse from Namur, in 1466, and ordered all the men and women inside killed. He burned Liège in 1468, and destroyed the rival ironworks there. In pursuit of his ambition to create one contiguous territory, Charles rampaged around the borders of France, Germany and Switzerland pursuing a series of personal vendettas. He spent so much time and money in these vainglorious pursuits, that in order to continue his attempt to conquer territory he raised credit from Italian bankers, the first time that bankers had funded a state military enterprise anywhere in Europe. Charles the Bold spent his borrowed gold on a large army of armoured knights on horseback, clearly thinking that something like Agincourt could never happen to him – which, of course, it did. In two doomed attempts to conquer territory from the Swiss Confederation, he ran his knights into an impenetrable porcupine of Swiss pikemen, who finally proved, to everyone's satisfaction, that the day of the armoured knight really was over. In a last frenzied attempt to gain the territory he needed, he laid siege to Nancy, where he was killed in January 1477.

At his death, much of the territory of the Burgundians reverted to France, whilst other territories took shelter under the arthritic wing of the Holy Roman Empire. Charles the Bold's sole heir was his daughter from his first marriage, Mary of Burgundy. She was nineteen, and Charles had been trying to arrange an advantageous match. After his death, she was offered the chance to marry the Dauphin of France, who was seven. Instead, she opted to marry Maximilian von Habsburg, the son of the Holy Roman Emperor. In order to assert his control over the vast Burgundian territories, Maximilian instigated fifteen years of internal conflict. Namur was besieged, and cannons were used against its fortifications, one of the earliest instances of effective modern artillery use in Europe. The scary ribalds and bombards had been replaced by proper cannons.

Five years later, Mary was dead, killed by a fall from her horse. But her children and grandchildren would ensure the political legacy of her marriage; she was the materfamilias of the Habsburg dynasty that was to remain in power in much of Europe, one way and another, until 1918. Her grandson was both Holy Roman Emperor and the King of Spain, Charles V. He also inherited the substantial remnants of the Duchy of Burgundy, including Namur and its ironworks. Namur was now part of the 'Spanish Netherlands', which became Belgium in 1830.

This, in my view, is why the de Marchants left Burgundy. Namur had become so important that it was being constantly fought over. Even at the height of Burgundy's power, it had been unable to prevent the rival city of Liège from destroying all of Namur's iron-working capabilities in the 1450s. By the time they were fully restored, the Meuse region was subject to Maximilian's depredations. The peaceful, highly civilised life offered by Burgundy was gone. The de Marchants were refugees from a seemingly never-ending war. You'd pick up your family, wouldn't you, if they were under constant attack? If your city was under siege? If political uncertainty meant that you had lost the means to make your livelihood? You'd pick them up, and take them somewhere else, somewhere safe. If your city was being bombed, you'd risk the sea-crossing from France to England, wouldn't you?

Especially if you had been invited.

The 28th February 1720. A fine day, frosty. My Wife and I went to my Cousin Marchant of Ditcheling. I bought 2½ bushels of flax seed of Young Jacob Hubbard at 17s to fetch it this week. We were at my Aunt Sarah Turner's.

The next day, 28 February 2020, we retraced our steps to the sea. We stopped again at the Auchan hypermarket outside Dunkerque, and stocked up on booze for Hilary, and a dozen tins of lentils in duck fat for me. We drove to the Dunkerque ferry port to wait for our boat, which was delayed by bad weather. We listened on the radio to a Dutch golden oldies station, which alternated between 'classic rock' and Dutch yoodle-diddly-doodle music played on accordions. I couldn't decide which I hated more.

Crossing the English Channel by boat is one of the great political issues of our time. The illusory idea that the Channel is somehow a barrier (when it is, and always was, a road) is at the heart of Brexit. Desperate and resourceful people, longing only for some hope and kindness, attempt to cross in their dozens in unseaworthy boats, because they are denied their rights as asylum seekers. Instead of kindness, they get fear and contempt. Their numbers are inflated ten-fold, in order to feed the slavering jaws of an electorate whipped into a frenzy of loathing by 'leaders' whose only interest is to take and hold power at all costs. Our political masters, pandering to those whose view of life is warped by their fear of strangers, are setting up a 'points-based' immigration system, which means that those who score highly, such as bankers, AI wonks and Russian gangsters, will get in no problem, whilst those who don't score points, such as the care workers who looked after my mother, can fuck off.

The de Marchants, and the 300 or so other iron families, would have scored highly, because they brought weapons technology. It was the first of the Tudor monarchs, Henry VII, who invited them. He wanted blast furnaces. And according to Brian G. Awty 'Henry VII's efforts to bring blast furnace technology to the Weald can best be explained by supposing that he had encountered it in Northern France during his exile.'

In 1485, Henry was at Rouen[14] preparing for the invasion which would lead to Richard III's death at Bosworth Field and subsequent burial in Leicester Cathedral's visitor car park. The area between Rouen and Dieppe is the Pays de Bray, which was the centre for French iron working using the Walloon method. Henry Tudor saw for himself the growing power of the guns. The Walloon method was so successful that there was a surplus of skilled workers – workers were a by-product of the process, like slag or cast iron itself – and the systematic destruction of ironworks (such as that by Liège in Namur, and Burgundy in Liège) meant there were plenty of displaced iron workers, hoping for a settled life, as do we all.

There is a lot of evidence of Iron Age and Roman bloomeries in the Weald. The Roman Channel fleet, the Classis Britannica, used large amounts of Wealden iron for shipbuilding. But iron production seems to have stopped after the departure of the Romans. In the medieval period, the iron industry had all but gone, until the arrival of the first blast furnace in England, at Buxted, in what is now East Sussex, in 1490. Historians are not sure why the industry disappeared for almost a thousand years. Most medieval iron was being imported from Lübeck (though an amount was being made by the bloomery method in the Forest of Dean). Sussex iron ore is not always top grade, but there was lots of it, which is all a blast furnace

14 There's a well-worth-visiting iron museum in Rouen.

needs. There was running water that could be stopped to form 'hammer ponds', and there was a seemingly inexhaustible supply of wood for charcoal. The Archbishop of Canterbury, John Morton, was the lord of the manor of Buxted, so he might have played some part in securing the innovative investment from the king, which brought the furnace and finery to his patch. What is certain is that, in 1491, Henry VII granted iron-working rights in the Ashdown Forest to Johannes de Peter and John Heron. The king, at his own expense, was to 'sende over the see for such and as many artificers and workmen as shalbe thought necessary for the gettying, melting, trying and making of such iren and barres of iren'. The king was to pay for recruitment, and the iron masters paid the wages.

And so they/we came. Lest there be any doubt, the move to England was not religiously motivated, because the Reformation was thirty years in the future. They came, the de Marchants and their ilk, because they were highly skilled workers; I think it likely that the de Marchants brought some capital, too. The first product the new immigrants started making in the Ashdown Forest were 'pellettes', i.e. shot and cannon balls. But as the furnaces multiplied, molten iron began to be produced in sufficient quantities to pour cast-iron cannons. From the start, the iron industry in Sussex was at the centre of the English arms trade. Henry VII invaded France in 1492, armed with munitions from the Weald. In 1496, for a war against the Scots, the king commissioned Henry Fryer, a Southwark goldsmith, to invite more artificers, founders and labourers to build foundries for the making of iron for ordnance. The Ordnance Office, reformed and modernised by Henry VII, bought munitions out of Sussex for the next 250 years.

The largest extant collection of Sussex cannons is in Bermuda, oddly enough. Hilary seemed to brighten when I told her this, and declared herself more than willing to visit them, which says a lot, I think.

I stepped out of the car into the storm-force wind and sleeting rain to see if the boat was in. Poor Hilary was in for another rough crossing. I wondered what kind of crossing my ancestors had. Better weather than this, I hoped. I can't know, and can only guess from where and to where they crossed. Hilaire Belloc, one of the great Sussex writers, and an experienced sailor who knew the Channel well, speculates in his book about the Pilgrims' Way,[15] *The Old Road*, on what Channel crossings were like in medieval times. He makes the point, a very good one I think, that there was no principal port into south-east England. At its narrowest point, the Channel is twenty-one miles wide, which doesn't sound a lot. The white cliffs of Cap Gris-Nez are visible from the grey cliffs of Dover. You might well stand in France, see England, and think, that's nothing. But as Belloc knew from experience, the winds and the tides are such that it is one of the trickiest sea crossings on earth. You might start off from Calais, Dunkerque or Boulogne, and, depending on the wind and tides, you might land in Ramsgate, Sandwich, Dover, Folkestone, Lympne or Rye. If they sailed from the Flanders ports, from Antwerp or Bruges, then they might have been forced round the North Foreland as far as the old Roman port of Reculver, now a caravan park outside Herne Bay. Belloc believed that it would make more sense to cross from Normandy, a longer trip, but easier and safer. This might mean that the de Marchants sailed from the iron-working centre of Rouen, up the Seine to Harfleur, and across the Channel; probably to Southampton, but perhaps even directly into Sussex, via Shoreham.

And I can't know much about the boat, though I can speculate in my turn. The traders of Burgundian Flanders and the Hanseatic League would have sailed in cogs, wide beam, shallow draught boats with a square sail, keel boards and a covered hold – those of northern

15   From Winchester to Canterbury, via Shalford.

France would have sailed in open-decked cutters with triangular sails and a deeper keel, better against the wind. Either way, the de Marchants would have shared the journey with traders' goods, mails, even livestock. It took huge courage and resolve, I reckon. But it was a journey taken in hope for a new and better life, exactly the hope that we have closed our doors to.

The ferry came in and started to load. The storms were back, or had never gone away. As we came close to Dover, Hilary was gagging. I held her head, and watched for the light on the end of the harbour breakwater.

'Nearly there,' I said. 'Almost there.'

It was 6 p.m., and dark, and southern England was hidden in fog. It was 28 February 2020. UK health authorities confirmed the first case of Covid-19 to be passed on inside the country. On the way out, we had run away from the consultant and his diagnosis. On the way back, we were running into something else again.

IV

WHO WOULD BE A GENT, LET HIM STORM A TOWN

I know that I don't want to run away from what is happening to me. After all, where would I run to? As I write this, in early April 2020, the world is closed. No. *Shikata ga nai*, as the Japanese say. It cannot be helped. The doctors tell me that my death is inevitable. Well, duh. Whined at or withstood, death is something we all have to live with. After all, as Thomas Cranmer wrote in the *Book of Common Prayer*, 'In the midst of life, we are in death.' You have to choose a path through life, even though we all know what lies in wait at the end. My path is that these days I find myself living increasingly in the *longue durée*, the long time. What happened then, is still happening now, if you pay attention and open your imagination.

The great historian G.M. Trevelyan wrote that 'the poetry of history lies in the quasi-miraculous fact that once, on this earth, once, on this familiar spot of ground, walked other men and women, as actual as we are today.' Now we need to remember that one day, in 300 years' time, other actual men and women will walk on this familiar ground, and that they will be our seven-times-great great-grandchildren, and that we need to start looking after their interests. The *longue durée* goes forward in time, as well as back.

As an example of the *longue durée* in action, Old Thom Marchant and I belonged, and still belong, to an organisation that has already existed for at least 1,400 years. We are Christians, but not just any old Christians. We are Church of England. Like everyone in England and Wales still, we live in a parish served by an Anglican church. We both sit, or sat, on a Sunday listening to the minister preach. We kneel to pray from the 1662 version of Cranmer's *Book of Common Prayer*, and stand to say together the Nicene Creed. We straightforwardly share a culture, one which has changed over time, of course, but which allows us both to say, if nothing else, that we are only here by the Grace of God.

The 1st March 1720. A very fine day, frosty. Will and Smith made an end of ploughing Tully's wheat earsh by Hollingham's. Terry thrasht with Banks at Brickhouse. Ned Burt workt in the garden.

On 1 March 2020, the Sunday after our return from Namur, I sat in St. Andrew's Church, Presteigne, and listened to my friend the Reverend Steve Hollinghurst preach on the temptation of Christ. 'If you are hungry, just turn these stones to bread.' Christ resisted resorting to miracles, and I am trying to. This is the thing – I'm not praying for a miracle cure, but for the forbearance and courage to help me face up to what is coming, to what cannot be helped.

After the service, I finished and filed a diary piece for the *Church Times* in which I owned up to my cancer diagnosis. Which meant that I would have to face up to telling my parents about my condition, even though they aren't subscribers, in any sense, to the *Church Times*. This wasn't fun. My mum had been struggling since she turned eighty with a series of chronic illnesses. She was blind, mostly incontinent, all but immobile, and had started to exhibit the first symptoms of dementia. Ralph Foxwell had been her main carer for five years. They hoped, always, that there would be a cure for death, and here was I, announcing mine.

> The 2nd March 1720. A very fine day, small frost. I
> were at Wanbarrow and at Brother Box's in the morning.
> Ned Burt worked in the garden with John Gun. I supt at
> Stephen Bine's with Mr Jeremiah Dodson, Mr John Hart
> and Mr Burry.

The next day, 2 March 2020, I had to travel to Surrey to record an episode of *Open Country*, the Radio 4 show on which I am an occasional presenter: subject, 'The Music of the Surrey Hills'. Producer Mary Ward-Lowery and I were conducting our first interview at Newlands Corner, and as she drove us up the hill from Dorking station, I started to feel – I didn't quite know what. Nostalgic? Angry? These are some of the prettiest villages in England: Abinger Hammer, Gomshall, Shere. Hidden among the trees, or hiding behind the hills, is a chocolate box world of villages, the villages where I had my beginning. I remembered all my mum's stories of the poverty that she grew up with, in cottages little better than hovels, unchanging in centuries. Thom had a hovel on Little Park Farm for the poorest of his hands. These hovels fetch what now? £750,000? Industrialisation forces this divorce from community, from the land. The houses aren't hovels any more, but nor are they lived in by agricultural workers, rather by commuters to the City. The people who have been driven from the villages by price have moved to Crawley or Woking.

Newlands Corner is a cafe, loo stop, car park and 250-acre place to walk the dogs on the old A25 between Guildford and Dorking. The view from Newlands Corner is a contender for the 'best view in England'; my grandpop Charlie and my birth dad Alan certainly thought so. All through my childhood, whenever we drove along the road, we would stop in the car park, and they would say, 'This is God's country,' and, 'This is the best view in England.' And for a long time, I believed them. This view from Newlands Corner became

my private ideal of England. To the left and to the right the Surrey Hills – Pitch Hill, Leith Hill, Box Hill, St. Martha's Hill, and, in the blue distance, the South Downs. Immediately below, the beautiful valley of the Tillingbourne, following its course to meet the Wey at Shalford.

Sometimes I think we live in the ruins of a great civilisation, which we can no longer understand. Below, church towers stand out from the enveloping woods, woods which seem to go on forever. The people who built the churches thought that would go on forever, too. Now, most people don't know who built them, or what for. Our descendants might stand up here in 300 years and wonder why we needed so many Porsche salerooms and artisanal gin distilleries.

My interview was with the musician Graham Dowdall, who had been Nico's drummer, and who currently occupies the stool for Pere Ubu. It is fair to say I was impressed. He had made a series of soundscapes in the Surrey Hills; five 'sonic reactions', based on field recordings, to hear what defines each separate hill.

I asked Graham what made the different hills sonically unique.

'Some have forestry, some deciduous woods. Each have different birds and insects. Some of the hills are chalk, others greensand – both kinds sound different. Some of the hills are still home to the wildwood, areas that haven't changed for hundreds of years; but they look down on Gatwick. It's a post-industrial landscape; the wildwoods that are left were lucky to escape being turned into charcoal.'

We stood side by side, and looked south, out over the Weald.

'Do you think it's the best view in England?' I asked.

'Couldn't say for sure. But it's not bad, is it?'

What might my earliest Sussex ancestors have seen if they stood here, in 1520, and looked out across the pre-industrial Weald? The historian of the countryside, Oliver Rackham, characterises the Weald as 'ancient countryside', '*a hedged and walled landscape dating from any of the forty centuries between the Bronze Age and the age of the Stuarts*'. His description cannot be bettered:

Ancient countryside, the *bocage*, is the land of hamlets,
of medieval farms in hollows of the hills, of lonely
moats in the claylands, of immense mileages of quiet
minor roads, holloways and intricate footpaths; of
irregularly-shaped groves and thick hedges colourful
with maple, dogwood and spindle; and of pollards and
other ancient trees.

If Thom had stood here in 1720 the view would have been very different. Charcoal smoke would be rising from the Wealden iron forges, the nearest at Abinger Hammer. The flames might have been visible, the smoke tasting at the back of his mouth, the sound of the great water-driven hammers ringing in the air. The Tillingbourne was an industrial river, its waters black with waste. In 1676, the year of Thom's birth, the diarist John Evelyn wrote to John Aubrey, 'I do not remember to have seen such Variety of Mills and Works upon so narrow a brook, and in so little a compass; there being mills for Corn, Cloth, Brass, Iron, Powder &c.' Powder in this sense means gunpowder; the Tillingbourne Valley was the largest manufacturing site for gunpowder in England for years after the Civil War. Paper-milling started a few years after Evelyn's visit; if Thom had stood there, in 1720, paper making would have been just getting going. The mills became known for the high quality of the paper they produced; such high quality that it was used for banknotes. William Cobbett, visiting in 1822, called gunpowder and banknotes 'damnable inventions', noting that the little Tillingbourne Valley, now so bucolic and quiet (apart from the roar of traffic and the contented purr of estate agents), was the place from which both had come.

We buried the ashes of Alan Marchant, my birth father, in Shalford, in 2010. His wish was that most of his ashes be buried in Shalford, but that the remainder be scattered into the Tillingbourne. It was an odd funeral, given that half of the people there (me, my half-sister, her mum) didn't actually like him at all. The others didn't know him. After the formal ceremony, I walked with what was left of his ashes down to the little bridge over the Tillingbourne, just above its confluence with the Wey. I tilted the box, and made to pour the remaining ashes into the stream.

'Goodbye Dad,' I said. 'You never knew how to live.'

At this point, I dropped the whole box into the water, without meaning to. I watched it bob along the little stream, and round the corner into the Wey. I reflected that a lot of ashes had been dumped into that river over the years, and one more box wouldn't hurt. Bit harsh, I now realise. After all, he was, if nothing else, the first Marchant I met.

Shortly after Hilary had discovered the family tree, and the link to Thom Marchant's diary, my granddaughter Cordelia, who was just eight, asked me:

'What was the name of the oldest Marchant?'

'Ah,' I said, 'that's a very interesting question. It's hard to be sure, of course; we come from the Ardennes, but there are various ancestors we might be able to trace back as far as the Pas-de-Calais in the thirteenth century ...'

'Just the name, Grandpop,' she said. I blushed.

'Jean-Jacques de Marchant.'

'Thank you Grandpop. That was all I wanted to know.'

Despite my bold assertions, it's difficult to find out for sure what the de Marchants actually did in Sussex. There are records of a Hugh Marchant working at the forges in Robertsbridge and Abinger Hammer, but whether he was an actual relative I'm not certain. The parish records show that Jean-Baptiste de Marchant was born in Namur in 1466, and was buried in 1540 in the Ardennes, the place where we all started. His father, Jean-Jacques de Marchant, Cordelia's oldest Marchant, was born 1435 in Namur and lived until 1518, so perhaps he came to Sussex too, or was the driving force in the decision to emigrate. We know Jean-Baptiste came to England because his son William, my twelve-times-great great-grandfather, was the first of the family to be born here, in Preston in 1520, and the first to drop the 'de'.

When Hilary first showed me the family tree I got excited that we had some Lancashire roots; but she disabused me of this conceit, pointing out that it was Preston village, then a farming community a couple of miles inland from the smouldering remains of the fishing town of Brighthelmstone, which had been burned to the ground by French raiders in 1514. Now, Preston is a suburb of Brighton, but St. Peter's Church is still there, where some of my ancestors were married and later buried. In 1986, my band played at the Brighton Urban Free Festival in Preston Park, about a quarter of a mile from the church, and I hope we didn't disturb the sleepers, or, at least, that they dug our groovy fusion of post-punk pop and free jazz.

Jean-Baptiste's wife (or perhaps rather the wife we know about) was called Habbine le Clercq. When they married he was fifty-two and she was eighteen, so I suspect she was not his first. The le Clercqs were another family involved in iron founding who emigrated to Sussex, but they originated from the Pays de Bray, between Dieppe and Rouen. On arrival in England, they changed their name to Clarke. She was twenty when William was born. Here, circumstantial evidence is stretched so far that it ends up on the fuzzy border between supposition and fiction, but let's do it anyway ...

There were several families called 'de Marchant', all originating in the Ardennes (and all related), many of them involved with iron working in its various forms. The most successful branch of the de Marchants came from Bouvignes-sur-Meuse, sixteen miles upstream from Namur city, but still in the old Burgundian county of Namur. Dinant, on the opposite bank, owed its allegiance to the bishops of Liège, rather than the counts of Namur, so the two settlements were in permanent conflict. But this branch of the family stuck around while we buggered off to Sussex. They specialised in making steel, difficult to make and highly expensive. Only the rich could afford a steel sword, and so the de Marchants became rich in their turn. So rich, that by the seventeenth century they bought the Château d'Ansembourg in present day Luxembourg, and changed their name to de Marchant-Ansembourg. They didn't just know how to make iron and steel; they knew how to invest in it. Because they stayed with the Holy Roman Empire, they were ennobled, and ended up as counts. They are still going strong, and are fairly high up in the pecking order of Belgian nobility. This much I know for sure.

I'm prepared to speculate that our de Marchants were related to those de Marchants; they were, after all, pretty much neighbours. So I suspect that old Jean-Jacques was alright for a bob or two, as my grandpop Charles Jesse used to say of the well-to-do. Jean-Jacques left Namur with his family because of endless political upheaval and war, and ended up in the Pays de Bray, Rouen, even. He was looking to invest, because he had some capital. In Rouen, he encountered the le Clercqs, and arranged a marriage between his fifty-two-year-old son Jean-Baptiste and the le Clercqs' eighteen-year-old daughter Habbine. The de Marchants, hearing of the opportunities opening up in Sussex, took their portable capital on a boat from Rouen into the port of Shoreham – and bought land in Preston, from where the family invested in the nascent iron industry. Here poor Habbine, aged twenty, sold by her family to a rich old man, gave birth to her son William.

This is the story I shall tell my grandchildren in future, anyway, whether they like it or not.

From the village of Preston, the Marchants worked their way slowly north. William's son Miles was born in Preston, but was buried in Edburton, a few miles north of Shoreham. His son Richard was something of an explorer, because he seems to have got as far north as Horsham, at least to be buried, but his land was in Albourne, about eight miles north of Preston.

Richard's son, Thom the Diarist's grandfather, was born in

Albourne in 1615. Inconveniently for my purposes, his name was Thomas; our Thom was presumably named after him. I don't know what his grandson called him, but I shall call him Mr. Thomas. In 1614, an unusual creature was spotted in the Weald a few miles north of Albourne: 'True and wonderful. A discourse relating to a strange and monstrous serpent or dragon, lately discovered ... in Sussex, two miles from Horsham, in a woode called St. Leonard's Forest ...'[16] Whether or not Mr. Thomas met dragons, I shall leave you to ponder, but he was born at the very end of the time when meeting dragons was a thing that was seen as at least possible.

Albourne is the neighbouring village to Hurstpierpoint, a mile to the west, the two places now divided by the A23. Mr. Thomas was a yeoman, which meant that he farmed land that he owned, and that he had the vote. Like other yeomen, like his grandson Thom in his turn, he collected taxes from his neighbours. In 1649, he collected taxes for the Parliamentary victors of the Civil War, which has led historians to suspect that he had Parliamentarian sympathies, but I'm not so sure. He was probably just keeping his head down, collecting taxes for the government, of whichever stripe. He was well off, that much is sure.

Sussex was largely bypassed by the main conflicts of the Civil War, not least because of its inaccessibility. The roads in Sussex, 'bad and ruinous beyond imagination', were regarded as the worst in England; the Weald was passable only with care. The armies wouldn't really be able to operate in such hostile terrain. In matters of religion, Sussex was split. Many of the working population, including the yeomanry, were Protestants, and Puritan Protestants at that. Between 1555 and 1557, seventeen Protestants were burned at the stake in Lewes. Iron master Richard Woodman was burned on 22 June 1557 together with nine other people; this was the largest number of people ever burned together in England. The Lewes bonfire celebrations on November 5th

16 *Admirable Curiosities, Rarities and Wonders in England, Scotland and Ireland* by 'RB', 1697.

celebrate not just the foiling of the Gunpowder Plot in 1603 and the landing of King Billy in Brixham, Devon, in 1688, but are also in commemoration of the martyrs, whose story has never been forgotten.

My grandpop Charles Jesse was a bit old to fight, and had very few war stories. I do seem to remember a story about accidentally setting fire to one of the huts at RAF Fairford. He may have told me a story about 'doping' wood and canvas gliders, but that may have been someone else. Clearly they were not great stories, or I would remember more. What I do know is that, as a child of people who were children during wartime, I grew up in the shadow of Hitler's War, which formed a large part of my imaginative landscape, as it seemed, and still seems, to form a vastly over-inflated part in the British view of what it imagines itself to be. War games with war toys, acting out stories we'd seen in war films; this was how we played. One of the lads in my class was called Wolfgang, and at breaktime he did a brilliant imitation of the scene in the film *Battle of Britain* where Goering is inspecting rows of Heinkel bombers, whilst the rest of us represented the Few, holding out our boyish arms and making noises to approximate Spitfires bringing down Wolfgang's Luftwaffe squadron.

Thom Marchant grew up in not dissimilar circumstances. His father William was born in 1648, when the Civil War was still being fought. William grew up in Cromwell's Commonwealth, and was twelve at the Restoration. Thom was ten when his grandfather died in 1686. Had he sat at the old gentleman's knee, and listened to the story of Hurstpierpoint in the Civil War? Of how Mr. Thomas came to acquire Little Park Farm as a direct consequence of the war? Maybe, even, of how Mr. Thomas was forced to fight? It would be very odd, if not. The story that Thom the Diarist heard his grandfather tell, so far as I can make out, went something like this ...[17]

17 As I say, something like this. Based on these facts, at least.

Hurstpierpoint gets its name from the Pierpoint family, who came over with the Conqueror. They imparked much of the land around the village, and hunted deer over it, somewhat to the annoyance of their feudal overlord, the Earl of Surrey. Their manor house was small, somewhere near the centre of the current village; they also built a small hunting lodge in their parklands. The park, known as Danny, was in two sections; 'the Great Park', of 400-odd acres, where the Pierpoints had their lodge, and 'Little Park', of 132 acres, which boasted a two-acre pond with carp and tench 'fit for the Lords's house'. The Great Park was dismantled in about 1570, but Little Park – the home park, in the centre of the village – hung on.

The estates in Hurstpierpoint (known by those who live there as 'Hurst') became embroiled in problems of succession, and in 1582 the descendants of the Pierpoints sold their Hurstpierpoint holdings to the Goring family. All four of the Gorings in Thom's grandfather's story were called George, which doesn't make for easy storytelling. The first two George Gorings built Danny House on the site of the old Pierpoint hunting lodge. In 1602, this passed to the third George Goring. Danny is still there, and it is a wonderful house. Built in brick and glass, it's in the shape of the letter E, in tribute to Queen Elizabeth, from whom George Goring the First had basically nicked the money to build it.

George Goring the Third was a bit of a one. He was, in one of my favourite expressions of the time 'as pert as a pearmonger's mare'. He appeared in a masque in front of James I in 1608, and swiftly became one of the king's favourites, mostly by acting as his chief fool. He was made a Gentleman of the Privy Chamber in 1611, and we can only imagine what that might have entailed, given James's fondness for a saucy lad. He was elected to Parliament, where he was seen as the mouthpiece of both the king and his favourite Buckingham. In 1625, George Goring the Third arranged Prince Charles's marriage to the Catholic princess, Henrietta Maria, the sister of the king of France, in return for which the queen made him her vice-chamberlain and Master of Horse. In 1639 he was also made Baron Goring of

Hurstpierpoint and vice-chamberlain of the king's household; by which time, the Wars of the Three Kingdoms had started in Scotland. Baron Goring was milking his posts to the tune of £21,000 per annum, because you needed money to maintain status at court. In addition to the now completed Danny, Baron Goring built Goring House, overlooking St. James's Park. You'll know the spot, because Buckingham Palace is now on the same site. He didn't spend much time at Danny, and seems to have made few improvements to the site, other than to plant a grand avenue of trees.

Baron Goring's involvement with Danny ended in 1629, when he settled it on his newly married son, George Goring, aka 'General George'. General George's wife was Lady Lettice, sister of Robert Boyle the scientist, but theirs was not a happy union. In 1636, her father, the Earl of Cork, wrote that Lettice was left to her own devices, and was 'solitary and alone in a country house'. They had no children, luckily for us, because then we'd have 'George Goring the Fifth to contend with.

General George was a wrong 'un. By 1633, he had run up debts of £9,000, which Baron Goring said 'almost broke my back'. Brave and reckless in battle, General George was more of a hindrance than a help to the Royalist cause, which never stopped him getting high command. It's at least arguable that he actually started the English Civil War. If I was a grandad telling this story to his grandlads and lasses, I'd say he did, anyway.

Political tensions had been rising throughout 1641 and 1642. Charles I had ruled by personal decree, without calling Parliament since 1629. But in 1640, Charles had recalled Parliament, because he needed to raise money for the war in Scotland against the Presbyterians, who objected to having the Scottish *Book of Common Prayer* imposed upon them. From the start, many of the MPs distrusted the king. There was a conflict of religious sympathy. Charles was Episcopalian, that is, he thought the Church should be governed by bishops appointed by the king ('No bishop, no King,' as Charles said), whilst the majority of MPs were Puritans, and sympathetic to the cause of the Scottish Presbyterians. Queen Henrietta Maria was a practising Catholic, and many suspected that the king had Catholic sympathies. In December 1641, Parliament voted in favour of 'The Grand Remonstrance', or, as we might say, 'the great big telling off'. It states, 'we do humbly present to your Majesty, without the least intention to lay any blemish upon your royal person, but only to represent how your royal authority and trust have been abused, to the great prejudice and danger of your Majesty, and of all your good subjects.'

The king took this as a threat, as well he might. The Remonstrance argues that increasing Catholic influence at court was the cause of unrest, and it ends by making a series of demands, all of which assert the authority of Parliament over the king. Charles was incensed, and feared for the safety of his family, so on 4 January 1642, he entered the House of Commons with an armed escort in order to arrest five MPs – who had been warned of his coming and were being protected in the Guildhall, at the heart of the City of London. Charles was forced to retreat without his hoped-for prisoners, and on 10 January 1642, he left London with his family, never to return, except as a prisoner.

From this moment on, armed conflict seemed highly likely. Some 30 peers and 300 MPs supported the Parliamentarian cause; 80 peers and 175 MPs sided with the king. Throughout the spring and early summer of 1642 both sides recruited armies. Parliament could rely on the militias, the so-called 'trained bands' of London, and also much of the Navy, because sailors deserted their ships and marched to London in support of Parliament. The Royalists, because they had the support of the aristocracy and many gentry families, could recruit cavalry regiments.

Meanwhile, General George Goring was holding Portsmouth, ostensibly in favour of Parliament. However, he was playing both sides. Parliament was on the verge of appointing him Lieutenant General of Horse, and sent him large amounts of money, most of which he spaffed away on gambling. But on 2 August, General George declared Portsmouth for the king, and offered it as a safe haven for the queen. No one was expecting this. Parliamentary forces at once laid siege to Portsmouth. Charles felt that open war was now declared, and on 22 August he raised his banner in Nottingham. A fortnight later, General George surrendered Portsmouth, and fled overseas.

At the same time that Portsmouth declared for the king, Chichester declared for Parliament. The king didn't want to lose the only city in Sussex, so he sent the High Sheriff of Sussex, Sir Edward Ford, to take it back. There was a gentry uprising, if you can imagine such a thing,[18] which opened the gates of the city. Together with a hundred horse, and some of the Sussex trained bands, Ford retook Chichester on 16 September. Flushed with this success, Ford decided that he had enough momentum to take and hold Sussex for the king; and so he set out to attack Lewes. In order to recruit troops, Ford ordered all men capable of bearing arms to join him, threatening that if they didn't he'd kill them and then burn their houses. Although he managed to get together a few unenthusiastic recruits from Mid Sussex, when they approached Haywards Heath on 6 December 1642, they were attacked by a smaller but highly committed Parliamentary force, which completely routed the Royalist forces, who lost over 200 men.

The place where this rout happened is now called Muster Green, a little oasis of blood-soaked history in the midst of the suburban sprawl of Haywards Heath. This was the furthest that any Royalist army was able to penetrate into Sussex for the whole course of the Civil War. To quote a historian of the period, 'The unhappy countrymen who had been pressed into service threw down their arms and ran as fast as their legs could carry them to

---

18 Such as you might get now if the local branch of Waitrose was scheduled to close, I imagine.

the neighbouring villages of Hurst and Ditchling, where we may suppose that their experience of the first fight on Sussex soil for many a long day lost nothing in the telling.'[19] This was surely one of the stories that Mister Thomas told his grandson Thom.

General George came back into England at about the time of the deadly skirmish in Haywards Heath, and fought bravely for the king, but stupid brave. He was at first under the command of the Duke of Newcastle, and he roundly defeated Lieutenant-General Thomas Fairfax at the Battle of Seacroft Moor, outside Leeds in 1643. At Marston Moor, a year later, General Goring commanded the Royalist left wing and led 2,000 cavalry against Fairfax, and seemed to have routed the Parliamentarians. General George was kind to his men, and, having overrun the Roundheads, let his lads keep going, to chase stragglers and do a bit of looting on the side. But Parliament was far from done; Cromwell led an attack on the Cavalier remnants of General George's forces, and drove them from the battlefield. The Royalists lost about 4,000 men; the forces of Parliament 300. Marston Moor was the moment when the king lost the North. After this, General George was deployed to the West Country, under the command of the Royalist MP Edward Hyde; who later, as Earl of Clarendon, wrote the first history of the 'Great Rebellion'. What did Clarendon think of General Goring?

> One whose course from first to last, devious, uncertain, and unprincipled, shed disgrace on the nobleness of his name and upon the honourable profession of a soldier. This man was Goring, than whom, on account of his private vices of drunkenness, cruelty and rapacity, and of his political timidity and treachery, scarcely anyone was more untrustworthy to be trusted with any important matters for counsel or execution.

19 *Sussex in the Great Civil War and the Interregnum: 1642–66* by Charles Thomas-Stanford, 1910.

But Goring was a charmer, to which vice the British public have always been susceptible.

In 1645, General George asked to be relieved of command of the remnants of his forces after a defeat by Fairfax at Langport in Somerset, and he went into exile. His father Baron Goring helped him find work as a mercenary on the Continent, where he died fighting for the Spanish king in front of Barcelona in 1652.

Meanwhile, his father, Baron Goring had enjoyed a fairly good war, even though money was always a problem. He had gone abroad with the queen in 1642 to raise funds for the Royalist cause, but returned in 1647 to play a prominent part in the Second Civil War. He had been ennobled while he was in exile, and was now the Earl of Norwich, but his behaviour at the Siege of Colchester was far from noble; even when the cause was lost, he refused to surrender. The people of Colchester, mostly supporters of Parliament, were starving because the Royalists had taken all the food. When the town fell, George the Third was taken prisoner and condemned to death by Parliament, but the sentence was rescinded and he went into exile to join the court of Charles II. At the Restoration, he was given a pension of £2,000 a year; he died in a pub in Brentford in 1663.

By then, the Gorings had lost everything. They had needed money throughout the course of the war, and began the break-up of the Danny estate. Little Park was 'dismantled' in 1643;[20] in 1644, Baron Goring instructed his Hurst lawyer, Ralph Beard, to split the Danny estate into lots, which were sold, or mortgaged and then remortgaged. Ownership was getting lost in a tangle of law, and the need for money was growing. In 1649 the Gorings had to sell their town house in Lewes to the soon-to-be High Sheriff of Sussex, a staunch Parliamentarian MP called Peter Courthope.

Peter Courthope was in his seventies when he arrived in Mid Sussex from the Weald of Kent. He had earned his money in

20   Which is to say, the fence around the park was removed.

iron and cloth, and was now looking to move closer to his Burrell relatives, who were well-established iron masters, based in Cuckfield. The Courthopes and the Burrells were intermarried, and both families seem to have employed the same long-term strategy to survive the financially disastrous interregnum: by purchasing lands from distressed Royalists and then arranging marriages with those same families to secure the estates for the future. For example, both families acquired land from the Campion family, and jointly compounded for his estate after Sir William Campion was killed under Baron Goring's command during the siege of Colchester. Old Peter's great-granddaughter Barbara married Sir William's grandson Henry. Thomas Burrell married the daughter of Sir Henry Goring, General George's brother. The Burrells have continued to do well for themselves; they own the Knepp Estate, ten miles from Hurst.

In 1653, Old Peter bought Danny House and 262 acres of the former Great Park. He didn't live long to enjoy his magnificent retirement home.[21] He died in 1657. His son Henry had predeceased him, so the estate passed to his grandson, also called Peter Courthope. At the time of his grandfather's death, he was an eighteen-year-old student at Trinity College, Cambridge.

Little Park, the old home park of the Pierpoints, was sold at the same time to the Juxon family. Sir William Juxon in turn sold Little Park to a Mrs. Anne Swayne in 1664, as part of the settlement of his uncle's will. Then, in 1677, Mrs. Swayne's son Richard sold the house and estate to Thom the Diarist's grandfather, Mr. Thomas Marchant of Albourne.

Mr. Thomas knew a good thing when he saw one, and set about rebuilding the old house, parts of which only dated back to the early seventeenth century, but were clearly in need of some renovation. That he could buy Little Park outright reinforces my point that there was money in the family. What's more, Mr. Thomas didn't buy it for himself – he had bought it, the house, the two-acre fish

---

21   Danny House is now a magnificent retirement home again.

pond and the recently dismantled deer park, as a wedding present
for his son William and his new wife Mary. A lead rainwater head
on the side of Little Park Farm bears the date 1677, and the initials
'W M M'; William and Mary Marchant. Their son Thomas, my
Thom, Thomas the diarist, was born in 1676, and so he knew no
other house. He inherited the estate and the house in 1706, on the
death of his father, when he was thirty.

As to what he inherited, I can do no better than the description
from the West Sussex County Council description of the house in
1957, when it was first listed:

> Early to mid C17. 2 storeys and attic. Red brick.
> Horsham slab roof. The west front has 2 windows and
> 2 shaped Dutch gables, also a massive brick chimney
> breast with half a crow-stepped gable. The attic
> windows in the gables have casement windows with
> diamond-shaped leaded panes. Sash windows below
> with glazing bars intact. Rainwater head with the date
> 1677. Door of 6 moulded panels, the top 2 panels
> glazed. The south front has 3 windows and another
> chimney breast now bifurcated on the ground floor
> with a recessed ogee-shaped opening cut through it
> which a sash window has been inserted. The front has
> mostly sliding windows. The interior has an early C17
> staircase and panelling with bench attached.

We have come a long way from the Great Oxygenation Event, 2,400
million years ago, but here we are. The Marchants have arrived at
Little Park Farm.

The 1st September 1720. A fine forenoon, showry after.
My Cousin John Lindfield sent me a teem to help in with
my barley and 6 people with it. Will Baker, the 2 Jarvices,
John and Thomas White, John Pierce, John Gun, George
West, Daniel Bide and our own people carry'd 15 loads
in all. I talked with Mr Jeremiah Dodson and Mr Richard
Whitpaine. Paid John Shashall jr 1s for bleeding me.

It is now 1 September 2020, and six months since our trip to
Belgium. It was unimaginable in early March that the whole nation
– indeed, much of the world – was about to be forced to stay behind
locked doors, with only their immediate family for company.

In my case, that meant me, my wife and my step-daughter; and
Thom, his wife and children, and his web of family connections.
Each day since I got back from Newlands Corner I have read Thom's
diary, and written as much as I could about what I found there.

In 1720, Thom wrote of carrying loads of barley with his
borrowed hands.

Today, in 2020 I wrote in mine:

A fine day. First chemo. OK so far. Saline drip to
open the veins, then a steroid drip, then chemo over
an hour. Then a saline flush. I was there 2 1/2 hours.
Read Wendell Berry on 'industrial fundamentalism';
'Our true religion is a sort of autistic industrialism.
People of intelligence and ability now seem to
be genuinely embarrassed by any solution to any
problem that does not involve high technology, a
great expenditure of energy, or a big machine. The X
marked on a ballot paper no longer fulfils our idea
of voting. One problem with this state of affairs is
that the work now most needing to be done – that
of neighbourliness and caretaking – cannot be done
by remote control on the largest scale.' In the evening,
bought 1 oz of pipeweed from (NAME ILLEGIBLE)

I can't read or write much more, not yet. I am more tired than I have ever been, and never more in need of neighbourliness and caretaking. And the company of family. The door is locked, the curtains drawn. The temporary lifting of lockdown regulations looks like it has been too premature. There's an empty chair beside the woodburner, a rocking chair. Come and sit with me, Grandsire Thom. We have a lot of catching up to do.

DISCERNMENT

in which the Author learns about time-keeping, why thermometers matter, Frost Fairs, strange appearances in the sky, how easy it is to lose one's pocket, dry hygiene and its consequence, how to grow your own underwear, the History of Fishes (and how to feed them with turds), rhubarb, village cricket, prizefighting, hare coursing, smock racing, turnips and why they matter almost as much as thermometers, how Dr. Johnson spent his time as an undergraduate, what to do with an advowson, how to collect a folk song and then sing it, the Divine Right of Queens, the fate of the Bishop of Bath and Wells, emmets, zenanas, mountebanks, what to do if your master is a man without honour, how failed rebellions end, why childhood inoculation is an age-old good thing, and sundry other remarkable persons and places; with pictures of several memorable passages.

V.

SAY NO ILL OF THE YEAR
TILL IT BE PAST

Mr. Thomas Marchant, of Little Park, Hurstpierpoint, Sussex, started keeping his diary on 29 September 1714. Thom had taken over the farm at the death of his father eight years before. He was thirty-eight years old, and married to Elizabeth Stone of Rusper, a Wealden village some twenty miles north, on the other side of Horsham. In 1714, she was thirty-five years old. She gave birth to eleven children between 1701 and 1717. At the time of the first entry, Thom and Elizabeth had two sons living, William, thirteen, and Jack, six – Will and Jacky to their mother and father – and three daughters, Elizabeth, ten, Mary, seven, and Molly, who was just four. Two more daughters were born during the time that Thom kept his diary; Ann, born in 1715, and Kitty, the last of them, born in 1717.

This is the first entry:

> The 29th September 1714 Wednesday, Michaelmas.
> A dry day. John Shelly went away. Sent 4 pigs to fatting
> yesterday. Lent Ja Reed 4 oxen. Paid John Gun a guinea.
> Went by Henfield to Stenning Fair and receiv'd 31s-6d of
> John Goffe part of three guineas I had lent him. I bought
> 5 runts of Thomas Joanes at £16. I drank with Thomas
> Vinall of Cowfold at John Beard's. Met with John Gold
> of Brighthelmstone at Bramber as we were comeing home
> and concluded as he should have a load of wheat at £7-10s
> deliver'd a Fryday senight next at the Rock but we agreed

for no barley because somebody had told him 'twas mow
burn'd. Ned Grey kept holy day. Took 22 pigeons.

It could serve as an example chosen at random, so like is it to many
other entries. The diary is a record of Thom's business, as much
as it is anything. It starts at Michaelmas because Michaelmas is
traditionally regarded as the start of the farming year. It was a time
of hiring fairs. That's why the first entry records the departure of
John Shelly. He would have been a farm hand, or a servant, and
at Michaelmas his contract would have been up. Perhaps he had a
better offer elsewhere, or perhaps Thomas (or Elizabeth) didn't
think much of him.

So Michaelmas was a time of beginnings, as it is still. The harvest
is home. By day, the weather is often sunny and warm, but there's a
refreshing chill in the evenings. Time to get started again, after the
work of harvest (or the languor of summer). It makes sense to start
a farm diary at Michaelmas. Except, why this Michaelmas? Thom
had been master of Little Park Farm since he was thirty. Why start
it now? I think that he started it at this moment because Britain
had just undergone a great political upheaval, one with far-reaching
consequences for Thom and his friends and family.

The Civil War was resolved, to a large extent, by the Restoration of
King Charles II in 1660. He died without legitimate issue; although
he had at least fourteen children by his mistresses. He was a good
father in his way and ennobled his sons, many of whose descendants
are still members of the aristocracy, including one of my neighbours,
Lady Louisa Collings. But Charles's actual wife was Catherine
of Braganza, who was unable to have children, so on his death in
1685, he was succeeded by his brother, James II of England and
VII of Scotland.

James II was a Catholic, and that was a bad thing. His nephew the Duke of Monmouth, the eldest of Charles II's sons and a Protestant, tried to take the crown by force, but was defeated at the Battle of Sedgemoor in 1685. These days, Sedgemoor is mostly known as a motorway service station on the M5, the first such that you get to after leaving Glastonbury Festival if you are heading north, a place of blessed relief for those who've been holding it in all weekend.

England was not a Catholic country. It was an Anglican country, on the whole, with a small Catholic minority, and a somewhat larger minority of 'Dissenters' (Baptists, Quakers and so on). The head of the Church of England had to be a communicant member of the Church, and James wasn't. He attempted to establish toleration for both Catholics and Dissenters, an honourable thing to do. Attempting to rule England without the benefit of Parliament, like his doomed father, Charles I, James II issued a proclamation, 'the Declaration of Indulgence', which would have ended the punishment of both Catholics and the Protestant Dissenters. In a speech in Chester in 1687 in support of the declaration, he said, 'Suppose there should be a law made that all black men be imprisoned; it would be unreasonable and we had as little reason to quarrel with other men for being of different religious opinions as for being of different complexions.' No one now would disagree with that; in 1687 the great majority of English people did.

James II had two daughters by his first wife, Anne Hyde. These were Mary and Anne, both Protestants, and therefore acceptable as heirs, but on 10 June 1688, James II's devout Catholic second wife, Mary of Modena, gave birth to a son, James Francis Edward Stuart, who would become known as the 'Old Pretender'. His parents were Catholic, and he was christened into the Roman Catholic Church. England did not want another Catholic monarch. This was the crisis that caused a number of Whig peers to invite James II's daughter Mary's husband, William of Orange, to invade England, and claim the throne for himself and his beloved wife. The invasion fleet, long in preparation, landed in Brixham, in Torbay, on

5 November 1688. The landing of King Billy is commemorated by the Orange Lodges of Scotland and Northern Ireland; they get their name from him.

William had an army of 15,000 men, but he was determined not to use them. He had 60,000 pamphlets printed and distributed, assuring the English that he was only here to uphold the law and the Protestant succession. James II rode out to join his Royal Army of 19,000 men gathered near Salisbury, but it quickly became clear that they didn't fancy it; many of them deserted to William's camp. Since James II had been Duke of York before ascending to the throne, this incident is a contender for the inspiration behind the nursery rhyme 'The Grand Old Duke of York'. James II, fearing for his and his family's lives, turned tail and fled from London on the day William arrived, throwing the Great Seal of the Realm into the Thames as he left.

So James II's daughter and son-in-law were joint monarchs, William III and Mary II. This is the event in English history known as the 'Glorious Revolution' of 1688, characterised (with some truth) as the moment of the peaceful transition from an absolutist monarchy to one that exercised its power by ceding it to Parliament. William had effectively been chosen by Parliament, rather than by primogeniture. In 1689 the Declaration of Rights, which aimed to put the rights of the people into the hands of Parliament, was enacted as The Bill of Rights, still a somewhat wobbly cornerstone of the unwritten English constitution, guaranteeing free elections, and the right of any citizen (including women) to petition the monarch.[22]

William and Mary never had any children, and the king refused to remarry after his wife's death from smallpox in 1694. This meant the throne would pass to his sister-in-law, Anne. Anne had struggled to carry a baby to term; only one of her seventeen pregnancies resulted in a child that lived beyond the earliest infancy, William Duke of Gloucester, who was born in 1689 and died in 1700 of complications

22 It also granted the right to bear arms, but only if you were a Protestant.

from hydrocephaly, a build-up of fluid in the brain. William III realised that after Anne's death there was nothing to stop the Old Pretender (then aged twelve) from claiming the throne. The death of the Duke of Gloucester galvanised William III, who came up with the person he saw as the only plausible non-Catholic alternative; the seventy-year-old dowager Electress of Hanover, Princess Sophia. She was the ideal candidate, he felt; a granddaughter of James I, a sound Lutheran Protestant, and the mother of four healthy sons. Parliament agreed, and in 1701 they passed the Act of Settlement, which made Sophia, Electress of Hanover, the 'heir presumptive'. If, as seemed likely, she was dead at the time of the monarch's own death, then her eldest son George and his descendants would become heirs presumptive. Rather sadly, Sophia died running to take shelter from the rain aged eighty, two months before Anne. Had she lived a few months longer, we would have had Queen Sophia the First, which would have been nice.[23]

Poor Queen Anne died in the early morning of 1 August 1714, ill, overweight, careworn, grieving. At 1 p.m. on the day of her death, the Royal Herald read a proclamation to a crowd in London:

> We therefore the Lords Spiritual and Temporal of
> the Realm, being here assisted with those of Her late
> Majesties Privy-Council,[24] with numbers of other
> principal gentlemen of Quality, with the Lord Mayor,
> Aldermen, and citizens of London, do now hereby,
> with one full voice and Consent of Tongue and Heart,
> publish and proclaim that the High and Mighty
> Prince George Elector of Brunswick-Lunenburg, is
> now by the Death of our late sovereign of Happy
> Memory, become our only Lawful and Rightful Liege

---

23 The Act of Settlement still applies. In order to be monarch of the United Kingdom, you
    still need to be descended from Princess Sophia and still not a Catholic.

24 One of the Privy Councillors in attendance was Charles Seymour, the Duke of Somerset.
    In chapter XIV we see Thom Marchant become his land steward at Petworth.

> Lord, George, by the Grace of God King of Great
> Britain, France and Ireland [...] God Save the King![25]

George I then became king. He was fifty-seven years old, and about as keen on the gig as I would have been when I was fifty-seven. He never learned English, and this is still held against him, but what fifty-seven-year-old bloke ever managed to pick up a new language? I can barely say a word of German, and doubt I'd pick it up even if they suddenly made me king of Germany. He made his reluctant way to England from his beloved home in Hanover, and was finally crowned on 20 October; in celebration of which there were bonfires, one of them in Hurst with Thom in attendance, as he noted in the diary –

> The 20th October 1714. King George's coronation day.
> In the evning went to bonfire and from thence to Danny.

The entry is laconic at best, because Thom was a Jacobite Tory, very much opposed to the fix that was the Hanoverian succession. He doesn't say he is, because that would be dangerous to write. I trust I will present enough circumstantial evidence to persuade you of this in chapter XIII; although I can't make a case that would see him hanged. But I think he started the diary on this particular Michaelmas day because he had found a political purpose. Things were stirring. Two days later, on 1 October, Thom first mentions his neighbour Mr. (actually Sir) Henry Campion, who was a Jacobite agent, and to whom I shall return. I think Thom started a diary in the same spirit that I blogged after Brexit; in anger, in pain, in an empty hope that writing might change something.

---

25 On 11 September 2022, I stood outside the Old Shire Hall in Presteigne, and heard the mayor read out the proclamation of the succession of Charles III, in exactly the same words.

Still, the diary has started, John Shelly has gone off for a new life, the pigs are fattening, and ploughing has begun. We know this because Thom lent Ja Reed a team of oxen. The Low Weald is a bowl of clay, surrounded by chalk hills. The water runs through the chalk and into the clay. The soil is therefore hard to work, even after prolonged dry periods, and a team of two heavy horses, which might be useful in Suffolk, would not be enough to turn the sod. That's why Thom had a team of oxen; he was clearly both rich enough to keep a team (unlike Ja Reed) and community spirited enough to lend them to a less well-off neighbour. Thom had money to lend; but reading the diary it becomes clear that he is borrowing it too. So local was their economy that people essentially served as one another's bankers, right at the moment that banking was being institutionalised. Like other topics in this first entry, I'll come back to this later.

I wondered about the journey Thom made to get to Steyning Fair from Little Park Farm. I told Ralph Foxwell, 'I can work out all kinds of things but, of course, what I can't really know is how long it took to take a horse by road from Hurstpierpoint to Steyning.'

Ralph cleared his throat. 'Well, my brother and I took three horses from Ditchling to Steyning Fair in 1948. We set off at the crack of dawn and the sale started at about one. So it took about seven hours. But we were walking with them, and Ditchling is a bit further off. Riding a horse, that would take four to five hours from Hurst.'

That's how I can know how long it took in 1714 to get to Steyning Horse Fair – because my stepfather actually did it, 234 years later.

Thom had business to conduct. There was drink to be taken, pubs to visit. The road from Steyning to Bramber is now the A283, and part of my Slow Road between here and there. We learn from the meeting in Bramber that in 1714 Brighton was still Brighthelmstone. We learn that reputation matters then as now, because John Gold refuses to buy Thom's barley, which he hears has been 'mow burn'd' – i.e. is a little wet and fermented. But he does sell John Gold some wheat, to be delivered at the Rock. The Rock? Why is it capitalised? Is this Black Rock in Brighton? I don't know. But though the location of the Rock may be unclear, we do learn that as well as a fortnight, there was once a senight, for those who couldn't be bothered to say 'week'.

Ned Gray kept holy day. Michaelmas is, from a liturgical point of view, the Feast of St. Michael and All Angels, which makes it sound very important – but it was always mostly only kept in England, rather than anywhere else in Europe. Ned Gray was one of Thom's men. Was he particularly devout? Or did he just fancy a day off? Clearly, for Thom, it was perfectly acceptable to 'keep holy day', either way.

In the last entry for 1714, the night before Lady Day (25 March, then New Year's Day),[26] Ned appears again. Here we learn: 'In the night, Ned Grey ran away. Mr Jeremiah Dodson's man Thomas King went to London with his master's horse today and I am apt to think Ned Grey met him on the road and went with him.' I am unable to answer the question as to whether Ned was devout, or a chancer who fancied Michaelmas day off, or both. But why did Ned Grey run away? Lady Day, like Michaelmas, is a time of hiring and firing. Perhaps Ned knew he didn't have to stay if he didn't want to. Perhaps Ned was a ne'er-do-well. Or just a young lad who fancied an adventure. But perhaps Thom was a hard master.

And to cap it all, after a long day of travel, drinking and business, Thomas walked his land, on this dry day, with a gun tucked under his arm, and a dog for company, as he hunted his twenty-two pigeons.

Themes that will recur as I get to know my family appear in this first entry. Day-to-day farming, local economies, travel, technology, faith, going down the pub for a laugh with your mates – it's all here. But it doesn't make sense to start at the beginning, and to read it at this pace.

26   All dates are in 'Old Style', unless stated otherwise.

My aim is to reanimate Thom, to enchant him back to life. I want to feel him breathing down my neck as I write. I want to make him stutter into almost life, like the hologram of Princess Leia, trying to get a message to me, to learn what he might say, what wisdom the grandfather of all my grandfathers might wish to pass on to me.

So I will approach the thing systematically, rather than chronologically, and I shall start with the two things that appear in every post: the date and the weather. If I am to draw as close as possible to Thom and his (my) family, I need to begin by taking neither for granted. Both are different now, from how they were then. He lived in different times, in every sense, and he breathed different air. Slower time, and colder air.

VI

DEATH KEEPS NO CALENDAR

> The 1st May 1727. A very fine hot day. I were at Lindfield
> Fair. Bought a barren heifer of Ed Hayler at 5s. Paid him
> for her. H Bull and I din'd together at an ale house.

Thom Marchant's diary is a record of the farming year; but it
doesn't map onto what is happening now, outside of our
windows, in our neighbours' fields. As I write this, the calendar says
it's 12 May 2021. Goldfinches mob in the hedges, out of the corner
of your eye the bluebells are in their pomp, the house martins and
swifts have returned, newts are in the pond and the apple trees are in
bloom. This was not the case on 1 May 2021, eleven days ago, when
I was anxiously watching the skies for the martins' return, when the
bluebells were just beginning, and the apple blossom hadn't started.
But in the Julian calendar that Thom uses, today is 1 May, because
they were eleven days behind. So, on May Day 1727, martins and
swallows filled the air, the bluebells were out and the apple trees were
in bloom. Much of the old weather lore, and therefore the traditional
farming year, is eleven days out.

The Julian calendar worked very well for a very long time, so
much so that there are two places in the British Isles which still keep
it, at least at Christmas. On Foula, the most isolated inhabited island
in the Shetland archipelago, and in the differently isolated Gwaun
valley in Pembrokeshire, they keep Old Christmas Day, on 6 January.
The Berber people of North Africa still use the Julian calendar for

practical purposes, because the Islamic calendar is lunar, and doesn't map onto the agricultural year as well the Julian calendar.

It's named after its instigator, Julius Caesar. Caesar knew that there was a problem, because the Roman civic year was around three months ahead of the solar calendar. So your calendar would say May, when outside the window it was quite clearly February. Caesar hired an Alexandrian astronomer called Sosigenes to sort it. Sosigenes advised the adoption of the Egyptian calendar of 365 and a quarter days, and divided the year into twelve months of thirty-one or thirty days, except February, with just the twenty-eight. He also introduced the leap day every four years. The new system was adopted in Rome in 46BCE. In order to make it work, there were three months of catching up to do, so 46BCE was the longest year on record, with 445 days. Sosigenes and the Egyptians had performed one of the most astounding calculations possible, without instrumentation; and they were close. They got the year 11 minutes and 4 seconds too long. Added up over 1,500 years, those 11 minutes came to 11 days.

Getting the date right mattered, and was largely in the hands of the Church. To keep track, literate people had illustrated books of hours, and, when printing arrived, almanacs. The Church needed to know the right date in order to work out the liturgical calendar, but so did the serfs. If you had to work for the lord of the manor two days a month, you wanted to know what dates those days were. Unlettered people got the date by going to church, so the Church took charge.

Pope Gregory VIII knew from the Vatican mathematician Christopher Clavius that the year was too long, so in 1582 he decreed that eleven days should be knocked off, and that the fourth of October should hence forward be the fifteenth. He also decreed that the first of January should be New Year's Day.

The fact that the Gregorian calendar was more accurate didn't convince either the Orthodox or Protestant churches. The Catholic and Orthodox churches had split in 1054 because they couldn't agree the date of Easter, so they weren't going to start agreeing what the date was now; Russia hung on to the Julian calendar until 1918.

And the Prots didn't want to adopt this new calendar; it was popish, and therefore a bad thing. Beautifully, Scotland adopted it in 1600, because they deemed it less popish than starting the year on Lady Day. For 152 years, England and Scotland dated things differently, and not until 1752 did the English fall in line with Euro-time. That year, Wednesday the second of September was followed by Thursday the fourteenth. There weren't any riots, despite the old story, but historians have had to keep an eye on those eleven days ever since. Documents from before 1752 are dated 'Old Style', so when I quote a date from the diary, such as Michaelmas Day, it should strictly be dated 29/09/1714 (OS). Why does this matter? Because I want to know what the world looked like to Thom. So I hereby decree that today is 01/05/2021 (OS), and the bluebells are open, and the martins are in the eaves, just as would have been the case 300 years ago.

Most mornings, Thom got up with the sun, as farmers do, and not according to the clock. There are exceptions, when he doesn't really get up at all; sometimes on Sundays, when he is too hungover to make it to church, and some days he writes that he has done nothing at all. But whether he paid much attention to it or not, Thom had a clock.

There was a tradition of clockmaking in Lewes and environs throughout the eighteenth century, with as many as ten clockmakers operating at any one time. Lewes was a rich town. It had industry, after all, and transport to the sea down the River Ouse (before Newhaven was a thing). It had wood for making cases, mild steel, metal working; even glass was made in the Weald. On 16 December 1714 Thom writes: 'Paid John Gatland of Cuckfield 5s for mending my clock.' John Gatland was the second of a family of clockmakers operating in Cuckfield, and his son continued the tradition into the second half of the eighteenth century. There are Gatland movements and clocks still in existence, most notably in Queen's Hall in Cuckfield, which has a one-handed longcase pendulum clock by John Gatland.

It seems a fair bet that Thom's clock was similar to this one;

certainly, it would only have had a single hand. Time was not counted in minutes, but in hours, halves, quarters and half-quarters. Seven and a half minutes was about as accurate as anybody needed. A single hand was what people were used to, after all – a sundial only has one hand, if you think about it, a shadow hand tracking the passage of the sun. Mechanical clocks would still have been set by the sun, but also by the best clock in the district – as Jay Griffiths writes in *Pip Pip: A Sideways Look at Time*: 'Before GMT, nine of the clock wasn't nine of all clocks, but nine of an agreed clock, a localised clock'.

If Thom's was a longcase pendulum clock of some kind, rather than the balance lantern clocks of his grandfather's day, then it would have been an expensive piece of hi-tech kit. Seconds first started ticking in 1657, with the invention of the pendulum clock by Christiaan Huygens. Huygens has been described as the first theoretical physicist, and, if you were odd enough to want to rank seventeenth-century scientists in order of importance, he's always going to be in your top four, along with Newton, Descartes and Galileo. The 'Scientific Revolution' of the late seventeenth century would have been known to literate audiences by 1714 (especially ones who regularly dined with members of the Royal Society, as Thom did), but pretty much the only fruit of that revolution that anyone would have in their homes was a pendulum clock. Huygens licensed out his system of using pendulums to regulate clock movements to manufacturers who paid him a royalty – theoretically, at least.

Pendulum clocks were sold as better timekeepers than the balance clocks, but this may not have been the case. Although probably easier to maintain and wind than the pre-Huygens clocks, there is evidence to suggest the old style clocks kept time to within a minute in twenty-four hours. The old clocks beat differently. They clicked along at fifty beats a minute, slow as an athlete's resting heartbeat. The royal pendulum takes two seconds to complete its swing, tick and tock, with a frequency of 0.5 Hz. To have such a thing in your home by 1714 would have been a sign of wealth.

It might have cost as much as five pounds to buy;[27] spending five shillings on the clock's repair was a fairly high price. Pendulum clocks were reassuringly expensive. So they may not have kept better time than grandfather's medieval contraption, but they looked better, and cost more. They were a sign that you had arrived, that you were up to date, and in touch with the latest developments. They tick tocked. When did time start? On one level, it started a few years before iron, at the moment of the Big Creative Bang, i.e. 14.3 billion years ago, but, in another sense, it started one day in 1657, as Huygens set his pendulum swinging.

Throughout 2020 and 2021, I heard economists and commentators say over and over again that Covid-19 caused the British economy to enter its biggest slump for 300 years. None of them said what caused the massive hit 300 years ago, but actually, it was a weather event, the Great Frost of 1709. Thom had taken over Little Park three years earlier, in 1706, so he farmed through it. The Great Frost was one of the consequences of the Little Ice Age; between about 1550 and 1700, temperatures were lower than at any time since the last glacial period ended, 10,000 years previously. Glaciers started to grow again, forcing Scandinavian and Alpine farmers to abandon uplands. Permanent snow appeared on Scottish mountains. Famously, the Thames froze over on a number of occasions, from 1536 (when Henry VIII travelled from London to Greenwich by sleigh) until as late as 1814. From 1608 until 1814, occasional Frost Fairs were held on the iced-up river. The 1683 Frost Fair boasted taverns, shops and even bull-baiting on the ice. Enterprising printers took their presses out onto the river, and made cards that skaters could buy to prove they had been there. There was a Frost Fair in 1715, right at the

27   About £600 today.

beginning of the diary; the river froze so hard that the ice rose four metres on a spring tide without endangering the festivities.

But in 1709, it wasn't fun. As an indicator of this, the Michaelmas wheat price went from twenty-four shillings a quarter in 1707, to eighty shillings a quarter in 1709. The harvest was catastrophic, and there was widespread famine in Northern Europe. England was not the hardest hit. In France, an estimated 600,000 people died of starvation in 1710. It took ten years for wheat prices to fall back to pre-Great Frost levels. In 1714, it was at thirty-two shillings a quarter. So John Grey's 'load' of wheat costing £7-10s would have been more than five quarters; in 1709, the same money would have bought just under two quarters.[28] A loaf of bread that cost 4d in 1707 would cost 9d in 1709; but was back to 4d by 1718.

Frost wasn't all. On the night of 26/27 November 1703, central and southern England was hit by the Great Storm, possibly one of the worst to ever hit the British Isles. It gave Daniel Defoe the idea for his first book. In *The Storm* he recounted stories and eyewitness accounts of devastation from across the south: trees down, roofs flying through the air. In Fairford, some of the famous stained-glass windows blew out and had to be reconstructed, like huge, jewelled jigsaws. Hardest hit of all was Brighton: Defoe wrote that 'Brighthelmston being an old built and poor, tho' populous town, was most miserably torn to pieces, and made the very picture of devastation, that it look't as if an enemy had sack't it.'

Thom watched the weather every day, but sometimes he just watched the sky. I should like to have seen the sky as he saw it. Out here in Mid Wales there are clear nights when you can see the Milky Way, but Thom would have seen it on most moon-dark, cloud-free nights. In a world where the brightest artificial light was a candle, there would have been no light pollution at all. Even now, the stars are so bright that sometimes you can see by them. Back then, when

---

28   A quarter is currently accounted to be 28 lbs. It may have been measured differently in early eighteenth-century Sussex, but the proportions would be the same.

people's eyes were more accustomed to the dark, starlight would get you home on a clear night — what wonders they would have seen. It's a view that we can only imagine, one that is lost forever in Britain.

On 7 March 1715 Thom wrote, 'Last night there were very strange appearances in the air, sometimes resembling fire, sometimes smoak, and most part of the night much lighter than usual.' The astronomer Edmund Halley wrote about this phenomenon in a paper for the Royal Society entitled 'An Account of the late Surprising Appearance of Lights seen in the Air, on the Sixth of March last ...':

> ... this wonderful Sight was seen; out of what seemed
> a dusky Cloud in the N. E. parts of the Heaven, and
> scarce ten Degrees high, the Edges whereof were
> tinged with a reddish Yellow, like as if the Moon had
> been behind it, there arose very long luminous Rays or
> Streaks perpendicular to the Horizon, some of which
> seem'd to ascend nearly to the Zenith ...

Halley's paper is one example of a change that was happening in the reporting of natural phenomena; he kept careful record of the movements of the 'corona', based on observation. What Thom had seen in Hurst became, in Halley's hands, an accurate account of astronomical events. Halley was one of the great scientists of his day, and Thom wasn't, but it's worth noting that Thom doesn't see the same event as any kind of supernatural occurrence.

This is the period in history when observation and instrumentation started to be applied to natural phenomena, such as the weather. One of the early scientists who urged this approach was called John Ray, and I'll be back for him too. Ray scorned the old weather lore, and insisted that only by observation and record keeping could any meaningful statements be made about the climate.

How do scientists know what the weather was like in the past, and therefore that climate change is occurring? How do they know the world was colder in 1714 than in 2021? Iwan the Flat Earther, permanent saloon-bar fixture in my local, asks this as an a-ha question.

'A-ha, but how do they know better than me Ian? It was cold in June, and you tell me there's global warming? Anyway, it's sunspots. The weather goes through cycles, it's just in one of the warmer cycles. Besides, the Holocaust, blah blah blah ...'

The answer, Iwan, is in the question. They are scientists. They use science. That's how they know better than you. First off, they know about, and carefully take into account 'natural variability', and can estimate its effect. To work out what was happening in the past, paleo-climatologists have a series of tools that they have evolved over time to reconstruct past climate conditions. They look at written records, like Thom's diary. They examine tree rings. They look at ice cores, lake and ocean sediments, and ancient pollen. They examine oxygen isotopes. They date uranium dust. Iwan the Flat Earther at the pub doesn't care, of course. He met a bloke at the golf club who says that a bloke he knows heard Nigel Farage say that it's all made up by Brussels and anyway chem trails blah blah blah.

Life gets a little easier for climatologists after the invention of the thermometer. Galileo came up with an early thermometer in the late sixteenth century. He thought it might be a big earner for him, which maybe it would, had it been any good. A heated glass tube, open at one end, was placed open end down in a bowl of water. As the air in the tube cooled, it sucked up water from the bowl. Having thus been set up, if the air in the tube warmed, the water level went down; if it got cooler, the water went up, so it was upside down from the way our thermometers are read. The problem was, because the tube was in a bowl of water, the level in the 'thermoscope' also made it act like a barometer, because the water level was affected by air pressure. A closed tube thermoscope was invented by the Grand Duke of Tuscany, Ferdinando II de' Medici in the 1650s. They were filled with alcohol with bubbles in, like a hen do in Torremolinos. The rise and fall of the bubbles showed temperature change, and were marked off on a scale of 360 degrees, like those on a circle. This is where the idea of measuring temperature in degrees had its origin. It was instruments like this that were used to take the first systematic measurements of temperature, starting in central England from 1659.

The problem now was that their use was limited without an agreed scale. Where is zero? Where is one hundred? How do you begin to make sense of the information you've collected, if the chap in the next town uses a different scale? How do you take a temperature so that it can be used as a measure of something, if you can't agree on the result? In order for measurement to mean anything, you need an agreed scale, and scales have got more exacting with time. A cubit, the standard measurement of the ancient world, measured from elbow to finger. But whose elbow and finger?[29] It won't translate from one building site to another. Now we use metres as standard, and they are as long as the distance light travels in a vacuum in 1/299,792,458 of a second – or, a little over two cubits.

Temperature is a different order of problem. A cubit or an ell, an acre or a gallon, are measurement of physical properties. But temperature is a quality. A thermometer measures 'hotness' and 'coldness'. You might sell a bushel of wheat, or a pint of beer, but no one can buy or sell 'temperature'. And yet, without thermometers that conformed to an agreed scale, our lives would not be possible. The vast Process in which we are caught up relies on chemistry; and without accurate measurements of temperature (and time), chemical investigations can't really get going. Huygens was interested in the problem of temperature measurement, and suggested that the scale should be drawn between the melting point of ice, as zero, and the boiling point of water, as one hundred, which, very broadly speaking, is how temperature is measured today, if you use the Celsius scale.

In 1714, the year Thom started his diary, Daniel Gabriel Fahrenheit invented the mercury-in-glass thermometer. Fahrenheit was from Danzig, but lived and worked in the Dutch Republic.

29 In Egypt, it was Pharaoh's elbow and finger.

Mercury works much better than alcohol, as it's more sensitive to changes in temperature. So it could be more accurately calibrated than the earlier closed tube thermoscopes. But, calibrated against what? Fahrenheit launched his scale on the world in an article in 1724. He used three reference points. The first was ice, water and salt, combined in a 'frigorific mixture', which he knew would settle at an even temperature (essentially, the moment when seawater freezes) – this, he marked as zero. Then, the thermometer was placed in a bowl of still distilled water on which ice was starting to form; this he marked as thirty. Finally, he marked as ninety the temperature of the human body, when a thermometer was placed under the arm, or in the mouth. A later refinement took advantage of the fact that, on this scale, water boiled 180 degrees above freezing point, and 180 is an easy number to divide.[30] During the course of the diary, therefore, modern chemistry was born. When Thom wrote on 1 May 1727 that it was a 'fine hot day', someone somewhere, probably in London, could have told him the temperature in Fahrenheit.

To emphasise the point: chemistry simply couldn't get going until the invention of the modern thermometer and an agreed scale. Fahrenheit changed the world. Steam engines could be run efficiently. Chemical processing on a large scale could begin. The Industrial Revolution had become armed with a powerful new weapon. Accurate temperature measurement, as well as making industrialisation possible, also shows that we're doomed, unless ... unless what?

The third warmest, fifth wettest and eighth sunniest year on record was 2020. This is the first time that one year has achieved a place in the top ten of all three criteria. I cried when I heard this. Life is in retreat. We know it isn't going to turn out right. Be in no doubt – what was foretold has come to be. The world's richest and most powerful people know that irreversible climate change is here, with terrible consequences for all of us. They believe that accruing obscene

---

30   So ice forms at 32 degrees Fahrenheit and boils at 212 degrees.

fortunes will shield them and their families from the worst of it. They are in power everywhere, and the majority of the Earth's riches is at their disposal. They command vast armies and uncountable numbers of nuclear weapons. They profit from the entire infrastructure of the global economy, which is committed to the consumption of resources which almost certainly don't exist; yet they believe that only industry can save us from the consequences of industrialisation. They are not trying to slow climate change; they are trying to work out how they can ride it out, ride it out on our backs. They must be stopped, but I know not how.

So I call on Thom, as respectfully as a child in need of help should approach their grandfather, and invite him again to sit with me, and to teach what he knows of love and life and loss, of the frailty we all share, and of the tenderness we each owe, one to another.

The rocking chair creaks. The lantern clock beats slow time, as deliberate and as quiet as a sleeper's breath.

VII.

GET THY SPINDLE AND THY DISTAFF READY, AND GOD WILL SEND THEE FLAX

There are no pictures of Thom Marchant that I know of, but I would recognise him for sure, because he looked like the Marchants I know, including the one I see in the mirror. He looked like my grandfather, Old Charles Jesse Marchant, or my birth dad Alan, or Aunty Madge, or my cousin Dominic or me. We look like large cheery monks, such as might be pictured skipping on the label of a bottle of Belgian beer, laughing, pink-cheeked, tankard raised, a rope belt wrapping the cassock around our ample bellies. Big in body and heart, jolly and generous people, as befits the descendants of Burgundians.

Thom was tall, therefore, but starting to run to fat. Blond, but losing it. Long-legged. Not handsome as such, but what you might call comely. He took the sun well, so was tanned in summer. He had a highly developed sense of humour, was quick to anger and quick to forgive; that shows in his face too. And Elizabeth was a looker, like all the Marchant wives I know, which, thanks to my birth dad Alan, have been a fair old few. It won't really do, but it's all I have to picture them by.

Some things step out of the realm of imagination. In May 2020, we had a chance to hear the world as it sounded for thousands of years, as it sounded in 1720, and hopefully will one day sound again, when the car has gone the way of all things. This was one of the most unexpected delights of the first lockdown – the chance to hear how a village or small town sounded without motorised traffic. We came close to the ancient peace of this country for the first time in over a century.

When the weather was good, as it was in May 2020, I sat in a chair outside the front door, smoking my pipe, chatting to pals out taking their permitted exercise, and generally just guarding the border between Wales and England, which runs down the centre of the River Lugg, fifty metres off. Farm vehicles still came by – tractors as big as a house hauling trailers overflowing with dung, late-twentieth-century pick-ups with a few bales of hay or a couple of sheepdogs in the back – but cars had pretty much stopped going past our house. In the normal course of things, it's usually possible to hear some surface noise from the Knighton road, almost a mile away, as sound travels up the valley of the Lugg, but in late spring 2020, there was nothing. In the high blue sky, 30,000 feet above our heads, occasional airliners still left their trails, but they flew too high to be heard. One afternoon I watched a hang-glider and a red kite compete for uplift in the thermals. My neighbour told me that a goshawk had been visiting his garden.

The street was loud with bird song – wood pigeons, chattering jackdaws, blackbirds, sparrows, owls at night, thrushes, house martins and swifts, who make a sound like far-off referees' whistles. At certain times of the year, you can hear otters screaming in the river. Trout rise to catch flies on summer evenings. From our neighbours' farm, on the English side of the river, I could hear lowing cattle and bleating lambs, and a cock who crows. The curfew bell in the church tower still rang at 7.30 every night. All this, Thom and Elizabeth would have heard at Little Park Farm in 1720. All that disturbed our eighteenth-century peace was Dai Drugs and his mates, who sat on the bridge getting wankered, as is their wont; and the RAF and USAF, who, once every three weeks or so, still flew exercises a few hundred feet above our heads. US F-15s, Chinook helicopters and huge C4 transporters flying low came screaming up the valley, turned before they got to the heights of the Radnor Forest and flew back down again, which wee jaunts I hope they enjoyed – I can't say I did.

One May evening, sitting outside listening to the world, smoking a pipe, I wondered to what extent Thom and I would have been seeing the same flowers, 300 years apart. We both would have seen snowdrops and daffodils, but his were wild, whilst ours are cultivars. The Radnor Valley was a centre for daffodil cultivation and breeding before Beeching closed our railway, so we get to see a wide variety, whereas Thom would only have seen one or two different types. Our neighbour across the river, Andrew of Bridge Farm, has an astonishing white magnolia tree. Magnolias seem to go well round here; Thom had most probably never seen one, since the first specimen only arrived in England from America in 1687. He'd probably seen a few tulips, but only a few. The tulip mania which gripped Holland in the 1630s was long gone by 1720, but the bulbs were still expensive and rare.

The house opposite from ours has roses climbing up the walls, pink as a maiden's blush, but they too are cultivars, hybrids using the China tea rose, which only arrived in the nineteenth century. The roses in Thom's hedges were less spectacular, but they were at least Shakespearean; 'sweet musk roses and eglantines'. If flowers were in Shakespeare, they were probably in Thom's garden – scented night stocks, columbines, heartsease, honesty; but mostly flowers would have been an afterthought. Gardens, like most things in Thom's world, needed to work for their living. There was a kitchen garden for vegetables, but the nearest thing that we would have recognised as a garden would have been for growing herbs, for cooking and for medicine.

A year later, May 2021, and I was back sitting outside, pulling on my pipe. The street had come back to life. Proper walkers with alpine stick things crossed the Lugg Bridge into England. Joggers came by in groups, wearing pink hi-viz jackets. Cyclists whizzed past in two flavours, Lycra-clad or electric-powered. Most days, once or twice a day, riders passed on horses, but the most frequent passers-by were dog-walkers. Some of the dog-walkers were grown men in shorts, and some of them had tattoos on their calves, but they never paused long enough to let me see what they were, though I assumed wanting people to admire their calf tatts was the reason the men are wearing shorts in all weathers.

Anyway, who was I to criticise another man's tailoring choices? I wear pretty much the same outfit every day. A Radio Free Radnorshire T-shirt (I have several), a wife-knitted sweater in winter or a poncy Laboureur jacket in summer, and a pair of Big Dude jogging pants. Cancer treatment– like my implant to block the production of testosterone, or a side order of steroids to help the chemo go down – has turned me from an overweight into an obese person, though I'm sure pork pies have helped me over the line too. Jogging pants are all I can get into anymore. Lots of people seem to wear jogging pants even if they don't have to. They are dreadful things for an old mod like myself to be seen in, but I started to see the funny side, because the ankles are elasticated. I was wearing knickerbockers, I realised. I was wearing breeches.

It's reasonably easy to work out what Thom wore because he writes about buying clothes in the diary. But because Elizabeth didn't keep a diary, I can only go on what costume historians write about what she might have worn. Because she was a well-to-do yeoman's wife from a gentry family, whose friends were mostly gentry wives, I'm assuming that she was a lady who was interested in fashion. Her hair would have been dressed, but quite close to the head (by 1720, high headdresses were out of fashion) and she would have worn a small cap (elaborate wigs for women didn't come into fashion until the 1750s). Getting dressed would have been something of a chore. First, she would put on a chemise made of linen, and then stockings, tied above the knee with ribbons. Next came a petticoat, and then would come the stays. Small waists and cleavages were in fashion, and stays would have been worn by most women. They came in two basic types, front lacing and back lacing. If you were well-to-do enough to have a lady's maid, or at least someone to help you into your full rig, your stays were laced at the back; if you had to dress yourself, then they laced at the front.

Then came a 'pocket'. This was something like an embroidered two-sided bum bag, but worn on the hips, and tied round the waist with ribbon or tape. I remembered when I was a nipper my Bulbeck grandmother teaching me 'Grandma's Pussy Cat', a nursery rhyme in call and response.

> *Rat a tat tat*
> *Who is that?*
> *Only Grandma's pussy cat.*
> *What do you want?*
> *A pint of milk.*
> *Where's your money?*
> *In my pocket.*
> *Where's your pocket?*
> *I forgot it.*
> *Oh you silly pussy cat!*

I was prepared to accept talking cats with money and the ability to carry a pint of milk, but how, I wondered, could you 'forget your pocket'? The old woman must be mad, I thought. Pockets are in trousers; does this mean the cat had forgotten its trousers? Lucy Locket, you may recall, lost her pocket, and Kitty Fisher found it. Not a penny was there in it, but a ribbon round it. Now I know what happened: the ribbons on their pockets came undone – which shows that if you're prepared to wait sixty years, some things begin to make sense.

The next layer was a petticoat with slits in the side so that you could get at your pocket, then a skirt and sometimes a stomacher, a triangular panel to cover your stays, and finally, a gown of some kind. In the 1720s, this could have been a 'contouche', a highly coloured loose overdress often made from smuggled cotton calico from India.

At first these were just for wearing about the house, but daring ladies started wearing them in society – much as, today, the velour leisure suit is fine for watching telly, but is increasingly seen around the shops.

Thom writes in the diary of buying broadcloth suits from a tailor and wigges from his cousin in Lewes, stockings in Lindfield, a greatcoat in Horsham. The early eighteenth century saw the advent of the three-piece suit, consisting of breeches, a long 'vest' (since shrunk into a waistcoat) and a frock coat, with the cuffs turned back and possibly decorated with embroidery. The cuffs of his chemise would be showing, perhaps decorated with lace. The suit would almost certainly have been russet brown in colour, like that of Cromwell's ideal officer. He would have worn a 'neck-cloth', not quite yet a cravat, but heading that way. The stockings would have been pulled up over the breeches, and tied with a ribbon. Thom usually wore riding boots, which he also bought in Lewes. We know he had hats, because Elizabeth bought him one in November 1714, from David Douglas 'in the Cliffe'.[31] If it was to be worn over a wig, it would have been on the large side.

By the end of the 1680s wigs were all but universal on men. The fashion was brought over from France by Charles II, and as a good Tory, Thom would have wanted to follow the king's example. The wig would be a full-bottomed one, such as you might once have seen on a hanging judge. Since Thom bought his wigs from his cousin Peter, it's fair to imagine he kept up to date with wig fashion, and had the new-fangled kind with the hair pulled into peaks, known as 'horns'. These were expensive items, so you had to be on your guard against 'wig-snatching' gangs, at least one of which used trained monkeys to pull off the heist. Thom would have worn the wig when he was out on business, which must have been fine in winter, but burdensome otherwise. The best were made from natural human hair, the second best from horse hair, but all kinds were heavy, hot and full of nits. At home, he could take off the wig and pop on a skullcap of some

31 Part of Lewes.

kind. We can imagine how great this felt. We know that his head was shaved every four weeks or so, often by Jack Parsons, who charged a tanner a time. Well and good.

But what about his underwear? What of Grandfather's pants? Few moments in a child's life are more horrifying than seeing your grandad's pants for the first time. Imagine you are staying at your nanna's, and there, rippling in the breeze on her washing line, are things so vast, so shapeless, so covered in ghostly stains, that they are, at first, unrecognisable, until, with growing distaste, you come to understand what they must be. You look away, hoping never to see such a thing again, little realising that one day, your pants will be like that too. And yet, here am I asking for your attention, as we examine Old Thom Marchant's under-shreddies. Because, you see, he grew his own pants.

Before I can take you into Grandfather's pants drawer, I need to ask, Why Wear Underpants At All? It might seem obvious, but underpants, like everything, have a history, and one which is pertinent to my task of reanimating my ancestor, because it will have an unpleasant consequence for our time together.

In classical and early medieval Northern Europe, no one wore underpants. Instead, people washed themselves. The peasants in *Monty Python and the Holy Grail* who sit shovelling shit, would have dunked themselves in the river after work. Apprentices would put their heads under the pump after a night on ye ale. The master of the house would take a weekly hot bath; then his wife, then his children, then his servants. Pity the poor scullion who got to go last. In addition, some bathhouses had survived from Roman times, and others were set up and run by returning crusaders, based on the hammams they'd seen and enjoyed after a hard day sacking Constantinople or Antioch. They were often built next to baker's shops, in order to take advantage of the waste heat. These urban bathhouses were widely used by both men and women, who enjoyed different shaped tubs.

They were known as bagnio, or bordellos, or stews, and, as the names suggest, they began to gain a reputation for sexual licence.

After the Black Death in 1347, they started to become less popular, because they were seen as sources of infection. Hot water opens the pores and allows miasmas in, it was felt. From the time of the Black Death on, medical doctors became increasingly sure that water was dangerous, and the arrival of syphilis in the early sixteenth century seemed to confirm this. By 1500, the bathhouses that were left were pretty much all brothels. Both the Protestant and Catholic reformations condemned the sexual licence of the 'stews'. According to John Stow's *Survey of London*, in 1603, there was just one left, which seems to have closed shortly after. The last of the bathhouses had gone, from all across Europe, along with the idea of washing with water, which didn't really make a return until the craze among elites for spa bathing in the mid-eighteenth century. Even then, the idea was to 'invigorate' the body, rather than to clean it.

For 200 years across Northern Europe, including England, no one washed except in dire need. This does not mean they saw themselves as dirty, because instead of water, people put their faith in what was known as 'dry hygiene'. King James I was one of the first to fully go for this – his hands were so filthy that his skin was described as being like soft leather. Although people dabbed their hands and mouths with perfumed water, mostly they relied on absorbent underwear to stay clean. An Italian designer of castles wrote in 1626 that 'the use of underwear ... today allows us to keep our bodies clean much more conveniently than the ancients did with water' – and that, therefore, a modern castle didn't need washing facilities. Knights of the Bath were pretty much the only members of the aristocracy (and thus the only aristocratic members) who took a bath, though it was only a ritual one, at their initiation.

Raffaella Sarti in *Europe at Home* writes: 'in a society in which cleaning primarily consisted of changing one's underwear, washing clothes was an important part of hygiene'. Collars and cuffs were originally part of the universal chemise or undershirt worn by both men and women, displayed peeping out from under the outer garments to demonstrate how clean and white their underwear was. This is why in seventeenth-century paintings, people wear cuffs and collars of dazzling white, because the whiter your underwear, the cleaner you were. When someone had the bright idea of making detachable collars and cuffs, less time had to be spent whitening the undergarments themselves. In practice, people could go months without changing their underclothes; to only have one set was regarded as a sign of poverty. The soap they used was mostly fairly horrible – the worst kind was just wood ash mixed with animal fat, which might be rancid.

Actual pants for men, such as Thom would have worn, grew in popularity over the seventeenth century, replacing the earlier codpiece and tights look.[32] They were knee-length drawers, with a flap at the front, made from linen. It would be a wife's job to make linen underwear for the whole family, and a husband's job to provide her with the cloth to do so. Flax does well in Sussex; Ralph Foxwell told me about a neighbour, at Manor Farm in Bishopstone, who grew a field of flax every year. 'People came over from Ireland to buy it,' Ralph said. So flax was being grown in Sussex as late as the 1950s for use in the Northern Irish linen industry, and is almost certainly being grown somewhere in the county now. It's magical stuff in the field, like a distant haze of blue sea.

There are two different uses for flax. One is making linseed oil, and one is making fibre. If you are harvesting for seeds, you cut the plants; if you are after fibres, you pull them from the ground, roots and all, because you want the fibres as long as possible. On 15 July 1720, Thom paid John Haslegrove, together with his helper, the delightfully named Goody Keg, 'six shilling an acre for pulling my flax'. Thom was therefore growing flax for fibre, about an acre of it. Flax is easy to grow, and takes a hundred days from seeding to being ready to harvest. In several entries, Thom refers to the crop as 'Will's flax', so perhaps it was a first project for the lad. Certainly, both Will and Jacky got to carry loads of the stuff about for days afterwards.

Flax needs processing, and after deseeding the first job is called 'retting'. The stems are steeped in stagnant water until the outer part

32 Knickers for women didn't become widespread until the nineteenth century.

starts to rot, at which point the fibres can be separated out. There is evidence of this in Sussex (a retting pond was found in a rescue dig in Crawley in 2005, for example), and Thom had several ponds at his disposal. But the weather in July under the Downs may also have been suitable for 'dew retting', where untied bundles of stalks were left in dew-moist grass for a few weeks. When the stalks had been in the water-slash-dew for ten days or so, they were ready for the next part of the process.

Getting them out was not fun. I was told at Thomas Ferguson's linen factory in Banbridge, Northern Ireland, that retted flax stinks to high heaven. When the stalks were dry, William and Jack spent a good few weeks winnowing it, separating the hard part of the stalk from the fibre, then 'scutching and hackling' to remove all traces of outer stem and to comb the fibres to produce the fine soft flax – which is the colour of flaxen hair, perhaps unsurprisingly. At this point, if it was Will's project, he would have handed over the combed fibres for spinning. Flax is harder to spin than wool, and involves the use of a 'distaff', as well as a spinning wheel. Thom seems to have outsourced it; he paid 14d per pound to have it spun.

In August 2021, I made another radio programme for *Open Country*, the first since I'd stood at Newlands Corner interviewing Graham Dowdall. This show was about a visionary project to grow, process and dye flax cloth in Blackburn, and then to turn it into clothing. The group who are doing this are led by Patrick Grant, one of the judges on *The Great British Sewing Bee*, a wonderful human being who is committed to making sustainable fashion. The group thought they might generate enough flax fibre to make a pair of jeans at this first pass. They also grew woad (somewhat less successfully, it must be admitted) to dye the resulting jeans indigo. The group found an abandoned piece of land in the middle of Blackburn, then raised a group of committed volunteers to clear it of mattresses and needles, cultivate it, plant seed and nurse it through a heat wave, until it was ready to crop. I rocked up on the day the volunteers were pulling the flax by hand, and it was a beautiful thing to see, though it would have been an unremarkable sight for Thom. I joined one of the lines, and had a go at pulling the flax myself. It came away from the ground easily, and with about thirty people working together it took about an hour and a half to clear the little field. This was a thrilling thing to be able to see and report on, an act of remembering, of an unwillingness to forget how things were once done.

Thom would have delivered the finished yarn to a handloom weaver, of which there were many in Sussex; in 1720 he paid one Stephen Reeve of Lewes 10s 6d for eighteen ells of linen cloth, woven from his own yarn. The weavers made cloth on a piece-rate, which Thom fetched home in 'druggets', and handed over to Elizabeth, whose task it was to make chemises, shirts and drawers.

I wish I could magic Elizabeth's diary into existence, the equivalent of Thom's but about how the house rather than the farm was run. A large part of her day would have been spent making and mending clothes. The house servants, of which there were always two or three, would have laid and lit the fires, cooked and cleaned and washed clothes, but very often Elizabeth would have been making chemises, undershirts and drawers for the family and servants. We know this, because it was a thing that women at all levels of society were expected to do for their families until the early nineteenth century.

Thom's drawers were pre-industrial pants. The whole family were involved in growing the flax and processing the yarn. Everyone had a part to play – Elizabeth the sewing, Will and Jacky the retting and winnowing, and Thom the sauntering about telling people what to do. The money they cost was six shillings for John Haslegrove and Goody Keg's couple of days pulling the flax, four pounds for spinning, and ten and six for the handloom weaver. There were processes to be got through to arrive at pants, but they were all within the family's control and understanding.

By the end of the eighteenth century, hot water became an ideal, rather than something to be feared. People could buy ready-made underwear as the processes were mechanised and cheap slave-grown cotton could be had from the American Empire. Textile production switched from the next village to factories in Lancashire and Yorkshire. These were industrial pants, manufactured from Manchester cotton in the English Midlands. I grew up in these pants. We knew where they came from, because in *Look and Learn* or on schools TV we'd seen pictures of still-functioning Lancashire cotton mills and cheerful ranks of smiling ladies behind sewing machines in a Nottingham factory. I must admit, I'm happy that our more recent ancestors went for the underwear and hot water model, rather than either/or, as previously.

Now I have post-industrial pants. I just go on the Big Dude website and order high-waisted XXXX briefs in packs of four, £18.99. These pants are ideal for my condition. Obese and with one's waterworks in some disarray, I need them to stay up whilst also comfortably housing an absorbent pad.[33] They are the best pants ever, and will horrify my grandchildren in years to come . . .

. . . but they are made in Bangladesh. Under what conditions? I think we can guess. And where does the cotton come from? Xinjiang? Why not? Slave-grown cotton is still cheap. Remember the coffee? Imagine the process which brings us pants. Thom and Elizabeth knew everything about the life of their pants, from seed to seedy. We know nothing; but our pants are better than theirs, I'm sure. It's a problem.

Anyhoo, the point is, Thom and Elizabeth and the boys stunk worse than retted flax. We would have struggled to sit next to them for long. They scraped the sweat off their skins, and sometimes rubbed themselves with damp cloths, like I used to do at Glastonbury, and which, I can assure you, has little or no effect. You know your teenage son, just in from football and before he's had a shower? When Will got in from cricket, he stayed like that until the next game in a fortnight. They used perfume and powder to cover the stink, in the same way as I once bought some patchouli at Glastonbury to make me OK to sit down next to in the Tiny Tea Tent. I still smelled like shite, but now also of patchouli.

33 Younger readers – I am your future.

Perfumes used musk, civet, castoreum and ambergris – the ingredients which give modern perfumiers 'animal notes'. So they smelled good and strong, even once they were perfumed up. Come to think of it, it can't have been much worse than the Lynx Africa your teenage son has sprayed on himself after the shower. Thom and his family were stinkers, but, of course, they might not have minded, or even noticed, because so was everyone else. This happens still; you might go into someone's house, and they don't think it smells, but it does. Little Park Farm really did. It stunk of pungent bodies, cooking meat, wet dogs and unwashed teenagers. And it stunk of candles.

Little Park Farm was well equipped with windows. Two windows were stopped up because of Window Tax in 1718, but there are still two large sash windows at the front, and three on each side. There are two leaded windows in the gable end of the attics, and two glazed panels in the door. It was a newly renovated house, thanks to Thom's grandfather, but the interior was oak panelled, which would have made it dark despite the windows, I suspect.

As dusk turned to night, the household gathered around the most important and consistent source of light, the fireplace, which would have been the focus of family and social life after dark. Thom sometimes bought a load or two of 'sea-coal'[34] from Brighton (again, from the Rock) which would have offered heat and a slow-burning bright light. But the main source of heat, and thus light, came from the burning of faggots. 'Faggoting', i.e., the making of faggots, is the most commented upon activity in the diary.

To make a faggot, you collect bundles of sticks and brushwood or coppiced wood, and bind them tight with strips of willow. The brush burns slower when bound tightly together (like the fasces in a fascist symbol); a house like Little Park would have used about two tons of faggots a year. Week after week, the boys and the farm workers spend days making them.

---

34 Sea coal means that it arrived via the sea, probably in Newcastle coasters.

Hedging rights for cord wood to make faggots was a valuable resource; if Thom or his men couldn't do all his hedging, he let the rights – which is to say, the contractor who did the hedging paid for the privilege, so important was it to obtain wood for faggots.

Ralph Foxwell was taught how to make faggots by his Field grandfather (who is also my great-grandfather on my mum's side – it's complicated). But by the 1940s the faggots weren't for burning, but sold as bundles of thatching staves.

As night fell – later if he was down the pub or supping with friends – Thom would go around the house, locking up. He seems sometimes to have had considerable sums of cash in the house. He would have had a locking coffer to keep it in, and double padlocks and bolts on the doors and windows. There were certainly dogs in the house, and at least one gun. I'm sure he would have used it at need: in 1720, a quarter of all violent deaths in neighbouring Kent involved guns.

The house secured, his wig on the stand, skullcap on, frockcoat off but still in his vest and breeches, his quill in hand, Thom would sit and write the diary by candlelight. It's easy to imagine that candles gave off a light a bit like we have, just less of it. But in fact a 40 watt electric light is a hundred times stronger than a candle. Eighteenth-century candles cast 'a faint presence in the darkness'. These were not candles as we know them. They were much worse. There were two kinds of candle. One kind was made from beeswax, which burned steadily and with minimal smoke, but they were very expensive, and kept for best. Fifty years later in the century, the great diarist Parson Woodforde wrote of an evening out, 'Mr. Mellish treated us very handsomely indeed. Wax candles in the evening.' When Thom or Elizabeth dined at Danny House, they might well have had wax candles on occasion, and probably had a few at home.[35] But

---

35 Stormy petrels contain so much fat that on Shetland, people used to push a wick down the throat of a petrel carcass and use it as a candle, which must have made for a fun evening for your guests.

like most people in England in 1720, they used tallow candles for everyday use.

Tallow candles are made from rendered animal fat, usually lamb or beef. They spat, smoked and smelled. As they burn down, the light deteriorates, and they spread melted animal fat about the place, which no one likes.[36] Between 1709 and 1834 candles were taxed, and it was illegal to make your own; Little Park Farm bought theirs from a Mr. Picknell, an Arundel tallow chandler and one of Thom's pals. Lighting a candle before dark was seen as profligate behaviour, and was known as 'burning daylight'. So even tallow candles might seem like a luxury to the very poorest; in 1820, William Cobbett claimed that his grandmother never burned a candle in her life, but used rushlights, which are made by dipping the pith from rushes in rancid animal fat. Some of Thom's workers would have had little else to light their hovels.

Where did Thom write the diary, in his skullcap by a dim candlelight? At the table, when everyone else had retired? Or in his chamber? If he took a candle upstairs, once he blew it out, it stayed out. There were no matches, and the only way to light candles would be to troop back downstairs and get a light from the fire's embers. So, by night, the customary way to get about was by touch, by feeling the oak panels under your fingers. An old Welsh proverb had it thus: 'a man's best candle is his discretion'. People knew where things were. Furniture was often arranged along the walls so people wouldn't bump into it. There's still a seventeenth-century bench settle built into the wall panelling at Little Park. There was a 'great chair' in the hall which must have stubbed a lot of toes, unless it was against the wall. And people would count the stairs. Thom was born in the house, and had counted them since childhood.

He hears a dog bark, and gets out of bed, feeling his way to the

---

36 It's not surprising that in warmer Southern Europe and the Middle East, where fat melted easily, they tended to use oil lamps rather than candles. They were hardly used in Northern Europe, except on St. Kilda, where they used lamps fuelled by an oil regurgitated by fulmars.

top of the stair. He stands in his chemise and skullcap, unseen, undetectable but for his smell. He speaks aloud.

'One-erum ... two-erum ... cock-erum ... shu-erum ... sith-erum...'
He is counting steps.

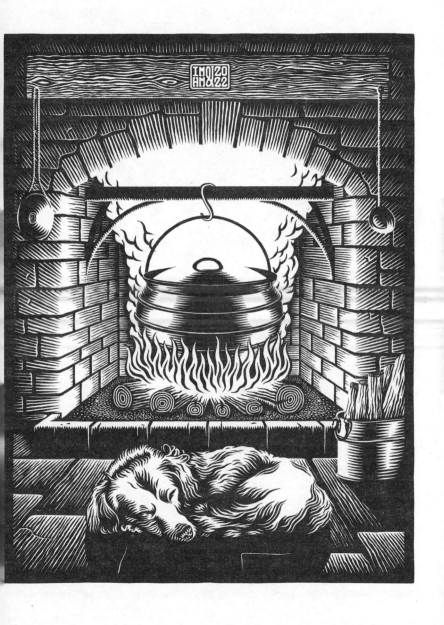

VIII.

SPEECH IS THE PICTURE
OF THE MIND

I call old Ralph Foxwell every night, just for a chat. We chat about Brighton's chances in the football, and England's in the cricket. We chat about Ralph's life with Mum. They were young lovers, who were advised not to marry because their mothers were cousins. This is why Ralph's grandfather is my great-grandfather on my mother's side. There is blood between us. He is my stepfather, my Real Dad, and my ascendant second cousin once removed. It's probably just as well that my mum went off and married my birth dad Alan, certainly from my point of view. It's also just as well she left Alan and married Ralph when I was ten. I get the best of all worlds. I got Alan Marchant's excellent Burgundian genes and a diarist for an ancestor, but I got to grow up with Ralph, and his persistent, never-doubted, utterly unshakeable love and kindness. I got to grow up with the gentle dawdling burr of his Downs country voice, telling me to get up and get going, telling me that everything was going to be alright.

Ralph's voice is all but unique now. He has a proper Sussex accent, like no one else I know. I don't. I speak what you might call 'received estuary'. A classless Radio 4 sort of voice, except my glottal stops are accidental. Most people from Sussex now speak like that. Even our neighbour Lady Louisa speaks like that, though she has no glottal stops, accidental or otherwise. You could probably tell we are both from the same part of the country, and that we both went to large Sussex comprehensives. My brother, known to everyone except our mum as Trapper, hardly bothers not stopping his glottal at all.

Gl'ol. Just very rarely can you hear the faintest rolling of the r's in anyone younger than Ralph – a couple of lads I was at school with had it, a little, but they are in their sixties, and I don't know how their children sound.

I asked Ralph about his grandfather's, my great-grandfather's, voice.

'He was broad. A broad ole country boy he was.'

'In the diary, Thom spells "Dorking" as "Darkin".'

'Yes, Grandfather Field said that. Daarkin!'

'How would he say, "One, two, three, four, five"?'

'Iden 'ow. It's been a long time.'

'Go on. I bet you used to impersonate him.'

'Wan tooo thrree foorrrr foive.'

If my great-grandfather Field sounded like that in 1935, it's a fair bet that Thom sounded much more like him than I do. Radio and television have put paid to regional voices. Between Thom and Grandfather Field, there would have been only a few changes in the way they spoke. Between me and Great-Grandfather Field, a world of change. Here is one of Thom's entries, from Christmas Eve 1714.

> Accounted with John Gun for thrashing 3 bushels of pease which is not set down anywhere. Sent home the gallon of oates I borrowed of Mrs Cathrine Beard by Ned May. Paid my Lord Treep[37] 1s for work on Willy's gun.

And here is a crude simulacrum of what I think Thom might have sounded like. For evidence I have used Ralph's voice, Ralph's impersonation of his grandfather Field's voice, and *A Dictionary of the Sussex Dialect*, by the Reverend W.D. Parish, Rector of Selmeston,

---

37 I chose this entry in particular because it marks the first real appearance of my Lord Treep. John Treep was a locksmith in Hurst and Thom's good buddy. Set in context, it is clear that Thom is giving Lord Treep his shilling in the Swan. He is Lord Treep in the way my pal Pete the Smith is Professor Smith, an honorarium between pals. His house is still there. It's called 'Treeps House' and it has a blue plaque on the wall.

1875. The Rev. Parish gives a useful guide to pronunciation, so here's my amateurish pass:

> Ecount'd with Joaon Gun far drres'n drey bush'ls of
> peasuh, wech is nart sit dowan any weirr. Sent ome
> t gollon a oao-tes oi barr'd of Mes Carth'n Birrd boi
> Ned Mai. Pay-ed Moi Lard Trip shil'n fer wark'n
> Welly's gun.

... which is no way for anybody to go on. Modern English sounds much more like the Midland dialect. South of the Thames, in Kent and the Weald, isolated from the rest of the country, accents were very different. We might have struggled to understand him, and Lord knows what he'd make of my voice, which would probably sound to Thom like an epicene alien trying to make contact in a high-pitched whine.

The Reverend Parish cites the sources for his dialect dictionary, the most venerable of which is 'Ray's Collection of Local Words'. 'Ray' is John Ray, and the book Parish refers to is called *A Collection of English Words Not Generally used, with their Significations and Original, in two Alphabetical Catalogues, The one of such as are proper to the Northern, the other to the Southern Counties. With Catalogues of English Birds and Fishes: And an Account of the preparing and refining such Metals and Minerals as are gotten in England*, published in 1673. W.W. Skeat, who edited the book in the nineteenth century wrote: 'It may be said that on the whole, Ray's is the most important book ever published on the subject of English dialects.' Many of the southern words are from Sussex, and were almost certainly collected in and around Hurstpierpoint in the 1670s, by Ray, when he was staying with his intimate friend and patron, Peter Courthope, at Danny House, to whom the book is dedicated.[38] Ray also published

---

38 'To his honoured friend Peter Courthope, Esq, of Danny in Sussex. Sir, Tho' I need
   no other Motive to induce me to present you with this collection of English Words,
   but that I might take Occasion publickly to own my obligations to you, as well as for

a collection of proverbs in 1670, called *A collection of English Proverbs digested into a convenient method for the speedy finding any one upon occasion*. Each of my chapters opens with a quote from Ray's *Proverbs*, which were being collected by John Ray at the same time he was collecting dialect words. So, astoundingly, we have a glossary of Hurst words and sayings in the 1670s, when Thom was born.

If this is something like Thom's voice, the next question I want to ask is, what did he talk about? Business, family, local affairs, national politics, are all there in the diary. But I think we can also work out some of the ideas about the natural world, ideas that we would now call 'scientific' that Thom and his social group would have encountered in Hurst. How might we know this, from a diary that is mostly about business and family? I want to say something about the intellectual life of Hurst in 1722, but I can't prove it, not as such. I must be true to my imagination, as William Blake insisted that we try.

I want to make a connection or two, using probability and common sense, as Lawrence Stone argued we must. I want to show that Thom had some understanding of the new way of looking at the world that was called natural philosophy, and is now called science; that he was not a 'mere' Sussex yeoman. And this is also because of John Ray, so let me introduce you properly, via the medium of children's television.

John Ray has at least two appearances in contemporary culture. John Ray Jr. is the supposed editor of *Lolita*; Nabokov chose the name because, as a lepidopterist, he revered our John Ray. The second is as the butt of a joke in the excellent BBC children's series *Horrible Histories*.[39]

Your long-continued friendship, as for the assistance you have some time afforded me in those studies to which I am, I think, naturally inclined; yet one circumstance did most especially lead me to make Choice of you for its Patron; and that is, that You were the first person who contributed to it, and indeed the Person who put me upon it; and so, it being in good measure your own, I have Reason to hope, that You will favourably accept it.

39 You can find a link to the sketch on my website, www.ianmarchant.com.

Scene: Restoration London interior. Samuel Pepys is
writing his diary, sitting at his desk as Secretary of the
Royal Society, when in comes Edmund 'Comet' Halley
for a bit of banter, before Sir Isaac Newton arrives,
and announces that he has solved all the problems of
classical physics in his book, *Principia Mathematica*.
Let's have a look, says Halley, who takes Newton's
manuscript, and says, By Jove! So you have! This will
be the most important book in the whole of science!
The Royal Society must publish it, Pepys! And Pepys
tells them he's spent all the Royal Society's money on
publishing a book called *The History of Fishes*. Who
needs a history of fishes? ask Halley and Newton,
dismayed. Fish historians, says Pepys. And how many
fish historians are there? One, says Pepys. Other than
the author of this book? None, says Pepys. Halley and
Newton tell him he's an idiot.[40]

On the cover it says Francis Willughby. But Willughby had been
dead for fourteen years when it was published in 1686; really, *The
History of Fishes* was by John Ray.

John Ray was born in Black Notley in Essex in 1627. After
grammar school in Braintree, he was admitted to Trinity College,
Cambridge when he was not quite seventeen, in 1644, slap in the
middle of the Civil War. Cambridge at that moment was controlled
by Parliament. The predominant question at that time was religion;
after all, the Civil War was, in large part, a war of religion. The
Parliamentarian commander, the Earl of Manchester, was forcing
students and fellows alike to swear allegiance to 'the Vow and
Covenant', which committed those who took it to support Parliament
and oppose the king, who had raised an army (it asserted) to promote

---

40   The rat at the end of the sketch tells us that Halley lent the money to the RS for the
printing of *PM*, and that Halley was repaid in unsold copies of *The History of Fishes*.

Catholicism; and also that those who took it will swear to 'assist all other Persons that shall take this Oath'.[41]

Ray was made a fellow of Trinity in 1649. Up until the Civil War, fellowship was only available to ordained men; but since only bishops can ordain priests, and by 1649 bishops had been abolished, John Ray got away with non-ordination until after the Restoration in 1660. He taught Greek, mathematics and humanities, and gathered around him a circle of young students who were interested in the new field of 'natural philosophy': Philip Skippon, John Nidd, Sir Francis Willughby – and Peter Courthope.

We left Peter Courthope as an eighteen-year-old student at Trinity College, Cambridge. He had come up in 1655, and he left in 1657 without graduating, upon his unfortunate inheritance of Danny – he seems to have been torn between continuing his studies under Ray and what he saw as family duty. But he continued as Ray's lifelong friend, sponsor and confidante.

Science, as we know it, is a consequence of the meeting of two great ideas from the 1620s and 1630s: first, that of using observation and experiment to understand nature; and second, that mathematics is the language best able to describe the world. Very broadly speaking, it was Sir Francis Bacon who advocated the idea that the world could not be known except by close observation and experimentation; and Galileo who proved the veracity of his observations by the use of mathematics. By the late 1650s, these new ideas were firing up Ray and his circle. He was supposed to be teaching them humanities and Greek, but instead he led his students on natural history expeditions around Cambridge. The old-school university fellows were not all convinced by this new way of looking at the world. It's easy, and wrong, to ascribe the difficulties they had with 'natural philosophy' to religious differences; in fact, the problem was one of authority. Previous to Bacon and Galileo and their disciples, it was held that if a thing wasn't in Aristotle or Ptolemy, it simply wasn't true. The

---

41 'Old' Peter Courthope, as a member of the Long Parliament, took this oath, so it's likely his grandson did too.

ancients knew how the world worked; the job of a scholar was to discover new works by ancient philosophers, and to interpret those that were already known. 'Natural philosophy' was an upstart field of study, which was slow to find favour.

Ray's circle of young scholars was engaged upon something new and daring. In a smart step from the sublime to the ridiculous, I knew what that was like when I was a young student; if you take 'the wisdom of the ancients' to mean Deep Purple, ELP or Pink Floyd, and 'natural philosophy' to mean the Sex Pistols, the Clash and the Damned. This may sound daft to the point of madness, but in 1976, when I started as a student at St. David's University College in Lampeter, there were only three or four other wannabe punks, and we shared a real sense of excitement, of us against the world. While all around us were listening to *Dark Side of the Moon*, we were listening to the Ramones' first album – and we knew we were right.[42] Ray and his tiny circle – they were punks, fired up by the new and contemptuous of the old. They knew they were right.

Ray's first book was the *Cambridge Catalogue*, published in 1659 (OS). It's a list of all the plants he and his students collected around Cambridge, and contains careful descriptions, not of the properties of the plants according to the old scholars, but based entirely on observations taken in the field. It's widely acknowledged as the first work of modern botany. Peter Courthope is one of three men mentioned by Ray in the preface, alongside Francis Willughby and John Nidd. He writes, 'we have been helped by them in no small measure in compiling this little work,' implying that Peter Courthope did some of the observations. He wrote in the copy that Ray presented him, 'Peter Courthope owns this book, given to him by a most erudite man. Author of the greatest part of it, his very

---

42 To push this creaky analogy to its limits, punk rock was something anyone could have a go at. You didn't need to be a virtuoso to form a band. Similarly, observing natural phenomena and recording what you saw could be done by any literate person – you no longer had to be Aristotle.

well merited friend, John Ray, Fellow of Trinity College Cambridge, 22/2/1659.'

This proves that Peter Courthope was what we might now call a lab assistant in scientific enterprise before the establishment of the Royal Society in 1660, and was therefore one of the first men in Europe to have a scientific world view. He was elected a member of the Royal Society in 1668, and so copies of the first proper scientific journal, *The Philosophical Transactions of the Royal Society*, would have been in the library at Danny House.

I called a friend since primary school in Newhaven, the entomologist Richard 'Bugman' Jones. Richard has written more books than I, including *Wasp* and *Mosquito* for the popular Reaktion 'Animal' series, and a brilliant book about dung entitled *Call of Nature*. He wrote the volume on beetles for the Collins New Naturalist series, which is about as good as it gets for a British writer on natural history. I asked him what he knew about John Ray.

'There's a thing that still exists called the Ray Society – I just bought a two-volume book on solitary bees they published last year. But his actual work is still really important. I'm writing another volume for the Collins New Naturalist series on shieldbugs, and one for Reaktion about ants, and I've been looking at lots of old volumes. One is by Thomas Muffet (whose daughter famously sat on a tuffet) called *The Theatre of Insects*, finally published in English in 1634. It's OK, it has some genuine observation, but much of it is rubbish, with loads of quotes from the ancients, like Pliny and so on. Muffet was especially shit on ants[43] – load of old nonsense.

'But John Ray's *Method and History of Insects*, the book that Ray was working on when he died, and published after his death, is a modern book, top notch, based entirely on his and Willughby's observations. The stuff from the ancients has all gone. It's difficult to use, sadly, because it's written in Latin, but Latin names weren't formalised till Linnaeus. Out of the fifty-five species of British shieldbugs that Ray writes about, I can only make out about eight.

---

43 'Especially shit on ants' would be a devastating Amazon review.

But the whole thing is based on observation. I've just been writing about ants, so I've been reading one of Ray's letters to the Royal Society, in which he wrote about how he obtained "spirit of pismire", which we call formic acid, by boiling up ants. Ray was a cutting-edge scientist; observation and experiment, that's what he did.'

In 1660, Charles II was restored to the throne, bishops came back, and ordinations became possible, and so Ray had little choice but to become a priest if he wanted to hang on to his fellowship. Which he did, for a short while. The thing that finished his career at Cambridge was the Act of Uniformity, in 1662, which made the new *Book of Common Prayer* compulsory in religious services, and restored episcopal ordination as the only route to becoming a minister. Fellows of Cambridge, as ordained ministers, had to sign the Act or lose their position. Ray thought long and hard, and wrote to Peter Courthope throughout his deliberations about whether to sign. If he did, he could stay in the Church and as a fellow of Trinity, but if not, what? In July, he wrote, 'I have already taken so many oaths and subscriptions as have taught me to discuss such pills.' He decided not to sign – and wrote to Peter Courthope in August: 'You and those like you, afflicted by similar circumstances, grant assistance to our situation; you are my only help and solace; you are the only consolation.'

Ray didn't want to be a clergyman or a teacher. He wanted to be a natural philosopher. But there was no such thing, not that you could make a living at. By refusing to sign the Act of Uniformity, he had made himself unemployable; and thus, it might be argued, on the way to becoming one of the very first professional scientists.

Two thousand clergymen refused to sign, almost all of them Puritans. This moment was known as 'the Great Ejection', and is regarded as the birth of 'non-conformity'.[44] Ray's biographers saw his refusal to sign as symptomatic of his Puritan sympathies, but there is no real evidence of this. Ray wasn't a Puritan, as such – he was

---

44 Baptists, Congregationalists, Presbyterians, Quakers &c.

simply sick of swearing oaths. From his letter, it's clear that Peter Courthope harboured similar doubts.

Courthope supported Ray financially for the rest of his life, but Ray's best-known sponsor was Peter Courthope's cousin, Sir Francis Willughby. Willughby was born at Middleton Hall, in Warwickshire. It's not far from Coventry, and is an excellent and most interesting place to visit, not least because it has a herb garden dedicated to Ray. Willughby arrived in Cambridge in 1652, an affluent son of the gentry. Most affluent students didn't actually take a degree (like Peter Courthope), but Willughby did. He was made a fellow of the Royal Society by the age of twenty-five. He was tutored in mathematics by Isaac Barrow, who also taught Newton. With an intense interest in the natural world, Willughby joined the circle around Ray, and became his colleague in the investigation of nature.

The historian of science John Gribbin wrote of Ray and Willughby: 'Both men were fascinated by the difference between plants, and unable to find anyone who could teach them to identify different species, they set out to provide their own classification scheme.' After Ray refused to sign the Act of Uniformity, he travelled around Europe with Willughby (at Willughby's expense) for four years, collecting and observing specimens, in order to understand difference in plants as the basis of their new classification scheme. They travelled through France, Belgium, Holland, Germany, Switzerland, Austria, Italy and Malta, and arrived back in England in 1666. Charles Darwin studied barnacles in minute detail for eight years; it was this intense work that made his name as a naturalist, and which was the bedrock of *On the Origin of Species* in 1859. Similarly, it was this earlier period of protracted and exact study that gave Ray the experience he needed to become the greatest British naturalist before Darwin.

After their return from Europe, Ray went to live with Willughby and his family at Middleton Hall, where he acted as family chaplain, so the pair could continue work on material. Ray depended on Willughby and Peter Courthope; in 1667, when Ray was elected a fellow of the Royal Society, they waived the fee because he was so poor. When Willughby eventually married, in 1668, Ray continued to live with his family. But in 1672, Francis Willughby died, and Ray was granted a pension of sixty pounds a year, comfortable enough to exist on, with help from Peter Courthope. In 1673, Willughby's widow remarried, and Ray was chucked out of Middleton Hall. He got married himself, and set up home in Black Notley, where he spent his time ordering and classifying his collections, and producing his books.

John Gribbin writes of Ray's work that, 'Most important of all, he established the species as the basic unit of taxonomy.' He gave the first working definition of species: 'members of the same species are never born from the seed of another species.' His taxonomic system, based on physiology, morphology and anatomy, paved the way for Carl Linnaeus, whose classification system of Latin names scientists still use, and much of which was based on Ray and Willughby's observations. In his *History of Plants* he classified over 18,000 plants, including rhubarb – he was the first person to suggest that the stalks of rhubarb might make good eating.[45]

Ray was one of the first scientists to take notice of fossils and to recognise them as the remains of once living plants and animals.[46] Because of fossils on top of hills and under sedimentary rocks, he was one of the first natural philosophers to cast doubt on Bishop Ussher's famous chronology, which dated the Earth as being created in 4004BCE. Ray wrote, 'It is a strange thing, considering the nativity of the World the age whereof according to the usual accounts is not yet 5,600 years.' Ray was the first person to attempt to date the Earth according to observation rather than biblical authority; he thought it had to be at least 30,000 years old, which is a bit closer to 13.7 billion than 5,600.

---

45 No one could like rhubarb more than me but it does have a somewhat dubious history. In order for it to become yummy, rather than medicinal (Parson Woodforde swore by it and doles it out liberally to his family and servants), it needs cheap, easily available sugar. Which then, and for many years after, meant slave labour.

46 But species can't go extinct because the Creation was perfect – Ray thought that the animals fossilised just hadn't been discovered yet.

In the preface to the *Proverbs* he wrote, 'All superstitions and groundless observation of Augury, Days, Hours and the like I have purposely omitted, because I wish they were quite erased out of the People's memories and should be loth to be any way instrumental in transmitting them to Posterity.' The old weather lore collected in dusty tomes should be forgotten, and new ideas about the weather based only on observation.

His most popular book was *The Wisdom of God Manifested in the Works of the Creation*, published in 1691, which avoids supernatural proofs of the existence of God. Rather, he uses science as Christian apology. In the world before the seventeenth-century Copernican Revolution, the explanations for the heavens moving or things falling were clumsy, inelegant, due to scientific ignorance; the new Copernican and Newtonian world view was simple and elegant, as befits the work of a Divine Architect. Ray argued that 'after comparing the vast multitude of different sort of creature to such contrivances as clocks and watches, pumps and mills', only the existence of a designing superintending deity can explain 'the Plastic nature' of living creatures.

London had not entirely taken over the economy and culture of England; people from somewhere like Hurstpierpoint could keep up with, and even be involved with, the early Royal Society. This was the time of Isaac Newton's domination of intellectual life; but Ray understood that in living beings there was the possibility of choice error and randomness, and that Newton's cool mathematical system of the world didn't always work with living creatures.

Ray, as I hope I've demonstrated, was a big beast, one of the giants upon whose shoulders Darwin stood. Peter Courthope was Ray's oldest living friend, his intimate and patron, one who had learned the scientific method from Ray at Cambridge and subsequently, as Ray made frequent visits to Danny.

Peter Courthope was also the leader of Hurst society. There are dozens of mentions of Peter Courthope and his family in the diary. The Marchants dine regularly at Danny and return the favour to the Courthopes. Mrs. Susan Courthope, Peter's daughter-in-law, seems to have been a pal of Elizabeth's mother, so often visits when she is staying at Little Park. They meet at other people's houses too, particularly that of Mrs. Catherine Beard, a Hurst lady of some consequence, whose late husband had arranged the sale of Little Park to Thom's grandfather. Thom acted as her land agent and Courthope consulted Thom on estate matters.

Peter Courthope's two sons both died in 1695. Colonel John Courthope, the eldest, died in front of Namur, during the siege of that city by the forces of William III during the War of the League of Augsburg. The younger son, Peter, died whilst a student at Trinity College, Cambridge, of an unknown disease – there's a memorial to him in Trinity College Chapel. This meant that Courthope's daughter, Barbara, was the heir to Danny and that ownership would therefore pass to her husband, Henry Campion, after Peter Courthope's death.[47] Barbara Campion seems to have been Elizabeth Marchant's closest friend and Henry Campion was another frequent visitor at Little Park.

Daniel Defoe described conversation as 'the brightest and most beautiful part of life', in coffee houses, in taverns and at dinner parties. What did friends in company do other than converse? Letters were seen as part of conversation. People didn't really keep intimate diaries until the arrival of the Romantic movement, at the turn of the next century. A diary was a journal, like Thom's, not a confessional. People confided their feelings in letters to their friends, as Ray confided his to Courthope. Later in the eighteenth century, somewhat elaborate rules evolved as to what might be conversed about but it was always the case that the most eminent person present would be able to speak without interruption. Did Peter Courthope talk about his old friend, the most remarkable person he had known, whose dictionary had been composed of Mid Sussex words, whose books were in the library at Danny, some of them dedicated to Peter Courthope himself? Of course he did. Thom may not have met Ray (though his father and grandfather may well have) but he certainly would have

47   In 1725.

known of him and his achievements, especially given that Thom was a fish farmer – another area of study for Ray – with an interest in medicinal plants.

There's a strange coda to the story of natural history in Hurstpierpoint. My Lord Treep, Thom's drinking buddy, was enough of a local character that his house is still called 'Treeps'. In the mid-nineteenth century, it was home to the family of the wife of the naturalist Alfred Russel Wallace and it was there, between 1868 and 1869, that he wrote *The Malay Archipelago*. That's why there's a blue plaque on the side of the house. This book concerned Wallace's journey to South East Asia, taken from 1854 until 1862. On this trip, Wallace and his assistants collected thousands of specimens, which he examined and catalogued in the great tradition of John Ray. In 1858, from Ternate in what is now Indonesia, Wallace sent Charles Darwin an article he had written, in which he proposed the idea of natural selection. Darwin had slowly been working away at *On the Origin of Species* for years, and Wallace's article panicked him, causing Darwin to present a paper to the Linnean Society of London, 'On the tendencies of species to form varieties', jointly written with Alfred Russel Wallace. *The Malay Archipelago* was Wallace's *Voyage of the Beagle* and *On the Origin of Species* knocked into one.

Although Darwin and Wallace agreed on how natural selection worked, they disagreed on the 'difficult problem of consciousness'. Darwin felt that the 'higher mental faculties' of humankind could be accounted for by sexual selection, Wallace that it could only be accounted for by 'the unseen universe of Spirit'. Darwin had started his career as a Christian, and ended it as an atheist, because of his work on evolution. Wallace was a convinced atheist who became, if not quite a Christian, then a Deist, for the same reason. I feel sure that John Ray, the father of natural theology, would have taken sides with Wallace.

John Ray died in Black Notley in 1705. You can still find his monument in the churchyard of St. Peter and St. Paul in his home village. It reads:

DISCERNMENT

John Ray Master of Arts
Once fellow of Trinity College in Cambridge
Afterwards
A Member of the Royal Society in London;
And to both those learned bodies
an Illustrious Ornament
What more did add to these bright gifts, we find
A pure untainted Piety of Mind
England's best Church so engroos'd his zealous care,
A truth his dying accents did declare.

Peter Courthope's eyes are rheumy; tears run easily, too easily these days. It is hard to be an old man, the last of your friends. He pulls down his favourite book from the shelf, and nods over the pages by the light of the fire.

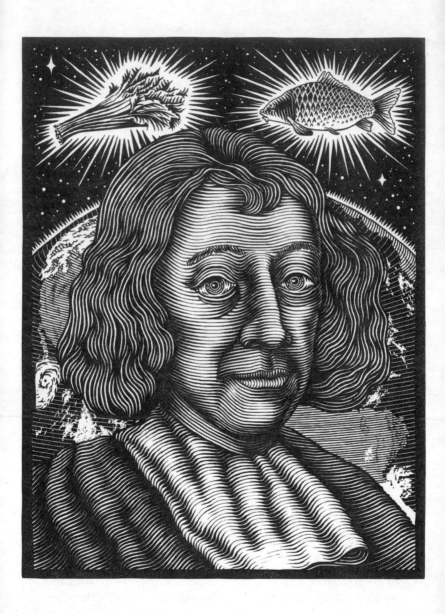

IX.

A MAIDEN THAT LAUGHS IS
HALF-TAKEN

Imagine if your seven-times-great great-grandchildren rocked up in a time machine, and told you that 300 years in the future you were in the history books – what would you want to be there for? Your extraordinary love life? Your world-changing inventions? Your work saving the planet from the damage wrought by industrialisation?

Thom and his boys Jack and Willy still appear in history books, current academic ones. Thom, it turns out, was an important witness to one particular part of social history. If I went back in time, appeared flickering in front of the fire at Little Park, and managed to croak over the fizzle of my not quite perfect materialisation, 'You'll be in the history books,' and they said 'What for?' and I said 'Cricket,' I imagine that they'd be quite surprised, quite apart from the fact of my being there.

But cricket it is. It turns out, Thom Marchant was the first writer to regularly record cricket matches. He didn't keep score, and we know very little about the games; but the history of cricket is continuous from 1717 onwards, because of Thom's diary.

I can't remember a time before cricket. My birth dad Alan and my Uncle Tony played for Shalford, where Alan was the dashing opening batsman, tall, blond, handsome, sociopathic. When we moved to Northamptonshire, he opened for Higham Ferrers, and after he and my mum split up he moved to Buckinghamshire, and played for many years for Lane End, where eventually, after his forced retirement from business, he kept for a time the pub that faced the village green. My Uncle Frank captained Ewhurst at cricket, and my mum had been a star of the village stoolball team, played on the same pitch.[48] Ralph opened for Glynde in a side that won the Cuckmere Valley League, and he helped set up a pub league in Newhaven, playing for the North Quay Social Club into his fifties. If Frank was short of a keeper, he called on Ralph to play for Ewhurst. His last game for Mum's village was when he was fifty-six; he took three catches, scored twenty-seven runs, and decided to call it a day.

When I went to watch the games, I would run around the boundary, play French cricket with my cousins, take tea with the teams and, after the game, help pull the great cast-iron roller over the wicket. At home, I would peep inside my dad's cricket bag with awe and wonder, and examine his bat, his grass-stained pads, his boots, his box. But, as a player, I feel that I have never been given a chance. I played once for the school team, when I batted at eleven for a stylish duck, didn't get to bowl and fluffed the only ball that came my way as I ambled about happily at long stop, or thereabouts. In 1978 I dressed as a cricketer to go to the Reading Festival, but was beaten up by some Sham 69 fans for my pains, which is the closest I've got to a game since school. But, inside, I know that I'm a cricketer. I can bowl imaginary off-spinners, and get you a knock of twenty imaginary runs batting at seven, I'm sure of it. Fielding, I admit, is the weakest part of my imaginary game, because of my poor hand–eye co-ordination and my inability to throw or catch a ball.

My Aunty Joyce would take me to watch Surrey, but only when they had a match in Guildford. Sometimes in summer, Birth Dad

---

48 After she married Alan, and moved to Shalford, she made the teas with the other cricket wives.

Alan would take me to watch Sussex in the one-day Gillette Cup games on a Sunday as a stop-gap access event until the football started up again. But, despite my inner conviction that I am, in fact, a cricketer, some of the finer points of the game are somewhat lost on me. My favourite bit of *Test Match Special* is the cake. I prefer going to village games, where home-made cake abounds. In England, in summertime, it's still a thrill to watch a game on a village green; not so much for the actual cricket, but for the enchantment of history.

Cricket is pre-industrial; that's why its truest expression is when it is at its least industrialised. In England, a cricket match on the village green is a true survivor of the world before industry. Its roots are deep. Its history is continuous from 1717 onwards; and that's because of Thomas Marchant's diary.

Sport was a bad thing, for a long time, unless it was done by the ruling elite. Aristocrats could hunt and joust and even play 'real tennis'.[49] Leisure was a thing to be enjoyed only by a very small minority. But people *would* insist on playing games, and so various monarchs legislated against it. Henry VIII famously banned ball sports, because he wanted men to practise archery. Football in particular was seen as dangerous, because it encouraged the forming of drunken, leery crowds. Hard to argue with, I guess; but until the nineteenth century, the drunken, leery crowds were playing rather than watching. Elizabethan Puritans in particular were against people enjoying themselves, especially on Sundays. A dispute about playing games on the Sabbath in Lancashire between a Puritan middle class and a large Catholic gentry with their attendant peasantry turned into a national problem. In 1618, James I attempted to resolve it, by issuing 'The Book of Sports', which permitted maypole dancing, archery and 'leaping and vaulting', but

---

49 A game somewhat like a cross between squash and tennis as we know it. 'Real' is a corruption of 'royal'. The tennis that is played at Wimbledon &c is now known as 'lawn tennis', but when it was invented (in Leamington Spa in 1874) it was called 'sphairistike'. Apropos of nothing really but a handy thing to know if you like a pub quiz.

banned bear-baiting and bowls. It was reissued by Charles I in 1633, who insisted that clergy read it aloud from pulpits, which inflamed Puritan sensibilities. So sport and games became pretty much illegal during the Parliamentary period.

No one thought to ban cricket, however, because it was just a children's game. The first time it's mentioned is as something schoolboys played in Guildford, in 1598. It couldn't be simpler to play: one boy stuck a stick in the ground, another boy tried to knock it over with a ball, and the first boy tried to stop this from happening by hitting the ball with another stick. Because no one had thought to ban it, and perhaps because kids had enjoyed it at school, it began to be played by adults in the early part of the seventeenth century. In 1611, two men were prosecuted for playing cricket rather than going to church, in the Sussex village of Sidlesham, near Chichester. That it was being played widely in Sussex became more evident as the century wore on, as men were fined for playing in East Lavant and Midhurst. It was being played in Kent, too; adult players were reprimanded by Puritan ministers for playing in Maidstone and on Romney Marsh. During the period of the Commonwealth, the adult game disappears from historical records for a number of years; but it was still being played in schools, certainly at Winchester and St. Paul's, where John Churchill, later the Duke of Marlborough, played it as a boy. Cricket makes a lot of sense if you see it as a children's game. You can imagine their mums saying, 'Play nicely. Take it in turns. It's time for tea, but you can play again later. It's time for bed, but you can keep playing tomorrow.'

Cricket is a product of the 'forest counties' of England: Surrey, Kent and Sussex. Because it is a team game, it became linked with what we might now call 'identity'. It was your parish against the next, your school against another. There were material differences from the modern game. The first description of a game comes from 1706. The bats were curved, more like a hockey stick than a modern cricket bat. Bowling was underarm, and the ball was probably a soft ball without bounce rather than a hard leather ball. There were two stumps with a bail on top. The leather ball rolled along the ground, and the batsman hit it, as a hockey player would, and ran to touch a stave that was held by an umpire to score, rather than between two wickets.

As England emerged from the period of the Commonwealth, so the adult game re-entered history. From fairly early on, there were often more people watching than playing, and this is because it had become useful as a medium for gambling, as the crowds could bet on the outcome. The game spread to London, and games were played in Islington, on the site of King's Cross station. Advertisements for games appeared in London papers from 1700 on. Each of the players would put in a certain sum of money, and the winning side would collect the pot, while the fans placed bets.

Now I need to quote a chunk of Derek Birley's magisterial *Social History of English Cricket* (1999):

> London cricket may have got more publicity but the game was more deeply rooted in the rural south. In Sussex, for example, there was a regular circuit of inter-parish matches played on village greens, on commons, or in parks belonging to local squires. There may well have been some betting by some of the players but, if so, it was incidental to the main purpose which was enjoyment laced with a keen local rivalry. *The Diaries of Thomas Marchant*, a small farmer, record laconically the matches played between his own village of Hurst and eight or ten neighbouring parishes, and the odd one unavoidably postponed. 6th June 1721: 'Will went to Steyning with the rest of our parish to play a cricket match, but the weather was so bad they could not.'
>
> On this infrastructure was overlaid a pattern of 'great matches' between the nobility and gentry leading teams drawn from their households, tenantry, village craftsmen and so forth. The highest-ranking of these innovators was the second Duke of Richmond.

> Twenty-two-year-old Charles Lennox, son of another
> of the illegitimate offspring of Charles II, who gave
> up the family parliamentary seat of Chichester when
> he succeeded to the dukedom in 1723. His first
> recorded game was a two-a-side challenge match
> in 1725 against Sir William Gage MP of Firle near
> Eastbourne, a gentleman of distinguished lineage who
> was already active in these matches.

The first time I read this, I was greatly surprised. It was pouring with rain, horrid cold winter rain. But I knew that if I looked out of the window long enough, our neighbour Louisa would come past, walking her covey of amusing dogs, and sure enough she did, on the other side of the road, head down against the rain. I called her;

'Louisa! Come and look at this!' She crossed the road.

'Will you come in?' I asked.

'Better not. The dogs are soaking. What do you want to show me?'

'This.' I showed her the book.

'I see.' (She is a patient woman, but wet and cold, and in no mood to discuss the history of cricket.)

'That's my seven-times-great great-grandfather, and your six-times-great great-grandfather, next to one another, in the definitive history of cricket. And there's your house –' I pointed, but I think she knew where it was '– and here's mine.' She admitted that it was rather amazing, but was clearly keen to get the dogs walked, and out of the rain. And so it is amazing. I'm not sure what it proves, but it must prove something. That history is sticky, perhaps.

Later in the year, when the rain had stopped, and we started feeling confident about taking tea in a neighbour's house again, Louisa came and chatted to me about Goodwood and cricket.

'We claim to have the oldest cricket pitch in the world,' she said. 'I remember being taken to watch a Duke of Richmond's eleven play at

Peper Harow,[50] to commemorate the first match. They all played in period costumes, with curved bats and underarm bowling.'

She smiled at the memory. 'It was a really nice day.'

I hate to disillusion you my friend. Peper Harow first played a Duke of Richmond team in 1727. The game was first played on Mitcham Green in 1731; that's the oldest pitch still in regular use. But the first place we can say for sure where cricket was played was on the Sandfield. At Danny House.

In 2017, a Danny House eleven played Hurst Cricket Club on the Sandfield to commemorate the tricentennial of the first time Thom wrote about cricket in his diary. Hurst CC claim Sandfield as 'the first identifiable cricket pitch in the world', and I'm sticking with that.

Thom writes about twenty-one matches in total, between 1717 and 1727. He is, I admit, no John Arlott or C.L.R. James. The first entry, on 31/5/1717 reads 'Willy went to see a cricket match.'; the last, on 29/6/1727, 'Will and the rest of our parish went to Patcham to play a cricket match, 'twas wrangled off.' The games were clearly social occasions, and Thom seems more interested in business than the actual games: 'Henfield boys & ours plaid a cricket match in our bankfield,[51] Henfield won. Paid J Lambert 28s at the cricket match for a calf, fetch'd today.' Thom also takes great pride in Will. So he was not just the first writer on cricket, but also the first dad of whom we are aware that went to see his boys play, even if he did sit about drinking and buying calves. Watching cricket had become the first mass spectator sport; 'thousands' of spectators were recorded in 1729 at the game played at Penshurst Park between Kent and a team of players representing Sussex, Surrey and Hampshire; presumably, many of them were there to have a flutter.

Cricket seems to have stopped at the time of harvest; none of

---

50 About five miles across the River Wey from Shalford, where I first encountered the game.

51 Sandfield was not the only cricket pitch in Hurst. Thom's 'bankfield' is the second oldest identifiable cricket pitch. Hurstpierpoint Cricket Club, who were founded in 1717, played there until at least the 1860s.

the matches Thom writes about took place later than the end of June. Thom and the boys, alongside all the day labourers and farm servants, would have worked long days throughout harvest time, between twelve and fifteen hours a day. But in the rest of the year, there was lots of time for jollities. When harvest was home, there were communal suppers. They 'kept holiday' at Christmas, Easter and Whitsun, on Ascension Day, Midsummer's Day, Candlemas, Lady Day, Michaelmas, All Saints' Day, St. Andrew's Day, Oak Apple Day and Bonfire Night. Often these holidays coincided with local fairs, and Thom and his family and workers duly took the day off to attend.

I am forming a picture of Will Marchant, my six-times-great great-grandfather. He was twenty-one in 1722, a hulking, good-humoured chap who played cricket, went hare coursing and went to watch horse racing and prize-boxing, mostly in Lewes. Sometimes he took Jacky with him, so I suspect he would have been a cool older brother in Jacky's eyes.

These were the early days of organised horse racing as we know it now. The Roodee at Chester is the oldest surviving racecourse in Britain, in continuous use since 1539. There had been racing at Newmarket in the mid-seventeenth century; Charles II was a patron.[52] Good Queen Anne kept a racing stable, and founded Ascot racecourse in 1711. But, as so often in this story, Thom was alive at a moment of change. The early eighteenth century was the moment at which modern horse racing could be said to begin, because of the arrival of three true Arabian horses: the Byerley Turk, who had served as a warhorse at the Battle of the Boyne in 1689, and who was sent to stud in 1697; the Darley Arabian, who was bought as a four-year-old in Aleppo, and shipped back to stand at stud in Yorkshire; and the Godolphin Arabian, born in Yemen in 1724, who was in the Godolphin Stud by 1733. From these three stallions spring the great majority of today's thoroughbred horses.

---

52   Louisa's eight-times-great great-grandfather.

My birth dad Alan loved the gee-gees, and going racing was another popular access weekend event for him. He adored Brigadier Gerard, a descendant of the Darley Arabian, and he took me with him to Goodwood to see his equine hero win the Sussex Stakes by five lengths, one cold and wet afternoon in 1971.

'I once won the placepot at Goodwood,' Louisa told me.

'Did you indeed?'

'I did. I was only seventeen, so I hid the fact from my parents, and threw a huge dinner party at our London house. They weren't amused when they found out.'

Thom was no Peter O'Sullevan, and so there is no record of the actual races at Lewes in his diary. He describes them as 'plate races', which is to say, they were run for a prize plate and a winner's purse. Sometimes the whole family attends, but more often Will went with pals or his brother. Although there was racing at Lewes from 1710 onwards, it's not until 1727 that the winners of horse races were recorded, and so we have no real idea of the outcomes of the races, but it's worth noting that Thom makes no mention of betting. Although it's perhaps too early for the Marchants to have watched what we would call thoroughbred racehorses, a plate race was clearly a spectacle worth seeing for its own sake.

A much more likely medium for betting was prizefighting, and Will seems to have been an aficionado, so perhaps he ventured a few bob; not much more than that if he did bet, because he wouldn't have had lots of money of his own. Thom records Will's visits to the fights, but doesn't seem to have gone himself. As Thom was no Harry Carpenter, we don't know for sure the results of the fights, but we do have some idea of what the fights were like. There were no gloves, no weight divisions, no referees and no rules until 1743. Large crowds would gather to watch two lads beat the merry hell out of one another. Since there were no rules, the fighter went in 'boots, fists and nut', as I once heard a young gentleman in the North Stand at Brighton describe an altercation with some Palace fans in which he had been involved. A round was declared when one of the fighters went down. If they could stand up and face their opponent, a new round would begin. Fights could go on for thirty rounds, until one or other of the fighters had had enough, or was knocked unconscious. The spectators would go home flecked with blood. Prizefighting enjoyed a long popularity in the Weald; the last ever public bare-knuckle prizefight in Britain took place in Wadhurst, south of Tunbridge Wells, in 1863.

Will's favourite pastime, however, was hare coursing.

In 1979, with a baby on the way and in need of an income (which was not being provided by the psychedelic post-punk band I was singing with, much to my sorrow), I got a job working as a boardmarker[53] for Mecca Bookmakers in Brighton. The first task each morning was to disassemble the *Sporting Life* newspaper, and stick it up on the walls for the punters to peruse. The sheets of the paper gave the runners and riders and form guides for that afternoon's horse races, but it also covered dog racing. Most of the time, this meant greyhound racing on dog tracks; but the *Sporting Life* also covered hare coursing, most particularly the Waterloo Cup, which was run in front of huge crowds at Great Altcar in Lancashire, on the northern fringes of Liverpool's suburbs, between 1836 and 2005. In its heyday it was seen as one of England's great sporting events, almost equal to the Grand National. The most famous champion dog was called Master McGrath, who won the Waterloo Cup three times in the 1850s. So great was his fame that Queen Victoria asked to meet him. Live hares were loosed onto the course, and the dogs chased after them; not necessarily to kill the hares, but to 'turn them', i.e., to outrun them on the straight, until the hares made a dash for it through the hedge. This, at least, was the view of hare coursing proponents – in practice, of course, lots of hares were caught and killed. It was made illegal in the 2004 Hunting Act.

---

53 This is pretty much the only job I've been trained for – my trade, if you will. A boardmarker was someone who wrote up the results of horse and dog races on a large whiteboard for the punters to follow the action. This is all done on screens now. My only skill in the workplace is obsolete.

Parson Woodforde, that good and kind man, loved to go hare coursing, and writes often about it in his diary, sixty years after Thom:

> Nov 5, 1788 – Soon after breakfast young Rose called
> here and desired me to lend him my Greyhounds,
> having found a hare sitting. Mr Walker and self took a
> Walk with the greyhounds and saw the Hare coursed,
> which gave great Sport indeed, but was killed at last.
> I never saw a better Course. I let Mr Rose have the
> Hare for a friend of his. After we had killed that Hare
> we went after another, and found one in about ah
> hour, but we had scarce little diversion with her, the
> Greyhounds scarcely seeing her, She soon got off.[54]
> Saw never another tho' we stayed out till 3 oclock.

Willy Marchant goes hare coursing regularly during the period of the diary. Was he coursing to kill hares for the pot, or simply for the thrill of seeing the hares run? Both, most likely. Does this mean he had his own sighthound: a greyhound perhaps, or, more likely, a lurcher? He must have done, but sadly there is very little about dogs in the diary; Thom was no Peter Purves.

Thom's favourite recreation, by far, was getting pished. Beer would have been made at Little Park and drunk at every meal. Thom grew barley and hops, and bought beer bottles and barrels. But away from home, he seems to have drunk mostly wine; two or three bottles some nights. This would not have been wine such as you might have a glass or two of with dinner. The Methuen Treaty of 1703 between England and Portugal ensured that taxes on French wine were prohibitively high, whilst those on Portuguese wines was very low. So when Thom says that he and a few pals

---

54 I once ate jugged hare, and I still regret it. It seems unthinkable now that such beautiful
creatures were killed for 'diversion'.

drank fourteen bottles of wine, it would have been port, Madeira or sherry. No wonder that he so often missed church on Sunday after a night on the tiles; or that he sometimes berates himself after an evening engagement that he had 'staid late and drunk too much'.[55]

Broadly speaking, there were four kinds of places you could buy a drink, and you might argue that this model still holds. At the top of the hierarchy was the inn, a place which offered food and beds as well as drink. Thom stayed at various inns; the Star in Lewes, the Half Moon in Petworth. This equates to your Michelin starred gastropub with rooms at £200 a night. Next, you had the tavern, where wine would be sold as well as beer; today, the equivalent would be a wine bar, or a cafe pub. Next, would be an alehouse which sold beer, and maybe cider, such as today you get lager on tap and Sky Sports on the big screen. All three kinds of premises would have had to be licensed, unlike the gin shop. Thom doesn't mention drinking gin; it was something for the poor. The modern equivalent of the gin shop is the supermarket, six cans of Carlsberg for a fiver, a bottle of Vladivar for £9.99.

I suspect Thom's local, the Swan on the High Street in Hurst, was a tavern, in view of Thom's taste in booze, but I could be wrong, given that he drinks with Messrs Hart, Whitpaine, Campion, Scutt &c in private houses after dinner, and my Lord Treep and various mountebanks at the Swan. So maybe he drank beer when he was down the pub. But I want it to be a tavern, so that I can quote Charles II's tutor, Bishop Earle, writing in 1628, still the best description of what a pub should be: 'A tavern is the busy man's recreation, the idle man's business, the melancholy man's sanctuary, the stranger's welcome, the inns-of-courts man's entertainment, the scholar's kindness, and the citizen's courtesy.'

---

55 What we would call 'port' didn't really exist in 1721, but its precursors, such as Thom and his pals were knocking back, would already be stronger than French wine. It was sold by the pint.

On Fryday 16 June 1721, Thom wrote: 'A fine day ... the mountebank at town. A smock race in our field.'[56] A smock race was a race specifically for women – 'young country wenches' according to Joseph Strutt in his *Sports and Pastimes of the People of England*, in 1801. William Hazlitt wrote in the 1820s that 'smock races were run by young girls in their chemises only'. Strutt describes the sport as 'not a very delicate one', due to the fact that the participants were running in their underwear. The chemise, you'll recall, was the bottom layer in a lady's costume; the runners wouldn't have worn knickers, much less a bra, and so I suspect smock racing was a popular spectator event with the dads. The prize was a smock, an outer garment of linen, embroidered and decorated with ribbons, which the winning girl pulled over her head after her victory. These races became more organised later in the century, and began to evolve into serious competitions; running seems to have been the first sport open to women.

At twenty-one, Will Marchant – a great big healthy man, with a fondness for sport, who was due to inherit an estate and a reasonable fortune – would have been seen as a good catch. The early eighteenth century was not a prudish time; that all came later. A contemporary French book on courtship noted that 'The rules of courtship required a man to tell a woman three times that she was beautiful. The first time she thanked him, the second time she believed him, the third time she rewarded him.' In 1711, Richard Steele wrote in the *Spectator*: 'Love, Desire, Hope, all the pleasing motions of the soul rise in the pursuit', and that: 'The passion should strike root and gather strength before marriage be grafted on it ... before marriage we cannot be too inquisitive and discerning in the faults of the person beloved, nor after it too dim-sighted and superficial.' Will would only have been 'innocent' if he chose to be.

But on 16 June 1721, a nice day has been had by all. Thom has brought a chair out to watch the girls go by. He's brought a couple of

---

56 The various mountebanks who came through Hurst will get special attention in chapter XV.

bottles to share with Treep and the mountebank. The winner was a very bonny lass, he thought. She looked fetching in the smock she had won, no doubt. The other girls were laughing, joking, pulling on their petticoats, teasing the boys. Will is standing there, grinning like a loon, like a big lunk – the winner laughs at him, takes hold of his arm, and pulls him away from the field.

X.

HE WHO HATH MUCH PEASE MAY PUT THE MORE IN THE POT

I've taught creative writing at pretty much every level imaginable, from infants to third-agers, and one issue that always comes up (alright, not with the infants) is class. The American students, especially, get confused about the English class system. They write about a road-mender who eats dinner at 7 p.m., a barrister who goes to the bathroom, or, heaven forfend, the toilet, and, because they equate class and money, a duke who drives a Rolls-Royce.[57] Then I start to explain some of the strange codes that people in England are subject to – the road-mender would eat tea and go to the toilet, the barrister would eat supper and go to the lavatory, the aristocrat would drive a shagged up old Volvo with 270,000 miles on the clock and so on.

The upper-middle classes ask questions to sound you out, such as 'Where did you go to school?' or 'How do you know Oliver?' (the correct answer here is, we were at school together). The aristocrat cares not for this stuff, and only wants to know one thing about you – are you fun? Like a good working-class boy, I try to find out as quickly as possible what football team people support, which, 91

---

57 The road-mender works away from home tarmacking motorways at night, works like stink, does all the overtime he can, and earns 60 grand a year; the barrister has a mortgage for half a mill, hasn't had a brief in months, has two sons to get through Eton and can barely afford to keep the heating on, poor love; and the aristo needs to raise 3 million quid to mend the roof, while visitor numbers have gone through the floor.

times out of 92,[58] is an excellent icebreaker. Football is still a working-class pursuit, despite *Fever Pitch* and all that. The middle classes like rugby and cricket, but they pretend to follow Arsenal or 'Man U'; the aristos like the gee-gees, though a few of them seem to support Villa, which is odd. And we all seem to have a stake in cricket, however slight. English people learn these codes at our mother's breast.

I have sometimes wondered what life might have been like if Little Park had passed down to me. Well-To-Do. Something in the City, first class on the 6.59 from Hassocks to Blackfriars. Would I have coped with being a hearty who went to a minor public school, whose favourite book is *Puck of Pook's Hill* and has ended up as captain of the Mid Sussex Golf Club? Would I have to have sons called Tristram and Giles? Is a Land Rover Discovery compulsory?

Or, might I have taken that other well-trod Sussex path, the one through the primrose woods to Bohemia? Might I drift around Lewes on a sit-up-and-beg bicycle, and wear a 'kerchief around my scrawny but tanned neck? Might I run a letterpress printing studio producing limited editions of my poems on thick creamy paper? Might I have a pot by Quentin Bell on my invite-laden mantelpiece, a pastel sketch of darling Leonard Woolf in the dining room?

Instead, here I am, a Newhaven-raised boy, one of the 'indigenous people of the Ouse valley' who Virginia Woolf described as 'white slugs'. When she walked into the floodwaters of the Sussex Ouse to end her life, it was my people who risked their lives trying to save her, despite her loathing of them. England is nothing without class division, like the mould in Stilton. But the first thing that has changed, on my discovery of the diary, is that I no longer claim to be 'working class'. I am better described as a distressed gentleperson. Class, in England, is an absurdist minefield.

Absurd or not, it still needs to be navigated, and there is something which I can't quite get hold of, entirely, which is Thom and Elizabeth's social status. English social historians use class as a predictor of how people might have lived, because, this being

---

58 The awkward exception is Crystal Palace, which sometimes causes ice to form.

England, English social historians are obsessed with it. There are very few early eighteenth-century documents by landless farm labourers, but by using various sources historians can have a punt at how people lived, ate, worked and played. And to do this, they use class as a marker. There might be very few documents, but those that exist are used to categorise everyone who is seen to share a similar class identity.

I'm not sure it works in Thom and Elizabeth's case. Thom was a yeoman farmer. This means, by one definition, that he owned and farmed his own land, and was therefore entitled to a vote in Parliamentary elections. By another definition, he was also an office holder, serving as churchwarden, tax collector and, eventually, the Duke of Somerset's land steward at Petworth House. The history books tell me that a yeoman was not quite gentry, but not just a peasant. E.V. Lucas, in *Highways and Byways in Sussex*, published in 1904, calls Thom 'a little squire'; Derek Birley in *A Social History of English Cricket* calls him 'a small farmer'. Thom had married into a gentry family, and spends much of his free time in the company of local gentry families, including the Courthopes; but he also worked his own fields alongside his workers, who included his sons. He seems to have had an interest in the welfare of his workers and house servants; the history books tell me this is 'paternalism', but the way I read the diary, he was genuinely concerned. When he was not dining at Danny House or Petworth, he spent a fair bit of time in the Swan with his pal 'Lord' Treep, often described as a 'tinker', or with the various 'mountebanks' who come through Hurst. Either he was uniquely unconscious of class and was just a sweetie who everyone loved, or, as seems more likely, class in the early eighteenth century had not begun to harden into the current musty ossuary of customs and attitudes that are piled up to exclude those who are Not One of Us.

The earliest reference I've found to Thom's diary is in *Glimpses of Our Sussex Ancestors* by Charles Fleet, published in Lewes in 1882. It must be remembered that he did not have access to the whole diary, but only to the parts of the diary transcribed by Reverend Turner, and published in the *Sussex Archaeological Collections* in 1873. I quote Fleet at some length:

> In social position ... Thomas Marchant, of Little Park Farm, Hurst, was a degree below the squires. Thomas Marchant was a yeoman. Yet they touched closely upon each other, and mixed with and were probably related to the same families; the Campions, the Courthopes, Dodsons, Scutts, Harts, Turners, Stones, Whitpaines, Lindfields, etc. For Thomas Marchant belonged to that higher order of English Yeomen who farmed their own land, and the house he resided in at Hurst was one of some pretensions. Little Park Farm is now (1882) the property of Colonel Smith Hannington, who acquired it from the last male representative of the Marchants of Hurst.
>
> It was a time of great material prosperity, but in country places, at all events, of little intellectual activity, and of peaceful pursuits ... The sword had been turned into the ploughshare. The campaigns of Marlborough were brought to a close, and the next 50 years were passed, with only rare exception, in profound peace, and in a state of material prosperity which has perhaps never been exceeded in England. But it was of a gross kind. This is reflected in the diary of Thomas Marchant, and others of the same period. They are redolent of eating and drinking and of the dealings connected therewith. People married, begat and christened children, eat and drank hugely, amused themselves in a coarse kind of way, bought and sold, died, and were buried. And all this went on in a uniform way as if there were nothing more in life and as if life would always go on in the same way. The education of the lower classes was utterly neglected,

and their morals did not improve. But they were fed
well to a large extent in the houses of their employers
who were not much superior to them in manners or
education. It was the period when the relations of the
farmer and the labourer were closest to each other.
The time was yet to come when they were to separate;
the farmer trying to maintain their position and
eventually rising on the scale; the latter sinking into
poverty and pauperism until poor rates threatened to
swallow up rents, and a reactionary movement set in
towards independence, which, assisted by new forces,
is going on in our day.

A closer reading of the whole transcription of the diary reveals
something else. Far from neglecting 'the education of the lower
classes', Thom and his mother were founders and patrons of the
primary school in Hurst that still exists. Jacky passed his exams and
went to Oxford. I have, I hope, demonstrated that Danny House in
particular was very much a centre of intellectual activity and political
foment. I have quoted Fleet at length, not just because he got
Thom wrong, but because it tells us a lot about how the Victorians
viewed the early eighteenth century. He is almost scandalised that
social class seems to mean not very much. 'A reactionary movement
... towards independence ... assisted by new forces' etc. is surely
referring to the repeated attempts by farm labourers to unionise. The
problem seems to be, not that they might be better paid, but that
they might get above themselves. For a Victorian, your social class
dictated everything about how you might expect to live your life.
Our annoying and debilitating code is only a far-off echo of what
it was. If it still matters now, in 1882 it clearly mattered a very great
deal more.

Another much better-known historian who seemed a bit put
out by the paucity of evidence for rigid class structure in the early
eighteenth century was E.P. Thompson. Thompson was a Marxist,
and for the theory to work, the lineaments of class division must be

clear and bold. But he can't quite make them out, not as clearly as a Marxist would like. In *Customs in Common*, from 1991, Thompson writes that there was 'some reciprocity in the relations between rich and poor; an inhibition upon the use of force against indiscipline and disturbance; a caution (on the part of the rich) against taking measures which would alienate the poor too far, and (on the part of that section of the poor which from time to time rallied behind the cry of "Church and King") a sense that there were tangible advantages to be gained by soliciting the favour of the rich.' There is, to judge from Thom's diary, a great deal of 'mutuality of relationship', as Thompson admits.

The blame for the division between the classes, which undoubtedly came into sharper focus later in the eighteenth century, is usually parked at the door of capitalism. I'm sure there's a great deal of truth in that. But in 1720, what we now call capitalism was only just starting to take shape. Central banks, joint-stock companies and new methods of credit exchange (such as banknotes) were in their infancy. Markets were strong in the late seventeenth and early eighteenth centuries, and there were agricultural surpluses, and so people got richer. Even the poorest were better off – their wages stayed at between seven and twelve shillings a week, but food was cheaper and more plentiful than ever before, so low wages went further. More capital spread across a few more hands is not the problem; the problem arises from the fact that, throughout the eighteenth century, Britain became increasingly industrialised, and it was in these industries that capital was invested. The poor had their land stolen by enclosure, and only the towns seemed to offer the chance of a better life; they found the factories and mines ready to swallow their hopes whole. But in 1720, we can point only to the two or three instances of industrialisation that I wrote about in 'Discoverie': coke-fired blast furnaces in Shropshire, inefficient and rare steam pumps in Cornwall, a few improvements to the tramroads in the north-east. Capitalism and industry had yet to make their destructive marriage; the English class system had not fully taken shape, because the Industrial Revolution had yet to begin in earnest.

The great historian of the eighteenth century Amanda Vickery points out that, although the big headline achievements of the Industrial Revolution were still thin on the ground in the early eighteenth century, there were thriving industrial processes which couldn't be undertaken in a homeworking context: she lists mining, shipbuilding, iron-smelting, pottery firing, glass-blowing, paper making, soap boiling and wool fulling as industries which were operating prior to the Revolution.[59] Over the course of the century, those processes which *had* been possible in a workshop adjoining your house, such as spinning and weaving, also became fully industrialised. In 1700, the population of Britain was a little over 3 million; a hundred years later it was a little shy of 6 million. The people coming off the land to work in growing industrial cities needed feeding. For the Industrial Revolution to really take off, it first needed another 'revolution', and that was in full swing, and evident at Little Park Farm, certainly by 1728. And, rather than coal, it was powered by turnips.

If the general reader knows one thing about the Agricultural Revolution of the eighteenth century, it is that Jethro Tull invented the seed drill. The reason the general reader knows this is probably because she is sixty-plus, like me, and remembers the band of the same name, and their singer Ian Anderson, a mum-scaring, goggle-eyed wildman hippie, standing on one leg to play the flute. If, like me, you 'did' the Industrial Revolution for O level, then you might be able to remember early lessons about the AgRev, and scrape up a few more names: Turnip Townshend or Coke of Holkham. Four-course rotation[60] might ring a faint bell; but that's probably as much as we could come up with. The Agricultural Revolution is a historian's way of characterising a series of changes which took place over at least 150 years, and so, as other historians are quick to point out, it was in no sense a revolution. Jethro Tull was bonkers,

---

59 Iron smelting, glass-blowing and paper-making were all Wealden industries.
60 Another good name for a band.

and Turnip Townshend and Coke weren't all they were cracked up to be. There are few 'Great Men' in the story, no Watt or Trevithick, no Wedgwood or Arkwright.

What there was, were lots of families like the Marchants of Hurstpierpoint. When Thom's grandfather bought Little Park, in 1670, it had been in recent memory an actual deer park, a mile and a half in circumference, with eighty fallow deer, '18 with antlers'. The mere fact that Little Park had been a park would have conferred status on the Marchants; in *Trees and Woodland in the British Landscape* Oliver Rackham writes that 'a park was a rich man's privilege and a not-quite-so-rich man's status symbol'. The definition of a park is that it was fenced by a 'park pale', an expensive-to-maintain palisade of oak stakes. By 1300, a quarter of English woodlands had been made into parks. For small areas (such as Little Park) this didn't make much sense – fallow deer are 'as strong as pigs and as agile as goats', as any country person knows who's had a few jump out in front of their headlights on a summer evening. Fencing deer in a small area is much like keeping water in a sieve. Although sheep and cattle may well have shared the ground with the deer, it's unlikely that Little Park had been used for arable, which means that the soil must have been untouched.

Thom's father brought Little Park under the plough. The deer were sold or let loose to live wild, and the fence taken down in the 'dismantling' in 1643. Although Sussex had begun enclosure in the sixteenth century (which is the legal process of enclosing common land and large strip farmed open fields into smaller fields with hedges, such as we recognise now), the Marchants didn't need to participate in this, as the land was already entire. So this is the first necessary condition of the AgRev; that more land was put under cultivation.

All farmers want one thing, and one thing only, which is to make a living from their ground.

Proper farmers therefore need to look after their soil. It's a fair assumption that the soil at Little Park was good (for Sussex) because it had only recently come under cultivation, but it still needed looking after. For hundreds if not thousands of years, one of the ways this was achieved was by 'three-course rotation'. One field would grow wheat, oats or barley, another legumes or clover, while the third lay fallow. Crops need nitrogen to grow, and clover and peas take it from the atmosphere and 'fix' it in the soil, so that the following year it would be fit for wheat, after which it would be left alone for a year. This meant that, at any one time, one third of arable land was unproductive.

In the early days of the diary, Thom is growing wheat, barley, 'pease', hops and flax. The last entries, in 1728, concern the growing and selling of turnips. This means that somewhere in the period of the diary, Thom has turned Little Park Farm over to four-course rotation, which meant that no fields had to be left fallow, and that, as the name suggests, four crops, or types of crops, could be grown in turn. The order was: wheat, turnips, barley and legumes.

Bread made from wheat was the staple of English tables, then, as now. Bread was particularly important to the poor, who couldn't afford as much meat as families like Thom and Elizabeth's; although, in this time of relative prosperity, most people would have been able to afford meat at least once a week. Seventy years later, the agricultural traveller and writer Arthur Young was disparaging about the poor's ability to cope with cheap food in the early eighteenth century, writing that 'whatever was gained by such cheapness was constantly expended by the husband in a proportionable quantity of idleness and beer, and by the wife in that of tea.' So wheat was sought after by bakers, and fetched twice as much as barley; but it couldn't be planted year after year. Thomas Coke of Holkham only allowed his tenants to plant wheat once every six years. It was hard to store and transport, so tended to be milled close to home. The early eighteenth century saw a glut of wheat production, which William III tried to mitigate by offering what amounted to the first agricultural subsidies, for exporting corn.[61]

---

61 Political life depended on keeping corn prices high until the Corn Law Reform Act of 1846. The reason is very simple: only landowners got a vote and their interest lay in keeping grain prices artificially high.

Barley, the other staple grain crop in the rotation, wasn't grown for bread, but for ale and beer. Malted barley is one of the three essential ingredients of ale – malt, water and yeast. Thom was brewing his own, and was clearly adding a fourth ingredient, because he was also growing his own hops, either in small hop gardens or in his hedgerows. Hops were a relative newcomer as an ingredient, not much more than a hundred years old – they add a pleasant bitterness, and help the ale to keep, but they are not essential; it's the ingredient that turns ale into beer. It's well known that English people drank a lot of ale and beer because the water was largely unfit to drink. But by 1700 there was a glut of barley too, more than brewers needed. Luckily, William III had an answer for that, too, which was the distillation of gin.

Gin only really needs two ingredients: ale (called 'mash' by distillers) and heat. The Dutch added juniper as a flavourant, but that's no more necessary than hops in beer – without botanicals, you pretty much just have vodka, or, if stored for at least three years in old sherry casks, whisky. The process is simple; you heat up the mash until it turns into steam, and then you tap off the resulting distillation. No one is certain when distillation first came to north-west Europe; there is some evidence that it was discovered as a result of alchemical experimentation in the sixteenth century. It was big in Holland. The first gin distillery on a commercial scale was the Bols distillery, near Amsterdam, which opened in 1575. The word 'gin' is derived from '*genever*', the Dutch word for juniper.

Until the Glorious Revolution of 1688, very little spiritous liquor was drunk in England (though whisky was being drunk in Scotland). The little that was drunk was French brandy, and that was mostly stocked by apothecaries for medicinal purposes.[62] But when James II was driven from the throne by his son-in-law and nephew, William of Orange, William straight away declared war on

---

62   19 June 1728: 'Jack Bartlet excessive drunk with brandy, which he did to put away an ague.' The brandy would have been smuggled.

the French and banned all trade with France. This meant no more brandy; hardly a move which would make a new king popular. But, like a good Dutchman, William's tipple was gin, and in 1690 he enacted a bill for 'encouraging the distilling of spirits from corn'. Not only did this Act allow for the unlicensed and duty-free production of gin, where the alehouses, taverns and inns had been paying duty for over 200 years on wine and beer, it also supported the landed gentry, who were thus guaranteed a market for their barley. It also had military benefits: William's general John Churchill, the Duke of Marlborough, encouraged his men to have a nip or two before going into battle – hence 'Dutch courage'.

The early part of the eighteenth century was a hard-drinking time, across all social classes. Gentlemen would have considered it impolite to rise from table in a state of sobriety – Thom, in this sense, was certainly a gentleman. Gin, free from excise duty, became the favourite inebriant of the poor, for whom it was a comfort and a consolation. It is estimated that, by 1733, 11 million gallons of gin were consumed per annum, and one in six premises in London sold gin; the slogan in some of these establishments was 'drunk for a penny, dead drunk for tuppence'. Straw was provided to collapse on for those who took the tuppenny route. The first attempt to tax gin, in 1728, the year of Thom's death, failed miserably. This great new industry demanded barley. If it could be moved efficiently to London, via the South Coast ports, then barley became a much more valuable crop than previously. And so the second grain crop of the four courses went up in price, which made it much more viable as a rotation crop.

Thom grew a lot of 'pease' throughout the period of the diary. These were not garden peas as we know them, but rather yellow peas, used now for little more than split pea soup. In the early eighteenth century, potatoes had yet to become a regular feature of English tables, though they were being grown and eaten in Ireland. So 'pease pudding' would have been a major source of carbohydrates. It is immortalised in the old nursery rhyme, 'Pease pudding hot, pease pudding cold, pease pudding in the pot, nine days old', and also in one of the UK's most obscure motorway service stations, Pease Pottage, right at the end of the M23, twelve miles due north of Hurst. Perhaps unsurprisingly, the name commemorates the fact that the area was known for the cultivation of pease. The next village to Shalford is called Peasmarsh, and just a few miles from Ewhurst is Peaslake, both names with a similar derivation. Pease pudding was clearly eaten throughout the Weald.

It's the fourth crop in the rotation which is the game-changer, and that's turnips. Turnips draw their nutrients from deeper in the ground than grain crops; they can be grown in rows, which makes it easier to weed (weeds exhaust the soil); and they are generally cropped in autumn, when harvest is done and labour is cheap. Their main use, apart from adding variety to the farmer's diet, was as winter fodder for sheep and cattle. If you pull your turnips, chop them up and put them back on the ground, you can then put your beasts onto the field, who eat well, shit on the ground and break up the soil with their hooves. This still happens now. In late autumn, huge trailer-loads of various root crops, mostly mangelwurzels these days, thunder past our house. Out in the winter fields, denuded of grass, muddied sheep eat the chopped-up beets, shepherded by electric fences.

So as the eighteenth century went on, more and better livestock could be grown, and meat and milk became cheaper and more widely available. Thom was clearly growing and selling large amounts of turnips, right up until his death. The penultimate entry in the diary reads:

> The 6th September 1728 Fryday. A wet day. Carry'd
> 13 bushels of turnips to J Byshop at the Comon and 24
> bushels to my Brother John Courtness's to be sold for
> me. Sold 4 bushels as we went.

Turnip Townshend didn't start growing them seriously until 1730. Defoe, travelling through England in 1722, remarked that turnips were widespread, but in many parts of the country, their cultivation as cattle feed wasn't fully accepted till the end of the eighteenth century. Thom, it seems, was an early adopter.

This seemingly modest, yet ultimately radical idea was first articulated in England by a man called Sir Richard Weston. Arthur Young regarded Weston as 'a greater benefactor than Newton' and yet his name is all but forgotten. His great-great-grandfather built Sutton Place, the house and park outside Guildford where John Paul Getty spent his last days, and which is currently owned by belatedly sanctioned Russian oligarch Alisher Usmanov.

Sir Richard spent some of his early life on the Continent, probably in Flanders; the River Wey runs through Sutton Park, and in 1635 Sir Richard was appointed commissioner to investigate the possibility of making the river navigable using 'pound locks', which were already in use in the Low Countries.[63] Sir Richard was a Royalist, and was driven into exile back to Flanders in 1644. Sutton Park was sequestered by the Commonwealth government for a time, but Sir Richard seems to have got it back, because by 1651 he was the main promoter of an Act to make the Wey navigable from Guildford to Shepperton, where it meets the Thames, and thus open up the best route from the Weald to London.

During his exile, Weston studied the agricultural methods employed in Flanders, where four-course rotation was already being used. Remarkable to think that the IndRev had deep roots in Wallonia, and the AgRev in Flanders, and so we probably need to blame Belgium for everything. On his return, and on the return of his estate, he began using the four-course method at Sutton Place. His aim was, above all, to be a good ancestor; he wanted to improve his land in order to pass it on to his sons in better shape than when he had inherited it. To this end, he wrote a letter to his sons from exile, extolling the virtues of four-course rotation, which he called his 'Legacie'. The letter found its way into circulation in manuscript form; it was called 'Discours of Husbandrie used in Brabant and Flanders'.

---

63   These are the locks that river and canal navigations use to this day.

Sir Richard's manuscript came into the hands of a remarkable man, in which the seventeenth century abounded. He was on the other side in the Civil War, and his name was Samuel Hartlib. He arrived in England from Danzig in 1628, escaping from the horrors of the Thirty Years' War. Ostensibly a merchant, he acted as a hub for scientific knowledge from across Britain, Europe and the American colonies, describing himself as an 'intelligencer'. Hartlib was an admirer of Sir Francis Bacon, whose 'new system of the world' and invention of what we would now regard as scientific method was the start of that other well-known revolution, viz. the Scientific one. Bacon held that knowledge should be useful, and that in order to maximise its utility it needed to be shared as widely as possible. Hartlib corresponded with hundreds of people; it's believed that across the course of his lifetime he received somewhere in the order of 11,000 letters, on such subjects as silk worm production (a failed scheme of James I), how to deal with mildew in wheat, the dunging of meadows, the keeping of bees, the difficulties of storing corn, the advantages of growing flax and hemp (of which I am very much in favour myself), how to make compost, how to treat foot rot in sheep, how to keep mice out of cheese racks, how to cure hogs of the measles and hundreds of others.

In order to spread the word, Hartlib published many of these letters; because, if careful observation of nature is one leg of scientific enquiry, the other is publishing your findings, for others to improve, or build upon, or refute. The *Philosophical Transactions of the Royal Society* is generally regarded as the world's first scientific journal, first published in 1665, so Hartlib's publications in the 1650s were ahead of their time. 'Hartlib's circle', as historians call his correspondents, formed part of the earliest scientific community, 'the Invisible College', sharing and publishing their findings. Hartlib was not a great one for asking permission to publish; he just thought it was right to do so. So it was that in 1650, an anonymous copy of the manuscript of Sir Richard Weston's 'Legacie' fell into the hands of Hartlib, who, seeing its importance, printed it without Sir Richard's permission. The following year, Hartlib found out that Weston was the author, and he wrote to ask if Sir Richard wanted to add anything. Although Sir Richard didn't reply, Hartlib republished a more complete version in 1651, and again in 1655 in his own book entitled *Samuel Hartlib, his Legacy of Husbandry. Wherein are bequeathed to the Common-wealth of England, not onely Braband, and Flanders, but also many more Outlandish and Domestick Experiments and Secrets (of Gabriel Plats and others) never heretofore divulged in reference to Universal Husbandry.*

It did well; but the seeds of Hartlib's downfall lay in the title – the Commonwealth of England was going strong in 1655, but with the restoration of the monarchy in 1660, Hartlib and his circle fell out of favour. When the Royal Society was formed in 1661, Hartlib and the great majority of his circle were excluded from membership, Hartlib's work was forgotten, and the Royal Society concerned itself with natural philosophy, rather than the practical arts of agriculture.

I don't know how Thom came to be a turnip enthusiast. Hurst is not far from Sutton Place. I don't know what books he read, other than the Bible and the *Book of Common Prayer*, but I know that he did read, and that he had access to the library at Danny, because he writes about lending books to friends, and about borrowing them from Henry Campion. If one was Hartlib's *Legacy*, I don't know. I like to imagine it was. Turnips are now regarded as a comedy vegetable, thanks to *Blackadder*. My wife and I can't even agree as to what a turnip is, since people from Scotland and Northern Ireland call swedes turnips. Thom's diary, however, is from a moment when growing turnips was at the forefront of technological innovation; and Thom is revealed, not as a declasse yokel to be condescended to by Victorian snobs, but as a forward thinker, a man who was ahead of the curve and prepared to try new ideas.

An essential part of the rotation was, and still is, the spreading of manure. One of the delights of country living in spring is the all-pervading stench of shite being sprayed in liquid form all over our neighbours' fields. When the Hurst History Study Group transcribed and published Thom's diary, they called it *A Fine Day in Hurstpierpoint*, but they might well have called it *The Dung Diaries*, since, from the first to the last, the most common entry is 'carry'd dung'. Sometimes, it's the sole entry, like that of 15/5/27; 'A gloomy day. Carry'd dung etc'. Time spent carrying dung is the best way to render any day gloomy, I would imagine, but a week never goes by without Thom listing it as a job that has been carried out. It came from the livestock and was collected and held in 'courts' until it was spread on the fields in spring. This is merely good practice, but it still needed writers like Samuel Hartlib to spread the idea that farmers should spread muck. King George III, 'Farmer George', wrote extensively on the subject of manuring the land, and so he would certainly have approved of Thom.

As well as dung carrying, Thom had the contract for collecting Hurstpierpoint's night soil, which he calls 'towne dirt', but which I will call, if you don't mind, turds. As Ray noted in his *Proverbs*, 'Money is welcome though it comes in a shitten cloth.' Emptying the cesspits and privies was not a pleasant task and was generally carried out by one of Thom's men rather than Thom or his sons. Dorothy Hartley writes in *Water in England* about the process in her home town of Ashton-in-Makerfield in 1900:

> The carts, which were nothing but great open
> tanks drawn by a cart horse, had to move slowly to
> prevent rocking and slopping the liquid. The tubs
> were hauled out (from the privies) with iron tongs,
> through wooden shutters set in the privy wall below
> the wooden seat. One man stood on the cart and
> hauled up, one stood below and heaved. There was
> a slobbering splash, followed by a thump, and the
> dripping tub was dropped down and shoved back and
> the horse paced on to the next privy. The stench was
> indescribably foul and the horrid sounds lasted a full
> hour. If the cart-men were delayed, the tank over-

filled and splashed onto the road, to lie another week
matted over with ashes thrown out by the inhabitants.

I doubt this system had developed much in 200 years. Night soil had some value in the towns, where it was used in tanneries, but there were no tanneries near Hurst. So what did Thom do with the turds after he had collected them? He would not, I think, have wanted them to go to waste. Burying them comes with many complications; they get too hot and contaminate the soil. Putting raw turds on the land was not a good idea; there's a reason why people don't like turds, not least of which is that they contain the eggs of parasites which survive muck-spreading and can be found on crops grown in turd-fertilised ground. In *The Structures of Everyday Life*, Fernand Braudel claimed that it was never done in Europe. So I believe it at least possible that Thom fed the turds to his fish.

When Mr. Thomas Marchant bought Little Park, there was already a two-acre pond; our Thom dug more. If you look at a modern Ordnance Survey map of Hurst, beside the little gothic words 'Little Park', which indicate an ancient monument, you can see the two surviving ponds. Look at the six inch scale map, published in 1952,[64] and you might be able to make out evidence for a further two or three. It's unclear exactly how many ponds Thom managed, but it's more than the two that survive:

> The 12th November 1720. A gloomy day. Fisht the
> middle pond. Put 142 of the lower pond fish into the new
> pond yesterday and 110 today of the middle pond. Put 48
> large tench into the Hovelfield stew. Put a great number
> of very small store carp yesterday into the Edgley Mead
> pond and about 150 or more today into the Churchfield
> pond.

64 Sussex Sheet XXXVI.SE, available through the indispensable National Library of
Scotland website, maps.nls.uk.

> The 14th November 1720. A gloomy day. Fisht the upper
> pond. Put 94 large carp into the new pond, 6 large carp
> and 10 large tench into the Hovelfield stew, 80 carp about
> 5 inches, 9 tench the same size and 16 small tench into the
> middle pond and 50 eels. Put 70 small eels into the upper
> pond again.

It sounds to me, therefore, that there was a network of ponds, as the evidence on the six-inch map would suggest: upper, middle, lower and new, as well as three other ponds which may or may not have been connected.

Thom is concerned throughout by the fishponds. He bought young fish, he sold mature fish, he built new ponds, he drained his ponds for cleaning. It doesn't strike me as hugely profitable. On 30 October 1714 he bought 244 carp for £6, and on 16 November 1714 sells 242 carp for £10. Thom seems to have been something of a dealer in freshwater fish, as he travelled between various Sussex fishponds to catch and then sell the fish, mostly carp, but some tench too. Carp was probably introduced to England in the fourteenth century. It was prized like venison, and became a dish of some status. Keeping fishponds therefore conferred a degree of social credit on the keepers; carp was often given as a gift to local aristocratic families. The monasteries kept extensive fishponds to provide them with 'white meat' on Fridays and during Lent. After the dissolution of the monasteries, the ponds were taken over by large landowners, who clearly gained some profit from them still.[65]

Thom's fish were taken to London, live, in tubs. The roads between the Weald and London were terrible, so it's possible they were taken to Brighton or Shoreham, and sent by sea. Thom says that the tubs of fish were put on a dung cart; they almost certainly used the same tubs for moving both fish and turds; Thom writes of borrowing 'courts' from his neighbours, including the eminently

---

65   E.V. Lucas, writing in 1904, notes that 'many of the old ponds are still dragged, and the proceeds sold in advance to a London firm'.

respectable Mrs. Catherine Beard. One can only hope that they were washed out first, although the fish may have gained some nutrients for the trip by cleaning up the water themselves ...

Feeding turds to fish has a long and honourable history, and would be an intelligent and even neighbourly thing to do. Certainly, monasteries in England were putting sewage into their fishponds. Some of the best archaeological evidence for this comes from excavations on the monastic establishment at Canterbury Cathedral.

Here's how it works. The turds stimulate the growth of phytoplankton and algae by releasing nutrients such as nitrogen and phosphorous. This increases oxygen levels, which makes fish able to swim in the wastewater, and to eat the phytoplankton and algae. After the fish have been caught and sold, the ponds are drained and the resulting sediment is put onto the fields. It takes skill to get the balance right between turds and fresh water; too much turd, and you get 'eutrophication', which means 'well-fed', and which overstimulates the growth of algae, generally a bad thing.

The ideal fish for this process is carp. Carp can come up to gulp air when oxygen levels are low, and studies in Germany showed they grow much faster if fed sewage than in ordinary fishponds. Tench is edible, but not all that nice, and full of tiny bones. The beauty of tench is that they are bottom feeders, in this case literally, and so process more of the food available from the turds. In Hanoi, where this system of sewage refinement is still used, scientific measurements in 1995 showed that the water that was released into the rivers after this process was well below the WHO's recommended level of contaminants.

There was an extensive network of fishponds for sewage treatment in Germany from the 1880s on. The system in Munich was in operation until the 1990s, and was only given up because the land was needed for development. Kolkata's sewage system still makes great use of fishponds to treat turds. A pond is fed with turds, which sits for two weeks. Then, water is released into a lower pond at a rate of one-to-four sewage to clean water, at which point fish are introduced. Eventually, the water is released into the rivers; again, studies suggest that the water can match modern cleaning processes for water cleanliness.

In the diary, Thom talks of spreading 'muck', which seems to be distinct from 'dung'. Modern organic farmers who use turds don't put them straight onto the ground; they use sewage sludge. If I am right (and the evidence is circumstantial at best, and admittedly highly conjectural, but fun to write), it was the sludge cleared from the ponds that was spread as muck, rather than the turdy night soil itself. The Little Park ponds feed into the headwaters of the Adur; fish-treated sewage would have meant less pollution in the river. It would be a good spot; Hurst's sewage is now treated at the Goddards Green plant, just three miles downstream from Little Park. It could not be done now, not with the same degree of safety, because our turds are far dirtier than those of our ancestors; they contain heavy metals and pharmaceuticals which fish can store in their bodies.

If turd water from fishponds went some way to clean up river water, chicken shit does quite the opposite, and is killing our local river systems today. Some of the major employers round here are huge battery chicken factories. There are an estimated 8.5 million hens in Powys, most of them on the hundred or so intensive units, which raise more than 40,000 head of chickens each. The chicken shit is sold as fertiliser, which is spread on the ground, and runs off into our rivers. Eutrophication is the result, and the River Wye catchment is greatly harmed by it. There is a community of Bulgarian people in Presteigne, a large family of whom live on our street, a few doors up from Louisa. They are very welcome, if nothing else because their children go to the schools; without these children, school rolls would be falling even further than they already are. But their main employment is in chicken factories. I suggest the factories try feeding the shit to fish in ponds, and selling the resultant sludge, rather than unrefined chicken shit.

By late August 2021, the harvest has begun, and the peace is gone. Tractors the size of elephants pull juggernaut trailers full of wheat or potatoes. There's a lot of agricultural plant thundering past the house whose function I no longer recognise. Is that a baler, a seed drill, a plough? It is hard to tell. In each machine, one man sits high in a cab, listening to music through headphones. The potatoes are to feed the maw of a nearby 'artisanal' crisp factory, which plumes steam night and day. Thirty-two-tonne Tarmac wagons scream up and down the lanes, carrying away, year by year, bite by dynamitey bite, one of the high hills in the Radnor Valley, to lie as hardcore beneath another new road. The water is being sucked out from the ground by a company selling plastic bottles full of fresh, lovely 'spring water' extracted from our aquifers, which are being polluted by the phosphate run-off from chicken shit spread over the ground, because the numerous huge chicken factories in Powys need to get rid of it, and they think you might like it back, since you ate the chickens.

One August afternoon, sitting in the sun outside our front door, as I like to do, I watched an elderly gentleman park his Suzuki Jimny on the grass verge by the Welsh side of the Lugg Bridge, and walk slowly towards the English side. He stood in the middle, straddling the border, and stared over the parapet into the river. I walked up to join him. Kids sometimes fish for trout from the bridge, and sometimes they catch one. It's a pleasure to sit on the bridge; when the mayflies are out you'll see the trout jumping, if you're patient.

'Are the fish rising?' I asked the gentleman.

He turned and looked at me.

'There are no fish,' he said.

'Oh, well, you see a few …'

He shook his head.

'It used to be, you had to be a bloody idiot not to catch fish off this bridge. You'd come down and fight to get a spot. See the water?'

I did. It runs clear in the shallows under the bridge, and then, as it deepens into a pool where the fish sometimes rise, it takes on colour, almost sea green.

'That used to be clear, right to the bottom. You could see dozens of fish.'

'What happened?'

'Algae bloom. Phosphate run-off.'

I walked with him back to his car.

'May I ask, what is your name?'

'Harry Powell,' he said. 'My name is Harry Powell, and I'm ninety-five years old.'

The same age as old Ralph Foxwell, born in 1926 to my maternal grandmother's cousin May. My paternal great-great-grandfather, Elkanah Marchant, was eighty-five and living in Burgess Hill, unknown to any of his descendants. Elkanah was born in 1841, the year that the railway between London and Brighton was completed; the nearest station to Hurst, just under two miles away, was Hassocks. The railways changed the Weald forever; before that, life had ticked along much as it had for the previous 150 years. Elkanah's great-great-grandfather was Thom and Elizabeth's great-great-grandson. The past is so close; all we have to do to see it is to shut our eyes and open our imaginations.

It had been a dry day, and now the night is clear and cold, and the moon is a week after full. Just as well the night is still bright, and the horse knows its way home, because Thom has been taking supper and drinking with his friends till late. He tiptoes into the darkened house, but the dogs bark as he comes through the door.

'Shhhh …' he says. 'S'good dogs. Shhhhh.'

Elizabeth has gone to bed, but she's left him a candle burning, so that he can write his diary. His handwriting is a little unsteady, and he needs to shut one eye to complete his entry …

The 25th January 1714. Mr John Hart, Mr Scutt, Mr Richard Whitpaine and I supt at Mr Healy's. We had a

trout for supper 2 foot 2 inches long from eye to fork and 6 inches broad, weigh'd 30½ lbs. He was caught in Albourne brook nere Trussell House. My Scutt said it was properly call'd a salmon pool. We staid very late and drank enough.

In the morning, he will have one of his heads.

XI.

A GOOD NAME KEEPS ITS LUSTRE
IN THE DARK

It can't be escaped. If you are going to live through a bad year – being locked down for months at a stretch, or diagnosed with incurable cancer, for example – then Presteigne is about the best place you could be. I'm sorry. It's an extraordinary privilege. Cancer and chemo meant that I was not just locked down, but shielding, yet when the weather was good, as it was in the early summer of 2020, I could still sit in the sun, smoking my old pipe, and friends would stop for a shouty chat as they passed over the bridge. When we took our permitted exercise, we could turn right and cross into England, walk along the banks of the Lugg through a small wood, back along a little used lane and home through the graveyard where I've booked a plot. If we went left, we could saunter along the excellent walking and cycling track that goes around the town. Straight ahead would take us past the church, we could walk along the Welsh bank of the Lugg, through the nature reserve and back through the community park. You could even borrow a pal's dog to take with you.

Most people lucky enough to find themselves here know how lucky they are to find themselves here. It's not a particularly rich town, just rich enough. It's a long way from anywhere, which has bred an ethos, a culture, a community. The population is about 2,000, which means everyone knows one another, at least by sight. When the first lockdown was announced, a group of friends organised a rota of High Street stewards, who stood in all weathers on the street in shifts, counting people in and out of the food shops. Since I was shielding, which meant the bulk of the shopping fell to my wife, this felt invaluable. Our little town got through it, together, in great good humour, because the spirit of the place encourages what you might call neighbourliness. For a Christian, your 'neighbours' are about the most holy thing there is, and, to judge from our non-Christian neighbours and their involvement with the community, this goes for pretty much everybody in Presteigne.

I know Thom, not just from the diary, but from my neighbours who fulfil the exact same functions, as school governors, church-wardens, and as people who run foodbanks and credit unions. If there is any hope in our cruel world, it is in neighbourliness that it might still be found.

One thing we know for sure about Thom is that he could read and write, and that, as a good neighbour, he worked to ensure that more people could read and write too.

There was, of course, a symbiotic relationship between the growth of printing and the spread of reading. The more books that got printed, the more people wanted to read. The wide availability of the King James Bible, published in 1611, and the Protestant insistence on the primacy of Scripture over priestly controlled tradition, meant that those who could read were deepened in their faith. John Bunyan's *The Pilgrim's Progress*, published in 1678, was the first bestseller. It's a good candidate for the first novel written in English; the theology guaranteed it a wide readership in Puritan circles, but many younger readers read it as their first adventure story. Cheap printed matter could be had through travelling booksellers, called chapmen; there were some 2,500 licensed chapmen by 1697. As well as religious and political pamphlets, their biggest seller was the *Almanac*, a cross between a calendar (including planting times, tide tables and weather sayings) and an astrological ephemeris. John Ray may have disapproved of old weather lore which wasn't based on observation, but lots of people disagreed – some 400,000 *Almanacs* were printed annually by the middle of the seventeenth century.

By 1715, it's estimated that almost half of men in England could read, and about a quarter of women. The reason for this disparity was education, or lack of it, a fact that some writers were coming to see as an injustice. Richard Steele wrote in the *Spectator* in 1711: 'The great improvements Women have made of Education, there being hardly any Science in which they have not excelled.' Steele clearly expected that the *Spectator* would have female readers. John Sheffield, the Duke of Buckingham, wrote in 1723: 'Women are thought generally by nature to be much inferior to man in understanding, but I believe the difference lies chiefly in education, by which they give us very great odds.' Some 30,000 children were in school by 1716, mostly boys, but with growing numbers of girls.

The fact that enthusiastic amateurs were able to transcribe the diary shows that Thom's handwriting was fairly legible, even after 300 years. If he had been writing 200 years earlier, it would not have been so easy, and this, somewhat paradoxically, is also because of the appearance of printing, and in particular the printing of 'how to' manuals.

There were two predominant handwriting styles in use in the late seventeenth century – 'italic' and 'secretary'. Previous to the Reformation, most documents and letters were written in the 'court hand', a lovely thing to see, but pretty hard to read. From the 1550s onwards, 'secretary hand' was developed for ease of use by a growing Civil Service and an upwardly mobile mercantile class, which started to be taught by 'writing masters'. In 1591, two writing masters published pamphlets detailing how to write the 'brakes and joins'[66] of secretary hand. To judge from Shakespeare's will, he probably wrote in secretary, which was being taught at Stratford Grammar

66 The 'breaks' are the strokes that make up the letters, whilst the 'joins' are the strokes that connect the letters together.

School when he was a pupil.[67] In 1650 Edward Cocker wrote and published a more up-to-date guide, which added to conformity and thus legibility; there is evidence that people were learning to write secretary from Cocker's book right up until the beginning of the eighteenth century. In the late seventeenth century writing masters began to print guides to writing in italic, an English version of 'the Italian hand', the ancestor of what we now call 'copperplate'. And although italic would succeed secretary, in the late seventeenth and early eighteenth century handwriting was in a transitional state between the two. Thom's writing looks more to me like secretary than italic, although it should be borne in mind that I am to palaeography what Elvis Presley was to veganism.

Paper for printing could be expensive, which is why the Royal Society had to choose between Ray's *History of Fishes* and Newton's *Principia Mathematica*. Writing paper, by contrast, was affordable to all, at roughly a penny for six sheets. A few sheets folded together would make a copybook, where pupils traced and repeated the strokes and letters from the writing master's books. They would copy pangrams – sentences which use all the letters of the alphabet, such as 'The quick brown fox jumps over the lazy dog.' Or, more likely in that biblically literate time, 'Job a righteous man of Uz waxed poor quickly.' They would copy aphorisms, such as those collected by John Ray: 'Manners often make fortunes.' Lines would be ruled with an inkless quill, so that the writing could be kept straight. The actual writing would be with a quill dipped in ink. This is pretty much how I learned to write, not with an actual quill, but with a nib on a stick, still dipped into ink. If we went wrong, our teacher would hit us; this in 1965, when I was seven.

Whether Thom actually attended the grammar school in Cuckfield, a two hour walk north of Hurst, I doubt, though I can't be sure; but it was well known for the excellence of its teaching of handwriting. Cuckfield Grammar was founded in about 1512, and shared a

---

67 There is good evidence to suggest that Shakespeare wrote his own will.

curriculum with Eton. Did Thom walk two hours there, and two hours back every day? Did he perhaps board with a family in Cuckfield? Or did his father, as seems most likely, hire tutors to come to Little Park to instruct him? Thom hired a tutor to teach Will mathematics (when Will was twenty-one, and much more interested in other matters). Thom also writes with pride about Jacky 'passing his accidence', which was a test of Latin grammar, but since the boys were also working on the farm, it seems unlikely that they went to school. Instead they had a live-in tutor, a twenty-three-year-old called John Hart.

There are currently two schools in Hurst: Hurstpierpoint College, a high-end public school (current fees for daybugs £8,495 per term, and £10,665 for boarders), and St. Lawrence Church of England Primary School, which is free, and was founded in 1714 by Thom and his family and friends. By 1700, there were around 500 grammar schools in England, but these were not seen as adequate in several respects. In particular, they demanded that prospective pupils be able to read and write before they started. The Society for Promoting Christian Knowledge was established in 1698 in order to solve this problem. The main way that they went about their business was the establishment of elementary and charity schools, as many as 6,000. Their work inspired other people to set up elementary schools, which would teach people to read and write. But not everyone approved. Bernard Mandeville wrote in 1723 that 'Charity schools and everything else that promotes idleness and keeps the poor from working, are more accessory to the Growth of Villainy than want of Reading, Writing, or even the Grossest Ignorance and Stupidity.' Thom clearly disagreed; he wanted the village children, poor or not, to be able to read.

John Hart was the first village schoolmaster. He dined with Thom often – not least because he took lodgings at Little Park Farm. He was born in Staffordshire in 1691, and matriculated at Clare College, Cambridge in 1709. Upon graduating in 1714, he took up the job as schoolmaster in Hurst. No one knows how they found him (or he, them); perhaps through the good offices of the

SPCK. Most villages had a 'dame school', where a lady would teach basic reading and writing, but in order to be a proper schoolmaster, you needed a licence. Thom and his friends were setting up a proper school for the children of the village, and so they wanted a proper teacher. The first entry concerning Hart is on 3 October 1714: 'Mr John Hart receiv'd the sacrament to qualify himself for a certificate from the Sessions.' Clearly, taking an oath to become a teacher was a serious matter. By taking the sacrament in church, he confirmed that he was a communicant member of the state-approved version of Christianity.

A few days later, on 8 October 1714, Thom accompanied John Hart to the sessions in Lewes, where 'Mr John Hart was sworn and had a certificate.' There is no record of what Hart actually put his hand on his heart to, but he would certainly have sworn that he didn't believe in transubstantiation, that the 'Bishop of Rome hath no jurisdiction in this realm of England', and further that he would uphold the succession of George I, 'and make known to His Majesty and his successors all treasons and traitorous conspiracies of which I know to be against him or any of them'.

After swearing such a solemn oath, which confirmed him in his position, he did what any young person might do on getting a new job: viz. he went to the pub and got pished. Unusually, he went with his new employers: 'Mr Nordern, Mr Richard Whitpaine, John Lindfield, Mr Hart and I came home together and drunk 14 bottles of wine at John Smith's.'

The next entry concerning John Hart was on the following Sunday, 10 October 1714, and I reproduce it here in full:

> A very fine day. Mr John Bateman preacht and read prayrs in the afternoon. After evning prayr Mr Henry Campion, Mr Hay, Mr John Bateman, a Frenchman, Mr John Hart and I went to Mr Richard Whitpaine's at Westtowne. Drank 3 bottles of beer and a small bowl of punch, and came home at 7.

I'm as sure as I can be that John Hart, just two days after swearing the oath that made him a licensed teacher ignored (at least) the part that read, 'and make known to His Majesty and his successors all treasons and traitorous conspiracies of which I know to be against him or any of them'. A few beers and a small bowl of punch were hardly enough to turn his head. The early eighteenth century was as febrile a time in British politics as now, more so, since civil war was about to break out again. There is no way that Thom and his fellow Tory school governors would have appointed a Whig.

It's not clear from the diary what Hart taught; or who, or how many. The curriculum would have focused on reading (probably the Bible) and, when pupils could read, writing and 'arithmatick'. Thom seems not to have educated either his sons or his daughters at the village school. The boys had tutors (John Hart one of them), and the girls went to 'Mrs Anne Beard's school', which may well have been on premises supplied by Thom.

Thom seems to have been the leading light in the school project, something approaching the chair of the governors. The diary entries concerned with it are mostly about school maintenance and the move to a new building in 1715. He writes (2 March 1719) that Mr. Scutt and Mr. Whitpaine contributed £7 each, whilst he contributed £4, and his mother a pound, which Thom promises to cover if she drops out. After Thom's death, Henry Campion seems to have taken on the role; he gave a rent of £5 per annum to set it up as an 'endowed school'; and this, despite a few changes over the years, is pretty much the primary school that still exists in Hurst.

Hart lodged at Little Park for the next six years, until 1722, and although Thom wrote in the diary about 'settling' Hart's account, it was Elizabeth who would have totted up what rent was owing. It's impossible to imagine that John Hart wasn't at least aware of Elizabeth's (and Thom's) High Tory sympathies.

In 1985, I lodged for three months in a council flat in Hangleton, a suburb of Hove, with a lady called Ros. In the evenings, we would sit in her front room and smoke our pipes, and tell one another about our disastrous love lives, which were equally but differently lurid. She would tell me everything, in particular about her appalling gentleman caller, who was called Tony. On nights he was due to visit, I would make myself scarce, because he scared the piss out of me. On days after his visit, Ros would sometimes have a black eye, and I would tell her off for putting up with him, and she would then tell me, in some detail, about how much she loved shagging Tony, so it was fine.

I always knew when it was time for bed, because Ros would offer me a line of speed.

'No, you're alright Ros,' I'd say. 'I'll probably just go to sleep.'

This always puzzled her.

'Can't you sleep after you've done speed?' she'd say.

'Oddly Ros, no.'

'I can!' she'd say cheerfully, before doing her line and tucking up for the night.

I knew everything about that woman. Landladies like to make a lodger feel at home. Hart knew, for sure, what Elizabeth was about.

I always thought I was the first person in my family to go to university, but this turns out to be untrue. My six-times-great great-great-uncle Jacky went up to matriculate at Pembroke College, Oxford in 1726. I identify somewhat with Jacky. I grew up amongst burly blond sporty types, and, although I loved them, I was not quite of them. I preferred reading to cricket. Hell, let's face it, I preferred reading to pretty much everything, which is how I got to university. When I got there I realised there were actually four things I preferred to reading, which were sex and drugs and rock and roll. Now, I'm down to reading again, reading and writing and smoking my pipe, all activities I could have undertaken quite happily as an early eighteenth-century parson.

There was never any doubt as to the boys' careers. Will, as the eldest son, would inherit Little Park; and Jacky would go into the Church. They both worked hard in the fields, but I have come to see them as different types. In my imagination, Will, the cricketer, the hare-courser, the race-goer, the fight fan, was a big burly blond

Burgundian, like his father, like my dad, my uncle, my cousin; whilst Jacky, the clever one, good at his books, versed in Latin, was dark haired and pretty, like his mother. No parents should have a favourite. Will was a proper lad, who took a greater part in the running of the farm across the course of the diary. Thom was proud of him, and always went to watch him play cricket, when he could. But I sense Thom's pride in Jacky's achievements, in a way because they are not his own.

The early eighteenth century was a time of decline in university admissions. Only somewhere in the region of 300 undergraduates were admitted into Oxbridge colleges in the 1720s, and only a few of them would have lasted the course. Only those intent on a career in the Church would bother graduating; the colleges were Anglican theological colleges as much as anything. The sons of gentry and aristocrats went only for a year or two, regarding them as finishing schools. The statistics on admittance make for shocking reading – between 1570 and 1630, more than half of entrants came from a 'plebian' background. By 1711, it was 27 per cent, by 1760, 17 per cent, and by 1801, 1 per cent.

Pembroke was a new college, founded in 1624 on the site of one of the medieval student halls, Broadgates. One of its first benefactors was James I, and Pembroke remained resolutely Jacobite. It took only twenty or so undergraduates a year, and the matriculation list notes the background of the students. You could be a gentleman, a commoner or a sizar, a student who waited table and cleaned up after his fellows. Jack is entered as a 'gentleman'. There was at this time a drop in gentry families sending their sons to Oxbridge, mainly because they didn't see the fees as a good investment in their sons' careers. Thom had enough money that he could send Jacky, and send him as a 'gentleman', which means he got to eat at high table, in return for higher fees.

There is no real record of how Jacky spent his hours at Pembroke. The chances are, that, since Thom and Elizabeth had invested in Jacky's future and since he knew he was destined for life as a Sussex clergyman, that he worked diligently at his books. Thom received a letter from him on 16 November 1727, and sent him a letter containing a guinea on 3 March 1727.[68] What we do know for sure is how long it took to travel between Hurst and Oxford; on 21 July 1727 'John Pelham set out to fetch Jacky from Oxford for 5s', and on 25 July 1727, Jacky was 'home from Oxford in the evening'.

The best account of undergraduate life at Pembroke at the time is from James Boswell's *Life of Samuel Johnson*. Johnson matriculated at Pembroke as a commoner in October 1728, a few weeks after Thom's last entry in the diary. The master at that time was Dr. Panting, who Johnson described as a 'fine Jacobite fellow'. Boswell collected accounts of Johnson's time there from his fellow students, and quotes the Bishop of Dromore, 'I have heard from some of his contemporaries that he was generally seen lounging at the College gate, with a circle of young students round him, whom he was entertaining with wit, and keeping from their studies, if not spiriting them up to rebellion against the College discipline, which in his maturer years he so much extolled.' Dr. Adams, who was a young fellow when Johnson was at the college, and who subsequently became master, told Boswell that, while he was at Pembroke College Johnson 'was caressed and loved by all about him, was a gay and frolicksome fellow, and passed there the happiest part of his life'. But this is a striking proof of the fallacy of appearances, and how little any of us know of the real internal state even of those whom we see most frequently; for the truth is that Johnson was then depressed by poverty and irritated by disease. Boswell wrote, 'When I mentioned to him this account as given me by Dr. Adams, he said, "Ah, Sir, I was mad and violent. It was bitterness which they mistook for frolick. I was miserably poor, and I thought to fight my way by my literature and my wit; so I disregarded all power and all authority."' Johnson described his fellow undergraduates as a 'nest of singing birds', because of the prevalence of poets among the undergrads.

This strikes me as a fair account of undergrad life even now;

68 A handsome gift, which illustrates Thom's wealth – a guinea in 1727 would be about £120 today.

lounging about with your mates, trying to persuade them not to go to lectures, frolicking about, putting two fingers up to the college authorities, being dirt poor, mad and violent. Worked for me, anyway. Johnson was unable to finish his degree; he left after three years because of a lack of funds. But poverty, for Jacky Marchant, wasn't a problem. Because Thom was rich.

As I argued earlier, the British economy took a catastrophic hit in 1709; and, like a proper historian, I quoted wheat prices at you, in order to establish this fact. But if I'm being honest, when I say the 'economy' I have no real idea of what I speak. The economy had largely recovered by 1720, but it was markedly different from ours, different in every respect. We have metrics, like GDP and the rest of it, inflation, Forex and so on. But in the early eighteenth century, such things didn't exist. The institutions that we might use to measure and regulate the economy were in their toddlerhood: the Bank of England was founded in 1694; Lloyd's Coffee House, where marine insurance could be bought and sold, in 1686; and, although joint-stock companies were first established in the early seventeenth century, stockbrokers were banned from trading in the Royal Exchange,[69] which was where most trade had been transacted since the time of Elizabeth. They also had to operate in the London coffee houses; the first systematic listings of stock prices were posted in Jonathan's Coffee House in 1698.

The main problem faced by the official economy was the lack of coinage. Until 1814, the pound was not measured against the gold standard, but against silver (hence pounds sterling). Silver shillings were minted from high-quality silver; such high quality that, if melted down into bullion and sold in Amsterdam, the price that could be obtained for the silver bullion in gold was higher than the face value of the silver coins. If you were clever, you could have your coins and still sell them for gold; clipping was a common practice.

---

69 Essentially, because they were a bunch of fucknuts who nobody could tolerate. *Plus ça change* and all that.

You skimmed off a bit around the edge of the coin, until you had enough to make bullion; then you sold the silver bullion, or had it made into new coins. Incredibly, the Royal Mint allowed private individuals to bring along their own silver bullion, which the Mint would then turn into coins.

Gold guineas were first issued in 1663, and valued at twenty-one shillings and sixpence. Isaac Newton was hired as head of the Royal Mint (in 1696, after his refusal to take Holy Orders lost him his fellowship at Trinity), where he instigated 'the Great Recoinage', which was hoped would solve the problem. All silver coins were supposed to be deposited with the Mint, who would then produce unclippable coins with milled edges, such as we seem not to need anymore – the only things I still pay for in cash are pipeweed and chippy teas. Newton also advocated revaluing the guinea down to twenty-one shillings, which is its value today.[70] What he should have done was make sure that each silver coin was cut with a base metal, so that its face value was more than its value as silver, because in India the value of silver was much higher than it was in England, so it still made sense to melt the silver, sell it for gold in India through the East India Company, get the Mint to turn your resulting gold bullion into guineas, and exchange these for silver coins, which were turned into silver bullion and so on. This process earned those who were able to pull it off something like 9 per cent profit per transaction. And so there was a shortage of silver coins, which meant that people had to rely on credit in order to buy and sell.

Apart from dung-carrying and faggoting, the next most common entry in Thom's diary is 'settled accounts'. There are hundreds of entries in which Thom pays, or is paid, for work done, or goods bought and sold, many of them on some kind of credit, such as promissory notes, or notes of hand. Essentially, Thom would deliver someone goods, fish or turnips, for example, and the recipient would promise to pay in a few months' time. Then Thom would use this credit to buy, for example, bohea tea, with a promissory note of

70   £1.05.

his own. When the turnip buyer paid up, Thom would pay the tea merchant and so on.

So far as I can tell, Thom acted as banker to some of his friends, lending them money on note of hand. Take the following five entries, chosen at random, as typical:

> The 2nd November 1716. A dry day. Paid the £50 and £6-5s for intrest, due to Mr Draper, deceas'd, to Richard Weedon for the use of Mr Holmes of Burpham and took in the bond.
> The 12th August 1717. A dry day. Reciev'd £6-10s of my Father Stone on John Cherry's account, part of the debt due to William Balcomb.
> The 23rd November 1717. A dry forenoon, very wet after. Paid Mrs Gratwick £5 in full for all the interest due to her to the beginning of August last.
> The 4th April 1718. A gloomy day. Jack Shave bought me an order to pay £150 to Mr Slade a woolen draper at the Gold Key in the burrough.
> The 29th April 1718. A dry forenoon, showry after. Nick Plaw was here in the evning. I gave him a bill of £150 on Mr Roberds for my Lord Dennet and a note for Mr Dennett to sign acknowledging the receit of it and promising the payment of the money when receiv'd.

Something is going on, but I can't quite fathom out what it is. Thom seems to be acting as an honest broker; perhaps even some kind of proto-banker. To untangle this stuff would take a friendly economic historian, and they are few and far between.

Moaning one evening to my stepdaughter Victoria about the near impossibility of finding out anything much about banking and credit before there were recognisable banks, she remembered that as a Cambridge history undergraduate she had been to several lectures by the economic historian Craig Muldrew, on credit arrangements in the early modern period. She found me his contact deets, and I fired off a quick email, in which I fluttered my eyelids and was generally just cute, begging for help. His generous reply was an a-ha moment; I hope he forgives my precis of his work ...

The way we view economic activity today is through the mutually incompatible lenses of Adam Smith and Karl Marx. In *The Wealth of Nations* (1776), Smith argued that the 'invisible hand' of rational self-interest regulated the market, rather than any moral purpose. In *Das Kapital* (1867), Marx argued that this resulted in exploitation of the wage-earning workers, who worked longer than the hours for which they were actually paid, in order that mine owners and industrialists and so on could profit from their labour; and that this is the immorality at the heart of capitalism. A 'free market' is impossible, because its functioning depends on loss of freedom for most of its participants. Craig Muldrew argues that neither model works when trying to understand the early modern economy.

For one thing 'the market', to whose supposedly amoral 'invisible hand' our political and economic masters pay obeisance, doesn't appear to have come fully to metaphorical life. Instead, there is a densely woven network of market relations in which all sections of society participated. Participants did not see themselves as primarily self-interested. Although profit was welcomed, it could not be achieved without the direct co-operation of neighbours, of fellow members of the network of relations. So buying and selling, rather than alienating us from our communities, bound communities closer together. It was, argues Muldrew, a moral economy.

Imagine that.

Almost all of this buying and selling was done on credit, at a time when legally binding credit did not yet have instruments to enforce it. The only time cash would be used would be in small transactions – or in the case where an individual's creditworthiness was unknown (or, presumably, when accounts are 'paid in full'). And creditworthiness was generated, not by a credit card company's algorithm, but by trust, by the debt you owed your society as a neighbour. The more you were seen as a straight dealer, as a person whose word really was their bond, the higher your creditworthiness. As Muldrew writes: 'Given the ubiquity of such actions, it seems functionally very unlikely that contemporaries would have used a language which stressed private desire for profit over mutual interdependence to interpret the meaning of what they were doing.' Buying and selling was seen in moral terms, rather than Smith's amoral self-interest. Social credit and economic credit were the same thing. One of the earliest modern economists, Charles Davenant, wrote in 1698 that: 'trust and confidence in each other, are as necessary to link and hold a people together, as obedience, love, friendship, or the intercourse of speech. And when experience has taught each man how weak he is, depending only upon himself, he will be willing to help others.'

As Ray had it in his *Proverbs*, 'He that has lost his credit is dead to the world.' Plain dealing, honesty and the keeping of promises were what made these market relationships possible. Given Thom's labyrinthine financial dealings, it can only be because he was trusted. Thom was straight, to be relied upon; a man who kept his word and was worthy of trust. This is a good thing to know about your seven-times-great great-grandfather. England has nostalgia in its bones, and there is little to be done about it; but at least we could be nostalgic about a time when there was very much such a thing as society. What I thought might be a somewhat dry (and amateurish) summation of Thom's business life has turned into a way to help me feel something of Thom's character. I owe Professor Muldrew a moral debt.

The poor, as you'll have no doubt noticed, are always with us, and they fall, now as then, into two distinct types, deserving and undeserving. Undeserving poor people include junkies, drunks, the workshy (such as me), chaotic families and asylum seekers (who somehow manage to cross the Sahara, spend a year in a hellish transit camp in Libya, give what money they have scraped together to pay unscrupulous smugglers to take them to Italy in a dangerous boat, before hacking up through Europe to live under an old cardboard box outside Calais port until, in utter desperation, risking their lives one last time to cross the English Channel in a toy inflatable, so they can claim £39.63 per week pre-loaded onto a debit card by the long-suffering British taxpayer). People don't like the undeserving poor, because they are poor in the wrong way.

The right way to be poor is through 'no fault of your own'. Even this isn't a great way to be poor. It might be no fault of your own that you are unable to find work, or you are disabled, or a single parent, or ill, or elderly, but you're still going to have to jump through a great many hoops to receive your pittance, which will then be subject to political control, by a party that has no aim other than to stay in power at all cost.

In 1720, whether you were deserving or not depended on your neighbours. Poor relief was administered through the parish, and Thom, as a churchwarden, seems to have acted as chair of the 'vestry meeting'. The vestry meeting was where local issues were decided; they happened in church, after a Sunday service. The main issues they dealt with were poor relief and highway maintenance. Given the state of Sussex roads, the relief of the poor would have been an easier task.

Thom, in his role as chair of the vestry meeting, collected Poor Tax from his neighbours; and rates were high. In 1721, Thom paid his father-in-law's Poor Tax to the tune of £6 8s; the equivalent of seventy-one days' wages for a skilled tradesman, or somewhere in the order of £750 in 2021. In 1701, an estimated £900,000 was collected nationally; a vast amount, worth hundreds of millions of pounds today. The great majority of Poor Law records from the early eighteenth century show that a very large proportion of propertied people seemed mostly willing to pay their assessed Poor Tax. There were two main reasons for this. Firstly, that it was felt that if the poor were not helped, they might rise in revolution. But secondly, and most importantly, there was a widespread feeling that it was something that the better-off should do for their less fortunate neighbours.

Poor relief helped the elderly, those with large families, widows and the disabled. Travellers were helped too, especially if they were pregnant women. ('5 December 1720, Lent a traveller whose wife lay in at the Swan 15s on the parish account.') It isn't always possible to tell from the many entries in the diary why people were being helped, but it is clear they were, week after week. It wasn't an ideal system. Many people fell through the gaps, and there were disputes and occasional bitterness between the rich and poor, but on the whole and by and large, by 1720, the system to some extent alleviated both poverty and social tension.

There were other taxes to be paid, including excise duties on imported goods. Perhaps the best known was the Window Tax, where home owners were assessed on how many windows their properties enjoyed. Home owners paid two shillings per window on properties with up to ten windows, and four shillings for between ten and twenty. This is why you can still find houses with bricked-up windows; if you had eleven or twelve windows, it was seen as worthwhile to block one or two off, in order to pay less tax to the king. On 22 December 1721, Thom was taken to court over a Window Tax issue, but, as he puts it, he 'got off'. He had paid up happily enough before, so the issue was probably not that he had been over-charged, but that the tax assessor had miscounted his windows, since he'd had two blocked off.

The main direct taxation was through the system of the Land Tax, which was paid by the land-owning classes, including Thom. The Window Tax was a bit mad, but the Land Tax was a very good idea, which should still be in operation, because it's based on taxing assets, rather than people's work. The Land Tax was administered by commissioners appointed annually by Parliament; but it was collected by hundreds of minor gentry and yeoman farmers – one of whom was Thom. No one much likes tax collectors now, but in 1720 tax collection was something that was done by your neighbours. Thom collects, but he also pays – in 1721, £9-11s-41/2d, maybe eleven hundred quid today. Once again, social obligation and economic obligation turn out to be closely related. Tax was not something you owed to an anonymous state, but to your neighbours. Theirs was a high-tax society.

Hurst in 1721 was a society where allegiance was owed to the community, and where neighbourliness was valued above all other public virtues. It was a place where the poor needed educating and taking care of; and where the well-off were prepared both to pay taxes and to give their time and energy to bring this about. Thom was at its centre; straight dealing, plain speaking, a trusted and trustworthy man. The more I get to know him, the more I like him.

Amongst the neighbours from whom Thom collected taxes was his friend, Mrs. Catherine Beard. I lost count of how many times he visits her, or dines with her. After Elizabeth, she is the woman who makes the most appearances in the diary. Mrs. Beard was a gentlewoman, and a landowner; Thom seems to have acted as her land agent, at least to some extent. They were in business together, on one occasion promoting a scheme to import pine from Norway.

And after supper at Mrs. Beard's, Thom strolls home through the darkness, looking forward to telling Elizabeth about the evening. He's whistling a tune.

'That damn'd air. Now where did I hear that?'

XII.

MUSIC HELPS NOT THE
TOOTH-ACHE

Music was only my third love, after girls and books, but it's a close-run thing. I suspect it won't be my last love, either,[71] but it will still be right up there, somewhere towards the end.

I actively listen to music for an hour or so most days, and have done for as long as I can remember. There was always music on at home, and all three of my parents were accomplished singers. When it comes to music, I am Mummy's boy. Her Nat King Cole/Ella Fitzgerald/Sarah Vaughan collection was always on the turntable – until Birth Dad Alan came home and put on records by the Clancy Brothers and suchlike. I knew from the age of six which I preferred. One kind of music featured very cool people singing great songs in astounding voices. The other was beardy old geezers going on about pubs and Irish nationalism and stuff. One kind had great piano, swinging rhythm sections, groovy horns and beautiful strings. The other had some bloke tweedling on a penny whistle. One had the jitterbug, the other country dancing, and you know what they say about that.

The transistor radio in the kitchen was always playing sixties pop, tuned to pirate station Radio London when Mum was in control. When Alan was home it was the Light Programme – the tedious *Two-Way Family Favourites* or *Sing Something Simple*, even duller than it sounds. He liked 'She Wears Red Feathers and a Hooly-Hooly Skirt' by Guy Mitchell, but didn't rate the Beatles,

---

71 That will most likely be diamorphine.

because hair. The Fabs were the first band I remember, doing 'She Loves You' on TV. And so on. Lives are marked out by pop music. Or mine is, anyway.

I've sung in dozens of bands. I joined my first band at eight. We were called the Marmites. I was in a band until 2016, when I lost my hearing. We were called The Same Tokens. I've sung opera, rock and rock opera. I've sung in church choirs, sixth-form bands, punk bands, ska bands, pop bands, soul bands, funk bands, funk/soul bands, punk/funk bands, nu-country bands, two anarchist collective bands, a comedy band and a high concept covers band doing Prefab Sprout songs. I've bellowed, crooned and rapped. I've sung in duos and with a twenty-eight-piece orchestra. And in all those years, and in all those iterations, I've never knowingly sung a folk song. But if I'm going to stand in front of the fire at Little Park Farm and sing a song for Thom and Elizabeth, like a precocious child singing to his indulgent grandparents, the moment has come.

In October 2019, I made a trip to Lancaster, to work for three days hosting a couple of stages at the Lancaster Music Festival; and to record a very old traditional folk song, for which I had tried to put all my long-cherished prejudices aside. In July, the Lancaster songwriter and guitarist Stuart Anthony had come to stay with me in Presteigne for a few days to work on the arrangement; now we were recording it in his studio. It was a huge honour to work with Stuart, who writes a lot with Larry Beckett, the Californian songwriter/ poet who wrote many of Tim Buckley's lyrics, including 'Song to the Siren'. Stuart had recorded guitar, harmonium and a pulsing drum, and all I had to do was to try to remember how to sing. At least my deafness meant I didn't have to stick my finger in my ear. The song is called 'The Turtledove'. This is the version I sang:[72]

> Fare thee well my dear, I must be gone,
> and leave you for a while.

---

72   You can hear this version via www.ianmarchant.com or see the QR code at the end of this chapter.

If I roam away, I'll come back again,
though I roam ten thousand miles, my dear,
though I roam ten thousand miles.

The sea will never run dry my dear,
nor rocks melt with the sun,
and I'll never be false to the woman I love
till all these things be done, my dear,
till all these things be done.

Oh say don't you see that little turtle dove,
sitting under the mulberry tree?
Hear him making a mourn for his own true love
as I shall mourn for thee, my dear,
as I shall mourn for thee.

Fair thee well my love, I must be gone,
and leave you for a while.
If I roam away, I'll come back again,
though I roam ten thousand miles, my love,
though I roam ten thousand miles.

I adapted them slightly from one of the best-known versions, because that has the words 'bonny lass' in it, and I had to draw the line somewhere. I did a pop songwriter's trick, changing 'my dear' to 'my love' in the repeated first verse, to add a bit of passionate emphasis.

'The Turtledove', also known as 'Fare Thee Well' or 'Ten Thousand Miles', is a folk standard, and has been performed by hundreds and recorded by dozens of singers over the years including Joan Baez, Mary Black, Eliza and Martin Carthy, Mary Chapin Carpenter, Marianne Faithfull, June Tabor and Alan's favourites Burl Ives and Liam Clancy. I was straying into his world, and it made me uncomfortable. No one knows why Alan was the way he was. He was not a cheerful Burgundian, hail-fellow-well-met kinda guy. He was a cruel, manipulative charmer. Turning into him is my biggest nightmare. Still – it's just a song. So I put my hands behind my back, and took a deep breath …

The village 'lost in the woods' is a common trope in gothic tales, but that's how I'd describe Rusper, even though it sits close to the end of the runway at Gatwick. The first time I visited, I got desperately lost trying to get back to Newhaven through the dark wooded lanes, so much so that I began to feel caught up in that gothic story. Whichever way I tried, I kept coming back to the village – it took three attempts to find the A24, all of three miles away. A village lost in the woods, from which there is no escape.

If ever you wondered why Kent, Surrey and Sussex are known as the 'Forest Counties', Rusper would be a good place to start. It is both the highest, and the furthest from the sea, of any village in Sussex. It's almost into the Surrey Hills Area of Outstanding Natural Beauty, and I remember standing at Newlands Corner, sixteen miles to the north-west, looking down on the Weald. Daniel Defoe, in his *A Tour Through the Whole Island of Great Britain*, published in 1724 but written from personal observation in 1712, calls the area 'the Wild'. The Wilderness. The nearest Defoe came to Rusper was Holmwood, just seven miles to the north.

> I saw neither town nor village for many miles, much
> less gentleman's seats, only cottages and single houses;
> but vast quantities of geese and poultry, which
> employs all the country in breeding them up. There
> has been large timber here, but most of it is cut down
> and gone, except that where there are any woods
> standing. The timber is still exceeding good and large.
> It is suggested that this place was in antient times so
> un-passable a wild, or over grown waste, the woods

so thick, and the extent so large, reaching far into
Sussex, that it was the retreat for many ages of the
native Britons, who the Romans could never drive
out; and after that it was the like to the Saxons, when
the Danes harrass'd the nation with their troops and
ravaged the country wherever they came.'

Rusper was Elizabeth Marchant's home village. Her maiden name
was Stone, an Anglo-Saxon name, so perhaps Defoe was right that
the invaders never penetrated this far into the wildwood. The Stones
seem to have been a gentry family fallen on hard times. Their house
was called The Nunnery. It was built on the site of a Benedictine
priory that was dissolved by Henry VIII, and in the only picture that
I have found of the old house (there is still a later house of that name
on the site), it looks to be a rambling pile of a place, built in brick and
pantile, with three bays, six chimneys and two storeys, with jettied
gables above. Maybe a century or more old when Elizabeth was
born, it looks very much like the professor's house in *The Lion, the
Witch and the Wardrobe*, and it's easy to imagine winding stairs and
hidden rooms in the gable attics. If I was an estate agent pricing such
a house in 2023, with great connections to London, and as close to
Gatwick as possible, what might I value it at? Two and a half million,
perhaps?

Elizabeth was born in The Nunnery on 16 May 1679 and was
baptised in St. Mary Magdalene Church, Rusper. When she married
Thom, in St. Mary's, Slaugham, on 10 September 1700, she was
twenty-one, and he was twenty-five.

Although Elizabeth doesn't have a voice in Thom's diary, she
is a towering presence. There are no real details of housekeeping
arrangements; but what there is is a clear sense from Thom that
Elizabeth was an individual with skills, opinions, and both a political
and a social life of her own. She was Thom's partner in every sense;
certainly, she kept detailed household accounts, as evidenced by
the fact that Thom leaves it to her to reckon up how much John
Hart owed for board and lodging. The diary surely doesn't do as

a detailed account book for the business, so it seems highly likely that there were proper double-entry accounts, and at least probable that Elizabeth was in charge of these. She had money of her own; we know this because Thom settles her accounts as often as he does anyone else's. Elizabeth went shopping in Lewes or Horsham with her friends, and often took supper with them too, without Thom. After these suppers, he quite often went to bring her home on a dark night. Her particular pals were Mrs. Barbara Campion, Peter Courthope's daughter and Henry Campion's wife, and Mrs. Susan Courthope, Peter's widowed daughter-in-law. So Elizabeth moved regularly in a slightly more elevated social circle than her husband, who mostly only dined at Danny in her company. There is no suggestion in the diary that Thom had a problem with this, or that he expected her to be at his beck and call. He never failed to note his wedding anniversary in the diary, which must have made him popular – unless, of course, Elizabeth had reminded him first. Thom doesn't seem to have left a will; so on his death in 1728, Little Park passed to Elizabeth, of which she seems to have been an excellent steward.

Based on this somewhat flimsy evidence, I have come to imagine that Thom and Elizabeth enjoyed a companionate marriage. To judge by the number of children they had (eleven in total), and the persistent seventeenth-century belief that women could only get pregnant if they enjoyed an orgasm, it seems a reasonable bet that their sex life was active. By the late seventeenth century couples were no longer marrying just for financial advantage, but because they liked, or even loved, one another. This shift towards marriage which provided emotional and sexual satisfaction was a step towards equalising marital relations between women and men. It became unfashionable for husbands and wives to address one another as 'Sir' and 'Madam', but rather by their first names. Thom usually refers to Elizabeth as 'my wife' in the diary, but given their propensity to call their children by pet names (such as 'Jacky' and 'Bett'), it seems at least likely Thom and Elizabeth addressed one another as such, rather than Mr. or Mrs. Marchant. According to Daniel Defoe, writing in 1727, wives and husbands should be 'first and dearest friends'.

This was a moment when women were beginning to argue that they were the equal of men. The woman regarded as the first feminist writer, a century before the better-known Mary Wollstonecraft, was Mary Astell. She wrote that men should look on women as Reasonable Creatures and not confine them 'with chain and block to the chimney corner'. In a series of publications, from 1694 until her death in 1731, Astell promoted women writers, the education of women and the spiritual benefits of female friendship. Astell was a committed Tory, so it's not beyond the realms of possibility that Elizabeth and her circle read Astell's works.

This is not to say that men and women were equal in the early eighteenth century; just that Thom and Elizabeth may have regarded one another as such. They were clearly not equal in the eyes of the law. Women had the right to petition the king, and had done so extensively in the seventeenth century, but not the right to vote. If a man murdered his wife he could be sentenced to be hanged, but if a woman murdered her husband she could be burned at the stake – the last time this was carried out was at Tyburn in 1725. William Blackstone, writing in his *Commentaries on the Laws of England* in 1765, said that 'the husband and wife are one, and the husband is the one'. When a woman married, all her property passed to her husband; including the children. It is telling that Elizabeth never remarried after Thom's death; perhaps because she couldn't replace her 'dearest friend', but also because she wouldn't have wished to give up the ownership of Little Park.

Thom spent a lot of time travelling between Hurst and Rusper, on the worst roads in England. If Hurst to Steyning on horseback took about four hours, as estimated by Ralph Foxwell, then the trip to Rusper would have taken something like seven. Thom helped his 'Mother and Father Stone' sell The Nunnery and move to Hurst. I suspect that part of the reason for the move to Hurst was that Elizabeth was worried about her parents and wanted them nearer; I also strongly suspect that the Stones' money had run out. So the marriage may have been companionate, but the arrangement must have had many advantages for both parties. The Marchants, well-to-do yeomen looking to improve their social position; the Stones, distressed gentlefolk, looking to restore their fortunes. It's therefore possible that the marriage settlement was modest. But Elizabeth did not marry empty-handed. She brought at least one tangible asset to Little Park, and that was the advowson for St. Mary Magdalene Church in Rusper.

And before you reach for your phone and start searching, an advowson is not a thing, but a right; the right to appoint a clergyman to a parish. The person, or organisation, that holds this right is known as the patron. This right is immeasurably old: 'The right of advowson is historically the survival of an originally much more extensive control exercised by the feudal lord over churches on his estates, which goes back in turn to the time when the pagan priest, in Teutonic Europe the predecessor of the Christian priest, was the feudal dependant of the lord.'[73]

This right has been kept alive since the Constitutions of Clarendon, in 1164. This was the legislation that Henry II passed to make clergy subject to the king's law, and, in opposition to which, Thomas Becket was murdered in Canterbury Cathedral. One of its clauses declared that all suits regarding advowsons be tried in the civil courts rather than Church courts, and so it remains, over 850 years later. The Palace of Clarendon, where the constitutions were drawn up, is now nothing more than a few crumbling walls near Salisbury. But this obscure point of law still stands; advowsons can be exchanged (though no longer sold), and there is little the Church of England can do about it.

Thom and Elizabeth sold the Rusper advowson on 6 November 1721 to Mr. William Martin for £700 and five guineas, worth today somewhere around £25,000.

It came with strings:

---

73   *Oxford Dictionary of the Christian Church*, second edition, 1974.

> The 6th December 1721 Wednesday. A gloomy day, frost
> thawing towards night. Mr Beard and Mr William Martin
> here. Mr Beard brought word that the living of Rusper
> was vacated by Mr Sixsmith.

This news seems to have precipitated something of a crisis, because the following day, Thom writes:

> The 7th December 1721 Thursday. A gloomy day, snow
> in the evning. I sign'd a presentation to Mr William
> Martin of Rusper liveing to resign when either of my
> Sons are in orders. Took a bond of him for it.

Mr. William Martin must have thought that it was a fair bet that neither Will nor Jacky would want to enter the Church, given that he'd only recently paid a large amount of money to get the living. But he must also have seen the justice of the arrangement, since he seems to have had no reason to sign the bond otherwise – we can imagine he was anxious when Jacky started his studies at Oxford, five years later. The arrangement in Rusper assured him of a reasonable living and an honourable profession. So Rusper was the family pueblo almost as much as Hurst. Elizabeth's childhood home, her family, the hopes for Jacky's future, all were part of the story of the village lost in the woods.

On 25 July 2021, I was staying with old Ralph Foxwell in Newhaven. He's not a churchgoer, so I borrowed his car and drove to a Sunday service in Rusper. I managed to get lost again, going twice round the Horsham one-way system, and got there with only a few minutes to spare. The date is relevant because the church is dedicated to St. Mary Magdalene, and the 22nd is her Feast Day. The 25th being

the nearest Sunday, I was therefore unknowingly at the patronal service, dedicated to the first apostle. At the beginning of the service, the rector, Father Nick Flint, pointed out that churches have earthly patrons, who get to choose the new vicar. He reminded the congregation that for the last fifty years, the patron has been the Bishop of Chichester, but that 300 years ago it was the Marchants; who were represented in Rusper church for the first time in a long time, by me. I waved a hello to the welcoming congregation.

The core of Rusper hasn't changed much. The church is at its centre, and there are two inns, the Star and the Plough. In Thom and Elizabeth's day, the Star was the sole inn, and this is where Thom would have slaked his not inconsiderable thirst. The Plough only became an inn in the nineteenth century; previously it had been a forge, where Thom could have left his horse while he had a crafty one in the Star. Yet the Plough looks about as olde worlde as a pub can look, as though it had been serving drinks since forever. On my first visit to Rusper, the one where I got lost trying to leave the village, I decided to eat dinner in the Plough. The ceiling was so low I had to bend almost double to find a seat by the open fire. That first time, I wasn't thinking about Thom, or Elizabeth, but the gentleman that my Field grandmother kept house for, at Leith Hill Place, just outside Ewhurst, some seven miles or so from Rusper. Mum used to complain about him, years later.

'Oh, nothing was too good for Mr. Vaughan Williams. Your grandmother loved him. In the war, Mum would always make sure he had plenty. She used to trap rabbits for his dinner.'

Even before the railway arrived in Horsham and Faygate, Rusper became in the nineteenth century a place where successful middle-class families started to build large houses. One of these families were the Broadwoods, the first family to make a fortune in the music business. John Broadwood and Sons are currently the oldest extant holders of a Royal Warrant, having been piano manufacturers to successive monarchs since George II. Haydn played Broadwoods, and one was presented to Beethoven, which became his preferred instrument. By the turn of the nineteenth century, they were rich enough to buy Lyne House, a fairly elegant Georgian mansion, built in 1716; it's just over the border into Surrey, but is part of the parish of Rusper. By the 1850s, the Broadwoods were so rich that they rebuilt Lyne House into a huge Gothic pile. They were very rich because in the 1850s, they were manufacturing and selling 2,500 pianos a year.

John Broadwood's grandson Henry ran the firm for most of the nineteenth century. Henry and his wife had eleven children; the youngest of whom, Lucy, was born in 1858. She was six when the family took over Lyne House in 1864, following the death of Henry's brother John. She was highly musical, and was a fine piano player. Under different circumstances, she might have pursued a concert career, but as the unmarried youngest daughter of a very rich family she was free to follow whatever course she wished. Lucy had become entranced by the folk songs she heard in the local area, from gardeners, innkeepers and, most of all, blacksmiths.

Her Uncle John, from whom Lyne House was inherited, is credited with being the first modern collector of folk songs. In 1847 he had a small number of pamphlets privately printed called *Old English Songs*. It was such an obscure publication that it appears it was not even known to the family. There were only fourteen songs, but what John Broadwood did was to write down both the music and the words of folk songs, which no one had done before. On the title page he wrote: 'The airs are set to music exactly as they are now sung, to rescue them from oblivion.' In 1943, Frank Howes, the chief music critic of *The Times*, wrote of him that he was the first to use the 'scientific method applied editorially to the oral tradition of English folk-song'.

Lucy had probably been noting down the songs she heard around the village, even as a child, but she was inspired, aged twelve, by finding a copy of her uncle's pamphlet in the library at Lyne. Without Lucy, John Broadwood's idea of collecting both music and words might well have been consigned to oblivion. Armed with his 'scientific method', Lucy began collecting seriously. Her first book, in 1890, was *Sussex Songs*, which included all of her uncle's songs, plus ten that she had collected herself. It was her second book, *English County Songs*, published in 1893, which brought her to national attention. She and her collaborator J.A. Fuller Maitland collected songs from each of England's counties, which they found by looking in old publications, by writing to folklorists asking for help and by collection in the field. The great folk-song scholar of our day, Steve Roud, says that *English County Songs*, together with Sabine Baring-Gould's *Songs and Ballads of the West*, 'really caught the mood of the time', and 'were responsible for attracting a host of new converts'.

The turn of the nineteenth century saw the resurrection of the idea of 'Merrie England'. It was the England of the revival of maypoles, of village green fetes, of many of our 'traditions', reformed in a vision of Ideal England, the one we saw from the warplanes rising over the Cotswolds. A vision that always and forever sees the countryside as bucolic Arcadia, rather than as a place where livings need to be made, crops grown, meat processed and cows milked, in the face of falling populations and a demographic that is sharply rising in age. The countryside is not just fields; it's 'the field', an object of curiosity, a curiosity that still operates, which claims to seek out an 'authentic way of life'; back to the land, off grid, grow your own pants, sing your own songs. I am subject to it myself, except for the songs bit, since I prefer singing Burt Bacharach. Actually, there are those who think that folk songs are just old pop songs with a memorable tune, rather than an authentic link to a lost culture. Will people be doing 'Delilah' or 'Don't Look Back in Anger' in 2321 folk club nights? Of course they will.

After the publication of *English County Songs*, Lucy Broadwood was viewed as one of the authorities on folk song in England, so much so that she was involved in the early days of the English Folk Song

Society. Founded in 1898, it was in the doldrums when Lucy, Cecil Sharp and Ralph Vaughan Williams revived it in 1904. For the next twenty years of her life (she died in 1929) she edited its quarterly publication, the *Folk Song Journal*, pretty much deciding what was, and what wasn't, authentic. In defence of her idea of this eternal question, she argued with Cecil Sharp, who left in 1911 to set up the English Folk Dance Society, which merged after Lucy's death with the Folk Song Society in 1934, to become the English Folk Dance and Song Society. It still exists, and still exerts influence over what is, and what isn't proper folk music. Its London headquarters, Cecil Sharp House, is named after Lucy's rival. But she is not forgotten in the world of folk – on the first of May every year, the Broadwood Morris Men come to Rusper, decorate her memorial in the church, and then dance about with sticks or something.

The Wedgwood/Darwin family bought Leith Hill Place in 1847. A daughter of the family, Margaret, the great-granddaughter of Josiah Wedgwood and the niece of Charles Darwin, moved back to the family home after her husband Arthur Vaughan Williams died leaving her with three small children. The eldest was Hervey Vaughan Williams, who lived at Leith Hill Place till his death in 1944 – it was for him that my grandmother kept house. The middle child was another Margaret, who set up the Leith Hill Music Festival, a choral competition that still runs. As festival conductor, she chose her youngest brother, Ralph. He was not particularly well known as a composer at that time; the Leith Hill Festival was his first big break, and he remained conductor till 1953, five years before his death.

Ralph Vaughan Williams is probably England's best-loved composer. He was certainly its nicest. He was a modest man, who believed in community music making. Lucy Broadwood was a relative and a near neighbour. It's not unsurprising that he picked up an interest in folk music, particularly the folk music of Surrey and the Sussex Weald. Another composer who fell under Lucy Broadwood's spell and into the English Folk Song Society was the Australian Percy Grainger, who, after hearing her talk in 1903 started collecting himself; most famously, perhaps, 'Brigg Fair'. His 'English Country Garden' was always on *Two-Way Family Favourites* when I was a lad, which is where I conceived a deep loathing of it. Grainger took the revolutionary step of using a phonograph to collect the songs, rather than writing them down; and both Lucy Broadwood and Vaughan Williams were impressed and supportive. The machine Grainger used was bought and owned by the EFSS, and this was the machine Vaughan Williams used to make his own recordings.

And so it was that Ralph Vaughan Williams turned up one night in 1907 at the Plough in Rusper to record the landlord David Penfold singing a song. Imagine the scene – gas lit, Vaughan Williams operating the hulking, heavy, fragile, clockwork-operated machine with its large horn for the singer to sing as loudly as possible into. The equipment is difficult to use; the recordings are often faint and distorted. The locals sat hushed as the landlord gave Vaughan Williams his song – which was, of course, 'The Turtledove'.

There is one more step to take. Steve Roud lists 'The Turtledove' as one of only forty or so folk songs that we can know for sure was being sung in the late seventeenth and early eighteenth centuries; he dates it between 1684 and 1702. Roud has categorised as many folk songs as he can, and given them a number, like Ludwig von Köchel did for Mozart. 'The Turtledove', for folk song aficionados, is Roud 422.

I present my evidence. Elizabeth was born and raised in Rusper, and continued to visit her family regularly, as did Thom. They held the advowson of the church, and had arranged for Jacky to become rector. Thom drank in the Star, and probably had recourse to the forge. In the nineteenth century, Rusper became a centre for folk music and its collection. In 1907, Vaughan Williams collected the 'The Turtledove' in the village, in the Plough, which had previously been a blacksmith's, which Lucy Broadwood knew was a rich source of songs; she had collected songs from blacksmiths in nearby Horsham and Dunsfold. According to Steve Roud, 'The Turtledove' is one of only about forty songs that can be positively dated as being sung in the late seventeenth century. Did Thom and Elizabeth know the song? I'm saying yes, of course they did.

What I can't know is if Thom actually liked 'The Turtledove'. Nick Flint told me that local legend has it that 'Bohemian Rhapsody' was written in Ridge Farm Studio, Rusper, where Queen were rehearsing in 1975; and drummer Roger Taylor confirms that they began playing it there. 'Bohemian Rhapsody' has attained the status of a folk song, no doubt. But how would I feel if my seven-times-great great-grandchildren could choose a song to sing to me, and they turned up in their time machine and sang BoRhap? I'd be gutted, is the answer, and I would chase them off with my stick.

But still, when I sang the song in Stuart Anthony's home studio, I forgot my long-held prejudices, and even my resentment of my father's musical taste. I closed my eyes, and imagined myself singing it for them, for Thom and Elizabeth, hoping that I might do the thing justice. I imagined that they might hear me, far off, and that they might sing along.

At the top of a forgotten flight of worm-eaten steps hidden behind an old oak door, she sits in her chamber, her white hair undone, the great-grandmother of my great-grandmothers, humming in tune with her spinning wheel.

Fare thee well my dear.

XIII.

WHO DRAWS HIS SWORD
AGAINST HIS PRINCE MUST
THROW AWAY THE SCABBARD

By December 2020, the chemo with a side of steroids had pretty much knocked me out. I sat, unable to think, unable to read and unable to pick things up, because I'd lost all grip in my hands. All I wanted to do was watch telly and eat. And when I say telly, I mean *Flog It!* and *Tipping Point*, not *Breaking Bad* or *Killing Eve*. Steroids make you hungry, like the caterpillar, except for cakes rather than lovely crispy, organically grown seasonal leaves.

Hilary would try to encourage me to walk every day. I was nursing an as-yet-undiagnosed pulmonary embolism, which was starting to make me seriously breathless. Some days I could get as far as the Assembly Rooms, a quarter of a mile away, and five minutes under ordinary circumstances. It was a bad time, a hard time. One day, I had got up to the Assembly Rooms and just about halfway back when we met our neighbour Louisa, my link to cricket's deep past. A proper person, is our Louisa, the sort of person you'd like living in your town. When she asks me how I am, I know she means it. She lives with her husband and four children behind a high yew hedge, right in the heart of the community. At least once a month she comes to church, often for the 1662 Prayer Book communion service. For 300 years, her family and mine have gone to the same kind of church and said the same words.

Hilary told her about the chemo I was having, and how it was made from the leaves of the yew tree.

'It might be made from our hedge,' she said. 'Cancer Research come and collect our clippings every year.'

'That's brilliant,' I said. 'Local, artisanal, organically grown docetaxel. We should start a business.'

The next day, she put a card through my door, saying that if I needed to get down to Sussex to see Ralph, she was driving down most weeks to see her mum, who was not well. Lockdowns and my increasing weakness meant that I couldn't take her up on her offer, but it meant a lot that she was on my side.

Three hundred years ago, there's a chance we would also have been on the same side; or, at least, the Marchants would have imagined themselves so. My ancestor kept a diary – hers was King Charles II. If things had been otherwise, I might have inherited an estate of several hundred acres in Mid Sussex. Lady Louisa Collings, née Gordon-Lennox, by a set of circumstances no less unlikely, might have been Princess Louisa, a member of the Royal Family. She is a Stuart. And the Marchants supported the Stuart cause. They were Jacobite Tories.

This part of the story was hard to puzzle out. Most of the evidence is circumstantial. With no academic libraries to sit in and do research, I was thrown back on my own resources. A 4,000-volume home library might seem adequate for the task, but large parts of it are about abandoned narrow-gauge railways, obscure parlour pubs and the doings of drug-crazed Freaks. The 1715 Jacobite Rebellion in Sussex hardly figures, and my first resource was my A level history notes, which I'd rescued from Mum and Ralph's attic a few years before. Even tinterweb could come up with very little. But I plugged away.

I am not a Tory, but I didn't want to argue with Thom. Once more I wanted to step into his shoes, and to understand both his politics and his faith; which, in 1715, were pretty much the same thing.

Lots of people have Tory grandparents; including me. My actual grandpop Charles Jesse was one, and I dealt with that fine. I just didn't want Thom to be one. What I mean by this, of course, is that I didn't want him to be the kind of person who would welcome shipping asylum seekers to Rwanda, or to defend ministers who lie to Parliament and give billions of pounds' worth of NHS contracts to pals that they were at Oxford with. I didn't want Thom to support corruption, but to fight it with all his heart. And what I came to see was that he and his allies *were* fighting against government corruption, and that the party who now call themselves the 'Conservatives' bear little resemblance to the Tory Party of Thom and Elizabeth and their friends and neighbours. The historian of the Conservative Party Robert Blake wrote that there is no meaningful link between the early eighteenth-century Tories and the Conservative Party of Peel and Disraeli. Similarly, there is precious little resemblance between the Conservative Party of Baldwin, Macmillan and Heath that my grandpop supported and the current gang of Ayn Rand fanboy libertarian accelerationists who have seized power both in this country and over the zombie corpse of their party.

Once I set aside my prejudices, I understood that, after all, we both share a cause, which is that we would both like to play a part in bringing down Their Majesties' Governments. I have come to understand that in 1715, I would have been a Tory myself.

Since everyone seems to 'do' the Tudors at school, watch films and telly shows about the Tudors, and perhaps even read Hilary Mantel's trilogy of novels about Thomas Cromwell and his relationship with the Tudors, I shall take for granted that readers can be spared most of the details about the English Reformation, Henry VIII's split with Rome, the rising and falling tides of Protestantism and Catholicism across the course of the sixteenth century, the Protestant martyrs and the coming to the throne of Elizabeth I &c. If not, see me after.

Elizabeth's first Parliament passed the Act of Supremacy and the Act of Uniformity. The first confirmed that the monarch was now the head of the Church of England, as under her old dad; not the Pope, as under her sister Mary. The second insisted that all churches use her half-brother Edward VI's *Book of Common Prayer*. Not everyone went along with this. English Christians at the end of Elizabeth's reign were split into three broad camps: the Catholics, who felt that monarchs of whatever stripe were subordinate to the Pope; the straightforwardly Protestant Calvinists, who were unconvinced by anything that smacked of popery, such as bishops and liturgies; and what I'm going to call the 'High Church' – people who wanted the Church to be Catholic-esque, with the monarch in place of the Pope, with bishops, but without too much nonsense about transubstantiation &c, and with the *Book of Common Prayer*.

After Elizabeth died in 1603, her cousin James VI of Scotland took over, to become King James I of England. He had had enough of the Calvinists who ran the Scottish Kirk, but he was a convinced Prot. So the High Church wing of the Church that wanted some of the trappings of Catholicism plus the *Book of Common Prayer* won out over the hard-line Proddy dogs, who were becoming known as Puritans. The Catholics shot their bolt with the attempted assassination of the king on 5 November 1605, gunpowder treason and plot &c, and were subsequently pretty much out of the picture. Catholicism became illegal, and the conflict focused on the differences between the High Anglicans and the Puritans, who were setting up their own churches run by elders, sometimes known as 'presbyters', separate from the national Church established by Elizabeth. Suffering persecution from the establishment, some of these churches fled to Holland, and one went further still, to America on the *Mayflower* to set up the Massachusetts colony.

King James felt that all churches should be run by bishops who he, as head of the Church of England, had the power to appoint and dismiss. He could do this because of his unshakeable belief in the divine right of kings, a belief that reached its dreadful apogee with his son and heir, Charles I.

This is an idea which, for all intents and purposes, England still holds to be true. A monarch in England is anointed by God, to this day. That's why it reads 'DG', on all our coins, which means *Dei Gratia*, by the Grace of God. Divine right was an idea that was central to the faith and politics of Thom and his circle, and one which has consequences for us still, so it's worth a proper look.

According to the theory of divine right, secular government is only lawful without papal or clerical confirmation because monarchs have a divine right to rule, direct from God. Parliaments didn't have this divine endorsement until after the Glorious Revolution of 1688, when many of the powers of the monarch were invested in Parliament. This is the situation that still pertains – Parliament rules on behalf of the monarch and has all the powers of the monarchy. So, in a sense, the belief that the King (and possibly his successors) are anointed by God means that his government in Parliament is too. Twelve Anglican bishops, theoretically at least chosen by the monarch, still sit as of right in the House of Lords. Although the law has been changed (as recently as under the Cameron Clegg government) so that monarchs can marry a Catholic, it is still illegal for the monarch to actually be a Catholic. Is this right? Should it still be the case? I don't think so. I would say that the vast majority of practising Anglicans are unhappy with this situation, whilst a large number of 'cultural' Anglicans think it's fine. Which is why, of course, disestablishment of the Church of England needs to happen. People who profess cultural Anglicanism can use it as a weapon against not just Catholics but other faiths too, mainly Islam. So long as the head of state is also the head of the state Church (in England only, it should be noted; not in Scotland, Northern Ireland or Wales), there will be those who claim that a follower of Islam couldn't be prime minister.

At the time of writing we now have a Hindu prime minister, who will have to excuse himself from discussion about Anglicanism, the first time this has happened. (Though, given the current rate of turnover, we'll probably have a Wiccan or a Baha'i prime minister by the time you read this.)

Disestablishing the Church of England might seem the very

least of our problems, but if a Progressive Alliance forms around the idea of constitutional reform, it might yet become a live issue. I'm going to get 'Disestablish Now' tattooed on my calves, and I'm going to ponce about in shorts, no matter the weather, until the job is done.

That only someone who has been anointed by God can be monarch, and that that can't be changed, might seem like a quaint anachronism now, but to those who, like Thom, felt that James II and his descendants were the rightful monarchs, it was the whole point. Charles I, awaiting execution, wrote a 'spiritual autobiography' and defence of divine right called *Eikon Basilike*, which was so widely read that Royalist sympathies didn't die during the period of Cromwell's Commonwealth but rather grew more entrenched. When Charles II was restored to the throne in 1660, he insisted that the Church canonise his father; so Charles I, king and martyr, is the only saint to have been canonised by the Church of England. I told Louisa that her many times great-grandfather was an actual saint, which seemed to freak her out a bit, as well it might.

Charles I's wife Henrietta Maria was a practising Catholic; fear of a resurgent Catholicism because of her influence was one of the undoubted causes of the Civil War. Her eldest son, Charles II, had the good sense to profess Anglicanism (although he converted to Catholicism on his deathbed), but his brother, James II, did not. His father had written in the *Eikon Basilike*, 'I know no resolutions more worthy a Christian king than to prefer his conscience before his kingdoms.' James was sixteen when his father was executed; little wonder that he followed his father's advice.

In 1687 when James II issued his Declaration of Indulgence, promising to protect the Church of England, but suspending penal laws against Catholics and Dissenters, six Church of England bishops (including William Sancroft, the Archbishop of Canterbury and Thomas Ken, the Bishop of Bath and Wells) petitioned the king to withdraw it – and when he refused, they in turn refused to have it read in their churches. They were locked in the Tower, and tried for disobedience to a royal command. When they were found not guilty people lined the streets to cheer them as they filed away from the court.

A few days before, James II's second wife, Mary of Modena, had given birth to the infant James, Prince of Wales (who would become known as the Old Pretender). Since his father would be raising him Catholic, the crisis, long in the making, had finally come. William of Orange set sail from Hellevoetsluis in the Netherlands and James II left for France. Parliament pragmatically declared that James had left the throne so it was vacant, and they offered it to William and Mary, who became joint monarchs both in fact and in law. It was, Parliament felt, the only workable arrangement. But while James had fled the country, he had not abdicated, unlike Edward VIII in 1936. He had run away from England but not, in his view, the throne. Many of his subjects agreed; they felt that once a king had been anointed and crowned, divine right meant that he, and he alone, was monarch until death. Divine right and the 'passive obedience' were cornerstones of High Anglican beliefs: subjects owed loyalty and obedience to the monarch whoever it might be and whether or not they were in agreement with his religious views. And so Roman Catholic James II was still king.

From the opposing point of view, although William III was not an Anglican but a Dutch Calvinist, most people in England were tired after 150 years of religious strife and didn't worry too much, so long as the king was Protestant. And, after all, William's wife Queen Mary was both James II's daughter and an Anglican.

But some 400 clergy (including William Sancroft and Thomas Ken), refused to take an oath of allegiance to William and Mary. This group and their followers were known as 'the non-jurors'. In the space of a few weeks they went from being imprisoned by James II to advocating for his return, so much so that they were prepared to lose everything. They could not go against what they saw as 'Divine Will'.

Thom's father would have sworn allegiance to James II. An oath was an oath. Your word was your bond or it was nothing; that was the basis of the moral, social and commercial economies of

Hurst in 1715. Contrary to popular belief, Christians don't really like taking oaths on the Bible. The last time I found myself in the dock, I chose to affirm rather than swear by Almighty God, mostly because I was quite clearly guilty, and it mattered not what the beak thought of me.

Numbers has it thus: 'Then Moses said to the heads of the tribes of Israel, "This is what the Lord has commanded: if a man makes a vow to the Lord or swears an oath to obligate himself by a pledge, he must not break his word; he must do everything he has promised."'

Christ, in the Sermon on the Mount, turned it over: 'You have heard that it was said to the ancients "Do not break your oath, but fulfil your vows to the Lord." But I tell you not to swear at all; either by heaven, for it is God's throne, or by the earth, for it is His footstool; or by Jerusalem, for it is the city of the great king. Nor should you swear by your head, for you cannot make a single hair white or black. Simply let your yes be yes and your no be no.'

Where did authority lie? To a Roman Catholic, it lay with the Pope; to a High Anglican, it lay with the king alone. No one had the right to rebel against this authority. That is why the Hurst Jacobites felt that they were rebelling, not against the legitimate king (the Old Pretender, in their view), but against a usurper, George I, who did not have what the Chinese call 'the Mandate of Heaven'.

In 1690, the non-jurors were deprived of their livings. William Sancroft crowned James II and was not going to turn his back on his past. He was replaced as Archbishop of Canterbury by John Tillotson, but Sancroft started to appoint and consecrate non-juring bishops. The non-jurors now became schismatics, and set up their own Church, which limped along until the 1790s.

And Thomas Ken, the saintly Bishop of Bath and Wells had to leave the Bishop's Palace in Wells, just about the nicest house in England. But he, at least, is not quite lost to the long memory of the Church. His lovely morning hymn 'Awake, My Soul, and with the Sun', is number one in *Hymns Ancient and Modern*, and we sing it once or twice a year. When we do, I say a prayer for Thom.

Thom was a churchwarden, which is to say, the Bishop of Chichester's representative in the parish. He had his own chair, he attended weekly vestry meetings to administer the church, the Poor Law and highway maintenance. Given his position in the church, he's unlikely to have been an actual schismatic. But we'll see that on several occasions he notes that he has been to hear non-jurors preach, and, on at least one occasion, one of these dines at Little Park. This would seem to match gentry non-juring behaviour. Of the one hundred or so families who supported the non-jurors, not all were strict in their observance, and many probably attended the established Church, like Thom. Many felt their obligations lifted after the death of James II in 1701; others after the Hanoverian succession in 1722. But as late as the 1720s Thom remained a non-juring fellow traveller; probably because it was consistent with his High Tory views.

Within living memory, the Hurst Jacobites had witnessed a Civil War beyond all imagining, the suppression of their religious beliefs under the Commonwealth, the restoration of the monarchy, followed by the forced abdication of the personage that they believed to be the rightful king; and then the assumption of the throne by two foreign princes, William III and George I. In order to avoid another civil war, they needed party politics. But they had ceased to believe in it, mostly because of the venal corruption of the Whigs.

The period after James II legged it saw the earliest beginnings of political parties, parties we now call the Whigs and the Tories. These were terms of disapprobation that each applied to the other. A Whig was a 'Scottish Presbyterian horse thief', one who claimed a right to exclude the monarch from the throne because Parliament was sovereign. They drew much support from non-conformists and the urban merchant class, who advocated for free trade and Empire. A Tory was an 'Irish papist outlaw'; albeit one who supported King James II, because they didn't believe that anyone had the right to remove the rightful monarch. The Glorious Revolution of 1688 somewhat modified the Tory view; they accepted a limited constitutional monarchy, but they opposed religious toleration, including that of Catholics. The best solution to the 200 years or so of religious conflict in England was that everyone should conform with the established Church. Their support came from country landowners, such as Thom, who were against free trade, and suspicious of 'foreign entanglements.'

In order to understand how these ideas played out in Hurst, we must turn to Thom's friend and neighbour, Sir Henry Campion. His father, Sir William Campion, had roomed with Peter Courthope at Trinity, and was MP for Seaford in the late seventeenth century. Henry attended Trinity for a year in 1697, and then Lincoln's Inn in 1698. In 1702, the year of his father's death, he married Peter Courthope's daughter and sole heir, Barbara – perhaps they were deemed as a suitable match by their respective fathers. Henry Campion brought £5,000 to the marriage, but since married women couldn't own property, on the death of Barbara's father, Danny would pass to Campion. Peter Courthope therefore invested Danny in a trust, so that it would pass to Henry and Barbara's eldest son, William.

In 1708, Sir Henry Campion was elected as MP for East Grinstead. He was classed as a Tory, and soon proved himself an ultra. In 1709 he supported an amendment to a bill to offer foreign Protestants naturalisation only on condition that they became communicant members of the Church of England. In 1710 he voted against the impeachment of Dr. Sacheverell, who had given an inflammatory sermon in St. Paul's Cathedral attacking Dissenters, Whigs, moderate Tories and just about anyone who disagreed with him.

Seventy-five thousand copies of Dr. Sacheverell's sermon were printed. Its modern equivalent might be Nigel Farage's shameful 'Breaking Point' poster during the Brexit campaign. Sacheverell's sermon was seen as an important element in turning the country to the Tories, who won the general election of 1710 in a landslide. At that election Henry Campion stood not for East Grinstead, but for the Cornish rotten borough of Bossiney, which was in the gift of

High Tories. It had previously been held by the two Sir Francises, Drake and Bacon, so it had some cachet.

The new Tory government was run by Robert Harley, the Earl of Oxford, whose family would come to own large chunks of Presteigne. Harley was what we would call a 'centrist', who wanted Tories and Whigs to work together to bring about peace in the War of the Spanish Succession, and to allow religious toleration, exactly what Dr. Sacheverell was against. It was also opposed by 150 Tory MPs, including Henry Campion. They founded the October Club, so called because they were reputed to drink strong 'October ale'. A contemporary equivalent might be the European Research Group, which harried their own side into granting the Brexit referendum, and then swallowed their party from the inside out, like a parasitic worm. The October Club wanted to pressurise the government to investigate the corrupt wrongdoings of the previous Whig administration; just the people whose support Harley needed to keep his centrist administration together. The October Club took Dr. Sacheverell's line in religious matters: Anglicanism, good; everything else, bad. This adherence to Anglicanism would prove to be their undoing; they opposed the Hanoverian succession, and insisted that James II's son James was the rightful king, on condition he became an Anglican, which he always refused to do. Case closed, really, let's be honest. But they never ceased believing that the Old Pretender might change his mind.

Jonathan Swift, the author of *Gulliver's Travels*, supported Harley's ministry, and met Henry Campion, who invited him to one of the October Club dinners. Swift refused, saying of the club members that they wished 'to have every Whig turned out and not to suffer that the new ministry should shake hands as they see they do with the old'. Campion was one of the leaders of the group. He spoke out in favour of measures to investigate the corruption of the old Whig ministry, and promoted a bill to prosecute bribery at elections. He was appointed by the House to be a Commissioner of Accounts, what we would now call a member of the Public Accounts Committee. A pamphlet was published listing the MPs who were seen as sound: 'A True and Exact List of those worthy patriots who to their eternal honour have detected the mismanagement of the late ministry'; Campion was one of those listed. The October Club was so powerful that Harley had little choice but to give in to many of their demands, on religious (in)toleration, for example. Swift published 'Some Advice Humbly Offered to the members of the October Club' in 1712, and finally many of the group, including Campion, took it on board, and started to co-operate with the government.

In the election of 1713, Campion was returned as one of the two 'knights of Sussex', where he continued his somewhat reluctant support of Harley's ministry. However, as Parliament wore on, he increasingly offered his allegiance to the leader of the High Tories, Henry St. John, Viscount Bolingbroke. I'll admit that early eighteenth century politics can seem a bit fustian, not because the conduct of politics was dull (riven as it was with duels, imprisonments, executions, invasions &c), but because the issues seem remote, remoter even than those of the Civil War. But Bolingbroke should be remembered as the father of one of the great institutions of our democracy, the idea of 'Her Majesty's Loyal Opposition', whose job, he felt, should be to oppose and challenge the government at every opportunity. Campion clearly agreed, as he opposed the offering of a reward for the Old Pretender, a project close to the queen's (and thus Harley's) heart.

Harley's administration collapsed after the death of Queen Anne, and there was some talk of Henry Campion becoming Chancellor of the Exchequer in a Bolingbroke administration. But it was not to be, because the Tories lost the general election of 1715 in a landslide. A Tory majority of 240 turned into a Whig majority of 130. The Tories would be out of power until Thom's son Willy was a grandfather. Campion didn't stand, because he had ceased to believe in party politics, but come to believe instead in its only alternative: the taking up of arms.

This election, 1714/1715, is the first record in the diary of Thom voting. Thom must have been hopeful of a Tory victory; on 12 January 1714 (OS) he wrote:

> I gave Mr Dodson 1s for which he is to give me 10s if
> both Tory candidates are chosen at the ensuing election.

Mr. Dodson may well have thought he was on to a sure thing, since he was offering nine-to-one against the Tories.

You know how these days, when you vote, you nip up the closed-for-the-day primary school or the village hall, or wherevs, and then you put a thing up on Facebook saying, 'I've voted'? In 1714/15, it was not so simple. The process began on 16 February 1714 with Thom fitting five hoops to his wagon so that he could cover it for a long journey together with other local voters to Chichester and back, a seventy mile round trip.[74] The next day, 17 February 1714, Thom describes as 'showry', so his passengers must have been glad of the cover. He and they got as far as Arundel, where they stopped for the night. Thom put up with Mr. Picknall, his tallow chandler, demonstrating his immunity to unpleasant smells.

On the eighteenth, they arrived in Chichester,

> ... with some people from Arundell, in all about 10 men
> to the election of the knights of the shire begun yesterday
> and ended to day. The candidates were Mr Bertram
> Ashburnham, Mr Everffield, Mr Butler and Mr Spencer
> Compton. The two latter carry'd it by a vast majority but
> as was suppos'd by all manner of indirect practices.

After voting, they stayed over in Arundel again, and arrived home on the nineteenth. Thom was clearly unhappy with the result, which he thought was bent. In short, the Whigs had carried the day, and Thom was gutted, not least because he'd lost a bob to Mr. Dodson.

Other than voting for the Tories, what is my evidence that Thom and Elizabeth were active Jacobites? It's somewhat circumstantial, as ever, though less circumstantial than the feeding turds to fish thing.

---

74 Thom and Elizabeth also kept a 'chaise', pulled by two horses. This is another sign that the Marchants were wealthy.

Firstly, there are five diary posts concerning 'a Frenchman', the earliest of which is the third entry in the diary:

> October the first 1714 Fryday. A dry day, only a short
> showr about 3 aclock. I was at Danny with Mr John
> Cheal, Mr Philip Shave, John Hill of Nut Knowle[75] and
> a Frenchman. Staid 'till 12 at night. Appointed to go to
> Nut Knowle a Saturday next with Mr Henry Campion.

Two days later, Thom notes that he assured Mrs. Susan Courthope (Campion's sister-in-law) that he 'will try to prevent the journey' to Nut Knowle. What was the meeting at Nut Knowle supposed to be about? Why was Thom appointed to go? And why did he think it unwise? Above all, who was the Frenchman? I don't know. To judge from the diary, the meeting at Nut Knowle didn't take place. A gnomic entry the following March doesn't help. Thom encountered Mr. Hill of Nut Knowle again, and writes:

> I told him what he had reported of Mr Henry Campion,
> but he positively denied it.

I can't make sense of this either; but there is no doubt that Campion was in touch at this time with James III's court-in-exile in France – historyofparliamentonline.org writes that he was a messenger for the Jacobite cause – and was preparing to take an active part in whatever came next.

On 10 October 1714, the Frenchman appears again, in company with Henry Campion, Mr. Hay, Mr. John Bateman and Mr. John Hart at Mr. Richard Whitpaine's house, where they drank beer and punch. A month later, on 12 November, Henry Campion and the Frenchman visited Little Park.

Did the Frenchman go back to France at this point? He's not mentioned again until 3 January 1714:

75   Nut Knowle is in Woodmancote, three miles from Hurst.

> My Wife and I and Mr John Hart and Willy din'd at
> Danny with Mr Healy, Mr Richard Whitpaine and his
> wife Mary,[76] Mr Bill and Mrs Whitfield and the French
> man. We staid late and drank too much.

There is one more mention of the mysterious Frenchman on 9 January when, 'After evning prayr, Mr Henry Campion went into Stephen Bine's and the French man.' Thom notes that he lent Henry Campion a pamphlet, which I would give my top set to know what it was.

It's very odd that Thom doesn't mention the Frenchman's name. Did he not know it? Could he not spell it? The Frenchman and Henry Campion are always in company with one another, you'll note. Was the Frenchman staying at Danny? Did Campion receive and send messages through the Frenchman? I think both fair assumptions.

Throughout May and June, Thom sees Campion on a number of occasions. Campion lends Thom a number of pamphlets, he drops by at Little Park, sometimes with his wife, sometimes with friends. On 10 June 1715, Thom writes:

> The Pretender's birthday. I went to Danny about 5
> aclock. There were Mrs Catherine Beard's family and Dr
> Woodward's. We staid 'till 11 aclock.

Did they drink a toast to the Pretender, or to 'the little gentleman in the velvet waistcoat'?[77] Again, I think it highly likely, given Campion's fanaticism; and in the light of the step he was about to take.

Thom met up with Campion throughout July, for dinner and to

---

76 Thom and Elizabeth didn't seem to much like Mary Whitpaine. On 17 October 1721, he refers to her in the diary as 'Flabberchops Brute' for trying to pick a fight with Elizabeth over Willy's dog.

77 A Jacobite toast, celebrating the mole who dug the hill that William III's horse tripped on, thus throwing his master and breaking his collarbone, the accident which led to William's death.

go fishing in Thom's ponds. On 22 July 1715, Thom notes that Henry Campion, Mrs. C. Beard and Mr. Osbourne went to Brighton 'but did not go a strugging because the sea was rough'. What 'strugging' might be, I have been unable to find out (going out in a boat?), but it's worth noting that Campion was by the seaside, and taking stock of conditions. On 24 July, Henry Campion was at church in Hurst 'forenoon and afternoon'. On 26 July Thom writes this:

> There was a great talk that the Duke of Ormond went off
> at Shoreham with Sir Harry Goring, Mr Middleton and
> one or two more who went off a Saturday as 'tis said, 'twas
> also reported that Henry Campion went with them but
> that is false whatever the rest be.

There is only one more mention of Campion for some time. On 18 September 1715 Thom writes that,

> Mr Henry Campion, Mrs Anne White and her niece
> Molly and Mrs Courthope were here after evning prayr.

In the period between 24 July 1715, when Campion attended church twice in one day, and his last diary appearance on 18 September, Campion had been back to his old stomping grounds in Cornwall, to prepare for an invasion fleet led by Bolingbroke and the Duke of Ormond. On 18 August, Bolingbroke (by that stage exiled in France) had written to the Pretender to tell him of the expected arrival of 'one of the most considerable and most zealous of your servants, 8 6 17 20 14 19 18', which was Campion's code name, less snappy than 007, but the same idea.[78] By October, Campion was in

78 Hilary broke the code, and sent me this explanation:

1	2	3	4	5	6	7	8	9	10	11	12	13	14	15	16	17	18	19	20	21	22	23	24	25	26
W	X	Y	Z	J	A	B	C	D	E	F	G	H	I	K	L	M	N	O	P	Q	R	S	T	U	V

The simplest alphabetic code would have 1 for A, 2 for B and so on. Looking at the sequence that denoted Henry Campion, the first two numbers were 8 and 6, which were the same distance apart as C and A would have been, but 5 places further on. If you write

Cherbourg, preparing to cross back to Cornwall to prepare the way for the imminent arrival of the invasion fleet, but long periods of bad weather in the Channel (and the non-existence of the fleet) meant that Campion was stuck in France, where he would stay in exile for the next five years.

The better-known part of the 1715 Jacobite Rebellion happened in Scotland. The Earl of Mar raised his standard in the Jacobite cause on 6 September at Braemar, and by October he had 20,000 men at his command. This army had largely faded away by the time the Old Pretender landed at Peterhead on 22 December, so when he arrived in Perth to meet up with Mar and his army, it only amounted to some 5,000 men, who were already preparing to retreat from the old town. The Old Pretender left British soil for the last time on 4 February 1715 (OS), sailing from the east coast port of Montrose.

In England, an army of Scottish borderers met up with Jacobite insurrectionists from Northumberland and recusant Lancashire. Some 4,000 troops occupied Preston, but after two days' fighting the Jacobites surrendered to government forces led by General Charles Wills. Other than a few minor skirmishes,[79] this was the last battle fought on English soil.

In Cornwall, which Campion had been trying to raise, only the town of St. Columb Major declared for the Pretender, when Mr. James Paynter proclaimed James III king in the market square. There were almost certainly government spies operating in Cornwall; the

out the numbers 1 to 26 and put the key letter J (for James/Jacobite?) at position 5, then start the alphabet with A at position 6, B at position 7, C at 8 and so on, continuing with all the other letters until you get to V at 26, then putting W back at the start of the line at 1 on to Z at position 4, the numbers 8-6-17-20-14-19-18 will work exactly to give you C-A-M-P-I-O-N.

79 Notably, Bossenden Wood in Kent, 1838, between forty or so Kentish farm labourers and a detachment of a hundred soldiers, where eleven men were killed; and Graveney Marsh, 1940, also in Kent, when the crew of a downed German bomber turned their guns on the detachment of troops sent to arrest them. Luckily, no one was seriously hurt and the German airman and the soldiers enjoyed a pint in the pub afterwards.

militia were called out to quash Mr. Paynter's uprising, a couple of local MPs were arrested and Mr. Paynter himself fled to London.

For this damp squib, Henry Campion seems to have been prepared to sacrifice everything. This was a deadly serious business. Some Jacobite prisoners were hung, drawn and quartered for treason, and thousands were imprisoned. Property was sequestered from Jacobite landowners; it was lucky that Peter Courthope was still master of Danny, or it might have been lost. The Indemnity Act of 1717 freed hundreds of Jacobite prisoners, but Campion clearly felt it was still better to stay in exile. He hung about on the Continent, aimless and rootless, though he seems to have collected military intelligence for Bolingbroke, and stayed for a time with the Jacobite Duke of Berwick near Paris.

It's been hard to find out much more about his time in France. Colin and Judith Brent, in their indispensable *Danny House, a Sussex Mansion through Seven Centuries*, seem to be the only other writers who noticed Hurst's Jacobite sympathies, and I am grateful to them for their account of Campion's post-Parliamentary activities. What is known is that, in May 1720, the Old Pretender wrote to the Duke of Ormond that 'honest Henry Campion' had just left him with a commission 'which will I hope settle such a unanimity and concert betwixt my friends in England and me, as will frustrate all the vain attempts of mine enemies on this side of the sea.' What this commission might have been, I cannot say.

On 29 August 1720, Thom wrote:

> The post has brought news that Mr Henry Campion was come to London. My Wife and Mrs Mary Whitpaine at Danny afternoon …

where, presumably, there was a great deal of excitement at Campion's return. Five days later Thom writes:

> Mr Henry Campion home this evning about 9, haveing been gone from Danny five years and six weeks. Mr

> William Martin, Mr Beard, Mr Richard Whitpaine, Mr
> Scutt and Stephen Bine went part of the way to London to
> meet him.

On 8 September, Thom dined at Danny to hear of his neighbour and friend's escapades; and, almost certainly, of the mysterious commission.

Right up until the end of the diary, Campion and Thom are dining together, doing business together, drinking together. Were they plotting together? Campion was still writing to the Pretender. In November 1721 he wrote to 'James III' complaining of the 'excess of caution and variety of schemes' amongst his 'several partners', whilst owning up to the fact that he was 'perhaps naturally too sanguine and impatient of delay in everything where I engage'.

After Peter Courthope's death in 1725, Campion took over the running of Danny, even though he was only one of four trustees of his son's inheritance. He settled down, as people do, and seems to have repudiated his harum-scarum past.

Given Thom's next surprising move, it seems that he too was not immune from the lure of the moderation that comes with the passing of the years. I know how this must feel. In my early twenties, I was a supporter of the Revolutionary Communist Party of Great Britain (Marxist-Leninist); at the 2019 general election, I campaigned unsuccessfully for our sitting MP, who was a Liberal Democrat.

It comes to us all, my dear old Thom.

XIV.

IT'S NOT THE GAY COAT THAT
MAKES THE GENTLEMAN

Like Henry Campion, Thom seems to have become reconciled to the political situation, so much so that in 1727 he took a job with Charles Seymour, the 6th Duke of Somerset, 'The Proud Duke', as his land steward at Petworth House. Twenty-five miles west of Hurst, Petworth House was built to astound, and it still astounds me, every time I drive past on my slow way from here to there. It was built in the style of a French chateau; Horace Walpole, who saw both, claimed that it resembled the Tuileries Palace, which was destroyed in a fire in 1848. E.V. Lucas, in 1904's *Highways and Byways in Sussex*, thinks it a bit basic – 'A Scene painter, bidden to depict an English park, would produce something very like Petworth.'

It's worth a visit if you are passing by on the A272. Not so much for the house (you can only get into the old kitchens), but for the art gallery, which houses by far the grandest collection owned by the National Trust, with pictures by Titian, Bosch, Van Dyck, Gainsborough, Blake and Turner, as well as a superb collection of sculpture, and a room full of paintings of 'Beauties at the time of Queen Anne' by Michael Dahl, eight portraits of the friends and cousins of the Proud Duke and his first wife, Elizabeth Seymour. Six of the eight were originally full-length; Thom, not I think indifferent to a well-turned ankle, would have seen them when they were newly painted.

Charles Seymour started life with few prospects. When his older brother was shot in a duel in Italy, Charles, aged sixteen, inherited little more than the title; a grand one, the second ranking dukedom in the land, but the family was hard up. His big break came aged twenty, when he married the fifteen-year-old heir to the dukes of Northumberland, Elizabeth Percy – as her third husband.

She was twelve in 1679 when she married fifteen-year-old Henry Cavendish, heir to the Duke of Newcastle; a sickly lad, he died in 1680. Husband two was Thomas Thynne of Longleat, one of the richest men in England. Elizabeth was fourteen, and Thomas was thirty. After the wedding she fled to the Netherlands; the marriage was in the process of being dissolved when Thynne was murdered by a group hired by one Count von Königsmark, who had a thing for Elizabeth Percy, and who thought killing her husband might win both her heart and her seemingly bottomless wealth. She controlled vast estates, and had several fine residences, including Alnwick Castle in Northumberland, Syon House on the Thames to the west of London – and Petworth. But people held that there was a whiff of brimstone about her, and that she wasn't entirely innocent of Thomas Thynne's murder; so in 1682, a few months after her husband's killing, she married penniless but high-ranking Charles Seymour, who was only twenty to her fifteen, and supposed to be a bobby-dazzler. His vanity, and the time he spent gazing upon his own loveliness, earned him the sobriquet 'the Proud Duke'.

The couple were active at the court of Queen Anne. He was Master of Horse and a cabinet member, and Elizabeth was made a Lady of the Bedchamber. After Anne fell out with Sarah Churchill, the Duchess of Somerset became 'the favourite', probably because she asked little of the queen whilst offering her genuine friendship. The duke was thought of as a man of some courage and audacity; he had stood up to James II when the king asked him to deal with the Pope's representative, arguing that contact with the Vatican was illegal. He switched allegiance to William III, and commanded some of his cavalry, but then voted against the idea that James had abdicated. William III dined at Petworth in 1693, by which time Seymour was taking his wife's money to turn it into the grandest and most modern house in England.

The Proud Duke was classed as a Tory, one who behaved Whiggishly, and he then became a Whig, one with Tory tendencies. In 1710, he conspired with Robert Harley; he thought he might lead a ministry of moderate Whigs; but then had to support Harley's moderate Tories. He may well have been at Queen Anne's side at her deathbed, and he was one of the Whig grandees who secured the Hanoverian succession.

The duke and duchess had an unhappy marriage. According to a contemporary, the duke 'treated her with little gratitude or affection though he owed all he had, except an empty title to her'. The same writer described the duchess as 'the best bred, as well as the best born Lady in England ... she maintained her dignity at court, with great respect to the queen and civility to others.' She was chief mourner at Anne's funeral, and died of breast cancer in London in 1722, aged fifty-five. As soon as she was dead, her husband pursued Sarah Churchill, telling her she had always had his heart. She spurned his advances (at sixty he was losing his legendary good looks, and growing in his legendary foul temper), so in 1726 he married Charlotte Finch, thirty years younger than him; it's she that Thom refers to as 'the Duchess'.

The duke was an artisanal, lovingly hand-crafted, organically grown shit, described by the nineteenth-century historian Thomas Macaulay as 'a man in whom the pride of birth and rank amounted almost to a disease.' The Earl of Hardwicke said of him that he was 'humoursome, proud and capricious'. The Earl of Dartmouth said: 'He was a man of vast pride, and having had a very low education, shewed it in a very indecent manner.' Anecdotes abound of his imperious nature; how he would only communicate with his servants by hand gesture; how he would order the roads to be cleared as he came by, in case he was seen by the hoi polloi. He liked to remind the second duchess that she could do nothing right, since his first wife had been a Percy.

Such was Thom's new boss.

Why did Thom want a job at all? He doesn't seem to have needed one. Perhaps it was for prestige, for connections. Perhaps he fancied a change; he was a funny age after all, just entering his fifties. Perhaps he wanted to give Will a run at managing Little Park. Perhaps he was flattered to be invited. Perhaps he wanted a look at one of his political enemies. The late seventeenth and early eighteenth centuries saw a rise in the use of land stewards by aristocratic landowners. The use of land stewards meant that aristocratic families could spend more time in London and at court, without abandoning their estates. It was a position of some power and prestige – perhaps that's what attracted Thom.

His entries on his time in Petworth form pretty much the only self-contained story in the diary, so I shall let him tell it in his own words. It seems only fair that I should reproduce, as fully as possible, edited lightly, at least one chunk of Thom's writing.

The duke had been trying to persuade Thom to come to Petworth since 1720:

> The 3rd January 1720. I went to Petworth with Mr Scutt.
> I were at the Duke of Somerset's in the evning.
> The 4th January 1720. A fine day. I talkt with the Duke of
> Somerset. He bid me £100 per annum and a house to live
> in to be his steward but we did not agree because I could
> not go immediately. We lay at the Half Moon[80] last night.
> The 10th January 1720. Sir Robert Fagg and I both went
> to the Duke of Somerset from Lewes. Staid all night.
> The 30th January 1720. I wrote to the Duke of Somerset.

There it seems to have been left. The next confirmed sighting comes in September 1727:

---

80   A venerable inn on Market Square under the shadow of the wall of Petworth Park, it was demolished in 1900. The NatWest bank now occupies the site.

> The 30th September 1727. Receiv'd a letter from Jude
> Storer appointing me to go to Petworth Monday or
> Tuesday next.
> The 2nd October 1727 Munday. A dry forenoon, wet
> after. Jack Bartlet and I din'd at Stenning and Mrs Sopkin
> Everfield and Molly, Jack and I went forward to Petworth.
> Hir'd one Holloway alias Hobly to guide us from
> Gretham thither, paid him 2s for his pains.

The road from Hurst via Steyning crossed the River Arun at Greatham Bridge; the road on through the woods to Petworth sounds as though it was bad, if Thom and party needed a guide. Now tarmacked and signposted, this road forms part of my Slow Road from here to there. A guide is no longer necessary, but it still passes through fairly wild country, heavily wooded and sparsely populated.

> The 3rd October 1727 Tuesday. A wet day. I talkt with
> his Grace the Duke of Somerset and agreed to serve
> him as land steward for which he is to give me £100 per
> annum, a house to live in and he is to keep me one horse
> in the stable all the year and an other at grass and I am
> not to go above 6 miles from home. We dined with
> Mr Elder.
> The 4th October 1727. We return'd from Petworth.
> Breakfasted at Peter Lutman's. Went down this morning
> to see the house I am to have of his Grace, which I found
> much to my liking.

It sounds as though agreement was made on the same terms offered in 1720. A salary of £100 per annum is not a great sum; worth maybe eleven grand now. But Thom took the deal, including the clause that he doesn't go more than six miles from Petworth without the duke's say-so.

A few months pass before anything else happens:

The 21st December 1727. Jack Bartlet[81] and I set out for Petworth.

The 22nd December 1727 Fryday. A gloomy day, very thick mist. I waited at the Duke of Somerset's all day but could not speak with him. There came 3 of the Duchesses brothers and others which was one reason I could not see him.

The 23rd December 1727. A gloomy, frosty, misty day. Mr Scutt and I return'd by Arundell late. Lay there, I at Jack Picknall's and he at the George. We supt at the George.

The 24th December 1727 Sunday. A very gloomy day and very thick mist. I return'd from Petworth, the worst journey I think that I ever rode.

Thom makes very few comments on his journeys, but after the state of the terrible Sussex roads, and the propensity of mist to loiter in trees, he must have been pleased to be home, in front of his own fire at Little Park.

The 3rd January 1727 Wednesday. A gloomy day. Jack Bartlet and I went to Arundell, thence to Petworth.

The 4th January 1727 Thursday. A gloomy day. Lay at the Half Moon last night. Waited at the Duke of Somerset's all day allmost but could not see him.

The 5th January 1727 Fryday. A gloomy day. Lodg'd the same. Waited as yesterday but at last talkt with his Grace and appointed to be there a Tuesday next at farthest.

The 6th January 1727 Saturday. A very wet afternoon, return'd home. Lay at Mr Picknall's in Arundell last night.

81   Jack Bartlet seems to act as Thom's servant throughout the whole stay in Petworth.

> The 8th January 1727 Munday. A showry day. Got ready
> for my journey to morrow &c.
> The 9th January 1727 Tuesday. A showry day. My wife
> and I, Nanny, Jack Bartlet and his father and Henry White
> set out for Petworth, went no further than Stenning.
> The 10th January 1727 Wednesday. A very fine day.
> We went to Petworth. Mr Booker went with us as far as
> Stoppham for which I gave him 2s-6d. We came to the
> Half Moon in Petworth about 2 aclock. Din'd at the inn.
> Went afterwards to Mr John Hart's and agreed for Nanny
> to board there at £12 per annum.

Nanny seems to have been a pet name for one of Thom and Elizabeth's daughters, but I can't work out which one. She would stay in Petworth town the whole time that Thom worked at the big house. Was this a common thing, or an unusual one? I can't work that out, either. And is this another John Hart? John Hart the village schoolmaster was living in Hurstpierpoint until 1731, when he was appointed head of Steyning Grammar School, so it seems unlikely that it was the same man. Thom's diary awaits a full academic reading, and so there are still places where I can only scratch my shaved head. But I like to imagine that Elizabeth said, 'Oh, job in Petworth with the Proud Whig Duke, is it? And who's going to help with the kids?' and that Thom replied, 'Well, Nanny can come with me?' A very modern conversation to explain something unexpected, but speculation is all I have at this point.

> The 11th January 1727 Thursday. A gloomy day. I
> din'd at my Lord Duke's and I was sent to look over
> Rothersbridge Farme where at present lives one Mr
> Rapley. Return'd and gave His Grace an account of it. Mr
> Fowler, one of my Lord Duke's baylifs, went with me.
> Sent my horse to my Lord Duke's stable per Jack Bartlet
> and the old mare to grass there.

The 12th January 1727 Fryday. A gloomy day. My Wife
went to look on the house I am to have but did not like
it. Return'd as far as Stenning with William Bartlet and
White. I did not see His Grace today.

See above. Thom doesn't seem to have Elizabeth's full support, to say
the least.

The 13th January 1727 Saturday. A very wet day. Went up
to the Duke's, din'd and suppt there but did not see His
Grace. I was informed by Mr Fowler that Mr E— was
playing an underhand game in order to have me sent home
again. I staid there till midnight.

Mr E— could be Mr Eades or Mr Elder. Either way, it sounds as
though the entrenched stewards were not keen on the upstart. After
the Petworth adventure ended, Mr Fowler comes to stay at Little
Park for a few days, where it's sure he told Thom what had really
happened.

The 14th January 1727 Sunday. A very wet day. I were
at prayers with the family in the lobbee.
The 15th January 1727 Munday. A gloomy day. I
were to look on Mrs Chessum's rooms and agreed
for 2s per week for my lodging there and paid her for
a week beforehand. Mr Fowler and I lookt again over
Rothersbridge farm, of which I gave my Lord Duke an
account in the evening and took orders for tomorrow.

Elizabeth clearly disliked the house that the duke had offered so
much that Thom didn't have the nerve to take up residence.

The 16th January 1727 Tuesday. A fine day. Harry White
brought a bed etc from home. Had home the white mare

and left the black horse in her roome. I rode to what they
call the Little Park[82] and lookt over several things.
The 17th January 1727 Wednesday. A showry day. I talkt
with my Lord Duke and pursuant to his orders went and
lookt over Gohanne and Joshurst Farmes that is under
William Keen's care. Sent in an account but did not see
His Grace.
The 18th January 1727 Thursday. A dry morning very wet
after. Paid Jo Litchford 46s in full for all our quarters
there. My Lord Duke's smith shood my horse.
The 19th January 1727 Fryday. A very wet day. Did
nothing but eat and drink and set by the fire: and hard
work too.

Thom usually works very hard, if the diary is any judge, but
this occasional delight in idleness is a link between our shared
Burgundian heritage and me. And my daughters.

The 20th January 1727 Saturday. A fine day. I went down
in the morning to Cowdersall Mill to view the repairs but
it was so much under water that no account could be taken
of it. After I return'd I rode out with his Grace into the
park and lookt over severall matters. His Grace order'd
me to take some of the timber there towards repairing
Cowdersall Mill.

Cowdersall Mill would be a consistent problem for Thom over the
next few weeks.

The 21st January 1727 Sunday. A gloomy day. I were at
prayrs in the chapel in the forenoon and in the lobbee in
the evning.

---

82 Imagine my despair on discovering another farm called 'Little Park', after all I've had
to suffer with four George Gorings, two Peter Courthopes and dozens of Thomases,
Williams and Johns.

The 23rd January 1727 Tuesday. A dry day. My Lord
Duke set out about noon for Guildford, in order for
London. I receiv'd severall orders and went with His
Grace to the farther side of Little Park. Fowler likewise
went so far with him and we came back together.
The 24th January 1727 Wednesday. A dry day. Mr Elder
set out for London, left some orders with me to view
Peter Woods's farm etc beside what my Lord Duke left. I
had my head shaved. Receiv'd a letter from my Wife.
The 26th January 1727 Fryday. A fine day frosty. I
met William Tester, a millwright at Cowdersall Mill,
view'd the repairs there and took a short account of it
and appointed Tester to come again tomorrow to set out
timber in the Park.
The 27th January 1727 Saturday. A fine day, smart frost.
William Tester came and we set out oak timber for
repairing the mill 261½ feet. Tester and I were afterwards
at the Bull to finish the account of materials etc. Peter
Woods came to me there and we went to my lodging and
we finisht the account of his repairs, only the house and
granery was not view'd but is to be view'd an other time.
Mr Eades came to us at the Bull to ask me why I stopt the
teems from fetching wood, which I did because I thought
His Grace would be angry, the frost being much thaw'd by
the fine sun shiney day and the way very sloppy.
The 29th January 1727 Munday. A dry day, frosty. We
got 3 teems fetch'd each of 'em 2 loads of wood out of the
grubb'd coppice and Farmer Mucher's teem helped carry
ice into the icehouse.

Cold weather like this, together with an efficient underground
icehouse meant that elite families could have ice pretty much all year
round.

> The 30th January 1727 Tuesday. A very cold day, frosty.
> Receiv'd a letter from Mr Elder per post.
> The 31st January 1727 Wednesday. A fine day, frosty.
> Receiv'd a letter per post from Mr Williams with
> directions from my Lord Duke to which I sent an answer
> by the same post.

For the next few days, Thom and Fowler were involved with moving timber for the repair of Cowdersall Mill. On Sunday 4 February, Thom notes that it is 'My Lord Duke's wedding day, two years'. On the 5th he rode out with the duke, and on the 6th he continued the mill operation with Mr Fowler.

> The 7th February 1727 Wednesday. A fine day, thawing.
> Did nothing. Were sent for into my Lord Duke's rooms
> and had orders with Mr Eades to go about the town to get
> votes for Mr Butler.
> The 8th February 1727 Thursday. A fine day. Mr
> Eades and I (by my Lord Duke's order) went to all the
> freeholders about Towne for their votes for Mr Butler
> and none refus'd that were at home. We din'd at Mr
> Goodyers. I did not see my Lord Duke.

Mr. Butler was the Whig candidate in the general election who Thom had bet a shilling against in 1715. Thom has clearly come a long way from Jacobitism; it's a sad symbol of the resignation that the Hurst Jacobites seem to have felt after Campion's return from exile. My former tanky pals in the Revolutionary Communist Party of Great Britain (Marxist-Leninist) might have said the same of me, if they had caught me leafleting for the Lib Dems.

> The 9th February 1727 Fryday. A fine day. Mr Eades
> and I were sent to Sutton to look on several matters of
> the mannor, took Farmer Neal with us. Went to Parson
> Thornton's and he promised his vote for Mr Butler and

248

to assist in treading the bounds of the mannor. We found some small encroachments.

For the next few days, Thom was concerned with the state of one of the tenanted farms, and with some fishponds on the estate, for which the duke had ordered him to get some drainage grates. No one in Sussex at that time knew more about fishponds than Thom; it sounds like the duke was planning to take no notice of this.

> The 14th February 1727 Wednesday. A showry day. I went and took a measure of the grates in Stagg Park. Talkt with His Grace and Mr Elder, askt leave for me to go to Stenning to morrow.
> The 15th February 1727 Thursday. A very fine day. Nanny and I went to Stenning. Mett my Wife there, din'd and staid 'till night and my Wife and I went to Hurst, Nanny staid there.

Thom returned to Petworth the next day.

> The 17th February 1727 Saturday. A fine day. I were sent to the people spreading gravel etc. Mr Eades and the millwright set out timber for the repair of Cowdershall Mill, as I had done once already …

(Mr Eades seems to making trouble, but most trouble came from the boss.)

> … I talkt with His Grace and he found much fault about the grates that he had order'd me to get made, but he was in a cursed humour about the dung-courts etc and sent the teem for hay to William Keen's at 7 aclock at night.

On the 18th, Thom took Nanny out for the day to Tillington, and did more nothing on the 19th.

> The 20th February 1727 Tuesday. A snowy day. I went
> with his Grace to North Chappel in his way for London. I
> had no orders to do any thing more, nor to forbare. I talkt
> with Mr Elder at Mr Dee's and he advis'd me to keep on.
> The 21st February 1727 Wednesday. A fine day. Begun
> board at Mr Hunt's yesterday night. Receiv'd a letter from
> my Wife.

So he went to stay with Mr. Hunt, rather than Mrs. Chessum; presumably the bed that had been brought from Hurst came too. For the next few days he arranged repairs and tenancy agreements at the 'Great House'. The duke wrote, and Thom replied. Although I am biased, Thom seems to be dispatching his duties efficiently; the qualities, we assume, which caused the duke to seek out his services in the first place.

Then the real world intervened again; Thom's entries are short, but his relief is palpable.

> The 26th February 1727 Munday. A dry day. My wife
> came from Hurst as far as Fiddleworth and staid there at
> night. I sent one of my Lord Duke's men to Stenning but
> he mist them.
> The 27th February 1727 Tuesday. A fine day. My Wife
> came to Petworth this morning early.

The next day, Thom is back trying to arrange timber for mill restoration. And then he learned the futility of his half-hearted canvassing for the Whigs, as I in my turn learned mine:

> The 29th February 1727[83] Thursday. A fine day. I went to
> Chichester to the election. Mr Butler chosen without any
> opposition. There were a great many people there. I went

---

83   1728 in the New Style. That's why there's a leap day in a year ending in seven.

and came with Peter Lutman, Mr Witcher and Thomas
Rice.

Estate business fills the next few days, though in the evenings Thom
gets to dine with 'my Wife and Nanny'.

> The 3rd March 1727 Sunday. A fine day. My Wife and
> I were at Petworth church. Sent a letter to Jacky with a
> guinea in it. Mr Nash's man carry'd it to the person that is
> to carry it, at Fiddleworth.

Thom and Elizabeth, Bank of Mum and Dad, are sending student
Jack a guinea; but getting a letter from Petworth to Oxford was
clearly not easy.

> The 4th March 1727 Munday. A fine day. Mr Eades and
> I view'd the repairs of Lutman's farme. Mrs Wacklife
> and her daughters to see my Wife. Paid Jo Lickfold all
> expenses of my Wife's last journey hither, being three.

Three what, Tom doesn't say. Pounds, I'd imagine.

> The 5th March 1727 Shrove Tuesday. A fine day. My
> Wife return'd to Hurst, Jack Bartlet with her on our
> Farrier's mare, and had home the old grey mare. Mr Mace
> receiv'd a letter from my Lord Duke wherein my Lord
> wondered I did not send in my bill for my wages.
> The 6th March 1727 Wednesday. A fine day. I were at
> the stables. Jack Bartlet return'd from Hurst, brought
> books, apples etc. Left the old mare at home. Mr Fowler
> and I supt at the Half Moon. Mr Mace showed me a
> letter wherein (as 'twas said in that letter) my Lord Duke
> desir'd an account of what was due to me because he did
> not think me fit for his service.
> The 7th March 1727 Thursday. A fine day. I went to

Rotherbridge in the morning with Mr Fowler and Martin, I din'd at Mr Hunt's and rode to Little Park. One of the grooms told me Mr Eades' grey horse was lame in the nere coffin joynt before. Mr Hunt came home allmost fuddled in the evening.

The 8th March 1727 Fryday. A fine day. His Grace return'd from London. I was at the house but did not see my Lord Duke.

The 9th March 1727 Saturday. A gloomy day. I saunter'd about the market, were up at the house, din'd at Half Moon with farmer Martin and Pike, a mason. Deliver'd in a letter in the morning of my demand for wages. Were at the house again in the evening. Staid late. Talkt with Mr Williams. He gave me the letter and John Buckland's account that I sent in it to Mr Elder pretending that Elder had not time to show it to His Grace.

The 10th March 1727 Sunday. A fine day. I were not at church. My Wife, Harry White and William Edwards came in the evening.

The 11th March 1727 Munday. A fine day. Mr Elder returned from London. Receiv'd £15-12s-4d of the Duke of Somerset by the hands of Mr Williams jr in full of my salary, due to last Wednesday.[84] I din'd with Mr Elder.

The 12th March 1727 Tuesday. Very fine day. My wife went home in the morning. I saunter'd about all day. Drank with Farmer Martin at the Half Moon and he promised to speak to my Lord Duke as I desir'd.

The 13th March 1727 Wednesday. A dry day. Took my horse out of my Lord Duke's stable and brought him to Mr Hunt's.

The 14th March 1727 Thursday. A gloomy day some rain. I were at Arundell Market. Din'd at the George with Mr Scutt and Stephen Bine.

84   Pro-rata salary for fifty-seven days, according to an editor's note in the diary transcription.

The 15th March 1727 Fryday. A gloomy day. I was at the Half Moon in the evening.

The 16th March 1727 Saturday. A dry day. I saunter'd about the market. Din'd at Mr Hunt's. Drank with Mr Gates jr and with Mr Milne at Half Moon.

The 17th March 1727 Sunday. A fine day. I were not at church.

The 18th March 1727 Munday. A dry day. Did nothing. Paid Mrs Hunt and Mrs Chessum all that was due to them.

The 19th March 1727 Tuesday. A gloomy day. I went up to the Duke's to take my leave of the family.

The 20th March 1727 Wednesday. A gloomy forenoon wet after. I came away from Petworth with Nanny and Jack Bartlet and all we could bring. Came to Stenning.

The 21st March 1727 Thursday. A dry forenoon, wet after. Lay at John Box's of Stenning last night. Return'd to Hurst today.

The 22nd March 1727 Fryday. A gloomy day some rain. Did nothing.

The 23rd March 1727 Saturday. A dry cold day. My birthday 51 years. I went to Lewes.

The 24th March 1727 Sunday. A dry day. We had a vestry after evening service. I were at Mr Henry Campion's in the evening.

Thom was a proud man, one who sauntered about Petworth market on numerous occasions after he had lost (or resigned) his job. He had nothing to hide, and fronted whatever had happened with aplomb. It's very hard to judge what went wrong, but going by his first suspicion, either Mr. Eades or Mr. Elder had taken against him from the beginning. Thom was, after all, nothing more than a yeoman, however skilled at his job; his expertise might well have annoyed the old hands. I doubt the Proud Duke liked being given advice of any kind, especially by someone who had made his own money. I doubt Thom was used to deferring to people who saw themselves as his social superiors.

It's an old story though; a fifty-one-year-old made redundant because of backroom plotting. Thom had taken a knock. And there was bad news from Oxford.

He sits by the fire, doing nothing.

He sits by the fire, drinking.

Sometimes Elizabeth sits with him and talks to him about how he had done no wrong in Petworth, and that he has many friends there who know the truth of what had happened, and that his good name is still untarnished, and how pleased she is to have him and Nanny home, and that tomorrow is Lady Day, a new year, a new start. But she knows of old that it doesn't help, and that he will sit now for days, doing nothing, nothing but drinking in front of the fire.

XV

APOTHECARIES WOULD NOT COAT PILLS IN SUGAR UNLESS THEY WERE BITTER

I'd been up and down like a bride's nightie for at least ten years, five or six times a night sometimes. Nocturia, it's called, and it's the biggest cause of disturbed sleep in men. The biggest cause of disturbed sleep for women is their male partners getting up to piss. I laughed it off. It's just a thing that happens as you get older.

But by autumn 2019, it had become relentless. I fell asleep dreaming of piss, and then woke eight or nine times to troop along the corridor to the bathroom. When I got there, my pisses were feeble things, hardly worth waking up for, but clearly my bladder was full to bursting. About half my piss went into the bowl; the other half leaked out onto the mat. I would try to clean up after myself, but inevitably the floor ended up pissed on. The landing too; in John Ray's words, 'Every path hath a puddle.' Then I had a few days of what felt like early onset dementia. I was vague, my memory was shot, I wept easily. Google suggested that the weepy vagueness plus the increasingly painful pissing added up to a UTI. I called the surgery, explained my symptoms and asked for an antibiotic. They agreed, so long as I took in a sample, which seemed a fair swap. I took the pills, and although the pissing continued unabated, frequent and little, the brain fog lifted a little.

Then the surgery called to say that, according to my sample, I didn't have an infection, and could I come in and see a doctor? I was apprehensive. I knew something was wrong. I was all but incontinent.

The doctor took a blood test, and put two gloved fingers into my anus. She didn't like what she felt, and I didn't like her feeling it.

Christmas came and went. I kept pissing myself, a couple of times on the car seat while I was driving. I went to the chemist and bought a piss bottle so I could piss in bed, and an extra-large pack of Tena Men, so I could piss in my pants.

In January 2020, there was a candle-lit evensong service for Epiphany in a small church in the benefice, three miles out of Presteigne. I managed to get through the service, and allowed myself to imagine I could get home – to no avail. We'd only driven half a mile before I had to stop, pull down my trackies, and try to piss in the hedge by the glare of the headlights. At this moment, of course, the vicar drove by, slowed down, lowered his window, and asked if I was OK, to which I assented, all the time spraying piss onto the verge, and over my trousers.

There is no escape from it. You never think this will happen to you.

Pissing became harder and harder in the first week of January. I wanted to piss all the time, but I had to force it out. It was a strain, like lifting heavy buckets from a deep well. I waited to hear from the doctors. The optimistic part of me still believed that I might merely have a grossly enlarged prostate, which was nice.

On 9 January 2020 I got the call from the doctor I had been waiting for, asking me to come in that afternoon. Turns out, the phlebotomist had taken a blood sample to test my cholesterol, rather than my PSA (prostate-specific antigen). Another set of bloods would need to be taken, but in the meantime my cholesterol was high, and I needed to start statins. This didn't come as a huge surprise. Most people can tell just by looking at me that my cholesterol level is too high, but I was glad of the statins, as I'd learned from endless *Daily Express* covers I'd seen in the Spar that statins are an unalloyed good.[85] So I waited some more. Pissing grew more terrible each day.

---

85   Also, that bad weather was due and that Princess Diana had been killed by MI5/MI6 – can't remember which.

My wife gave me this gift; she treated it all as normal, not a problem. An entry from my diary captured the situation perfectly – 11/01/20. 'Wet horrid day. Went shopping in Leominster and pissed the car seat. Got the shits. Everton 1, Brighton 0.'

On 16 January, my doctor told me that my PSA was very high, and that she was referring me to the urologist. The optimist in me remained sunny throughout. After all, according to the interweb, cycling could raise your PSA and I had been cycling only the decade before. On 30 January, I got called to the urology department at Hereford County Hospital. Here, a consultant repeated the fingers up your arse thing.

'Goodness,' he said, aloud, not meaning to.

As he pulled off his glove, and was washing his hands, he said, 'I've felt a lot of diseased prostates, Mr. Marchant, and I can tell you that you've got cancer. We need to do scans to see if it's become involved with your bones.'

Funny way to pass your days, I thought. Fancy getting all those A levels and spending years at medical school, and at the end of all that you spend your life feeling about in old geezers' arses. Still, I valued his hard-won expertise.

Over the next month, I underwent a variety of scans: CT, MRI, and a weird bone one that makes you radioactive. They did that thing where they put a miniature camera up your old chap.

The consultant said, 'It might hurt a bit as the camera goes past your prostate', and he was right.

He said, 'Do you want to look?' The inside of my bladder was up on the screen.

'No, you're alright,' I said, and closed my eyes.

'You'll be pleased to know there's no sign of bladder cancer!' he said, and he was right again.

'Camera coming out now. Might sting a bit as it comes by the prostate ... there.'

I was so grateful, I said, 'You're the first man whose ever touched my penis.'

'It was me, actually,' said the nurse.

I felt that I couldn't let this moment pass without us being introduced. His name was Tony, and he was a lifelong Crystal Palace fan. I told him that I, in stark contrast, supported Brighton and Hove Albion. We both agreed that we were glad we hadn't shared this before our moment of intimacy.

Every day the pissing got worse. I would lean against the bathroom wall and shout with pain as I tried to empty my bladder. Diarrhoea was a blessing, because hard turds needed to force themselves past my swelling prostate. It went like this; I shit a little hard turd, which enabled me to piss an eggcup, which allowed another pellet of hard turd to pass &c.

As a last hoorah, two days before the trip to Namur, I had a biopsy on my prostate, which would confirm what sort of cancer I had. Here, I'll draw a veil, but if male readers haven't yet reached for the phone to call the doctor to get their PSA checked, let me tell you this. A biopsy on your prostate gland is something you need to try to avoid.

On the same day as the biopsy, the Macmillan nurse had given me a pill to take, a testosterone blocker. That first night, I sat looking at the pill. I had a glass of water ready to take it with. I wept longer and louder than I have for years. I ululated with grief at what I was about to lose. I sat there for an hour. Then I took the pill. Metastasising bone cancer needs hormones to grow, so I shut off the supply. Death is the price of sex. By killing my sex, I might live for years. If I hadn't taken it, I would be dead already.[86]

Then, on 12 March 2020, back from Belgium, back from Surrey, a few days before the first lockdown started, I got called into Hereford County for an appointment with the Macmillan urology nurse, who told me the news. I had the most aggressive cancer there was. It had become involved with my bones, and I had two 'hotspots', in my left

---

86 I now have a testosterone blocking implant every three months. They shrink the prostate and have thus made pissing at least OK, thank you for asking. The chemo shrunk the tumours in my shoulder and hip. The Tena Men pads sit largely unused. In the immortal words of DJ Pete Tong, 'We continue.'

hip and my right shoulder. She gave me a booklet, called something along the lines of 'So You've Got Prostate Cancer'. She had dog-eared the last chapter, chapter five, entitled, if memory serves, 'Basically, You're Fucked, Mate', so that I didn't have to bother myself with reading the earlier, less gothic chapters. Chapter five in the prostate booklet also assured me that the testosterone blocker was as effective as a castration, and so it has proved.

'You are no longer a urology patient,' she said. 'You're now under oncology. They'll call in the week to make an appointment.'

The nurse said, 'It's incurable – but it's manageable.' I heard 'incurable' as 'terminal'. Have mercy upon me, O Lord, for I am weak. O Lord, heal me, for my bones are vexed.

All of the men on the family tree that my wife sent me are dead, except one. What's more, I know when all of them died, except that same one. During my initial conversation with the oncologist, she got hold of the wrong end of the stick. I asked her, 'How long ...' and she said 'two to five years', but I think I was asking her something else; I can't remember what. Two to five years; time added for good behaviour, it now seems. If that didn't make you think about your own death, then I'm not sure what would.

The families of patients often talk about 'brave battles against cancer', but honestly, all you do is lie there and eat hospital cheese sandwiches while the doctors and nurses and administrators do the battling. A cancer patient's body becomes a battlefield, and all you can do is watch the fight and hope the day goes well. In the seventeenth and eighteenth centuries, there were no admin staff to smooth your path, and no nurses to do the actual treatment. There were, however, medical doctors, and because medicine in the early eighteenth century was pre-scientific, they were all but useless. The marriage between medicine and science has had its ups and downs, like all marriages, but it has served humankind well. If you doubt this, then how do you account for the fact that you're reading a book by someone who is only alive as the result of that union? It can't be fecking 'wellness'.

Charles II died in 1685, when Thom was nine. Charles Spencer, writing in 2017's *To Catch a King*, tells the stomach-turning story of what the poor king's doctors did to try to save his life, which will serve as an account of the state of high-level medicine at the time. Charles II became unwell on 1 February 1685; the following morning, looking ill and unsteady on his legs, he started to fit, and to have powerful convulsions whilst his servant was giving him his morning shave in a chair by the window. The physicians were called, and ordered that the king be bled, at once. Sixteen ounces of blood were drawn from his arm, and he was muzzled to stop him biting off his tongue during the convulsions. The physicians decided that the king needed stimulation, and to this end they burned his shoulders with boiling hot cupping glasses, and then took another eight ounces of blood through a series of minor incisions. Next, they needed to drive out the poisons they felt were giving him fits. They gave him emetics, a laxative and an enema. They shaved his head so that they could put plasters on his head that were soaked in a liquid which would cause blistering. Other parts of his body were cauterised; still the fits continued. They gave him another enema, and rubbed hellebore root in his nose to burn the nostrils.

Only now did they move him into his bed at which point the king rallied a little, and managed to speak. He told them that in the night, feeling rough, he had gone to his bathroom to take a few 'King's Drops', which were made of human skulls ground up in alcohol. This hadn't helped, disappointingly, but after all the shit they had put him through, he felt a bit better, thank you. That evening though, the royal physicians, the greatest medical doctors in the land, started at him again. They put plasters packed with revitalising pigeon guano on his feet, and applied more plasters containing organically grown cowslips, lovingly blended by artisanal hand with hydrochloric acid and ammonia. On the upside, he was allowed to drink as much 'light ale made without hops' as he fancied.

The next day, the doctors felt that the worst was over, so they only made him gargle with extract of elm bark, and drink some cherry juice mixed up with lime flowers, peony, lavender and crushed pearls. Just to be on the safe side, they bled the king of another ten ounces. And again the next day; more bleeding followed by a laxative, which included white tartar and senna leaves. This didn't improve matters, quite the contrary, so they gave him forty drops of 'spirit of human skull'.

Good Thomas Ken, the Bishop of Bath and Wells, appeared at the king's bedside to offer him final communion, but the king said that he wasn't quite ready. Meanwhile, the king's current favourite, Louise de Kérouaille, Duchess of Portsmouth,[87] was arranging his deathbed conversion to Catholicism; his brother, on the cusp of becoming James II, was by his side as the king was received into the Roman Church by Father Huddleston, who had helped Charles escape after the Battle of Worcester in 1650. Charles survived another night, perhaps helped by the powdered goat's intestines that his physicians urged upon him, washed down by a draught of 'Raleigh's Antidote': herbs, spices, animal parts, ground up coral and pearl in white wine. The next morning, he asked that the curtains be opened so that he could see the sunrise for the last time, fell into a coma and died that afternoon.

Such was the state of top-level medicine in late seventeenth- and early eighteenth-century England. Charles II's doctors weren't to blame for what they put him through; by their lights they had done all that they could. The problem was the paradigm under which they operated. Their view of the human body was close to utterly totally and completely wrong, as it was based on the idea of 'humours', which had held sway over medical thinking for hundreds, if not thousands, of years. Put crudely (the system became more highly developed over time, though no less wrong), the body contains 'four humours', which

---

87   And our Louisa's many times great-grandmother.

both symbolised and actualised the state of health of an individual. These are blood, phlegm, black bile and yellow bile. Illness and disease were caused by having too much or too little of any of them. Health could be achieved only if the four humours were in balance.[88] The king was purged to rid him of the various kinds of bile, burned to expel excess phlegm and bled to get rid of excess blood.

The theory and practice of blood-letting can be traced back to Hippocrates, he of the oath. It starts from an observed fact, that of menstruation in women. Hippocrates wrote that this loss of blood cleansed women of bad humours, and that therefore everyone could do with losing lots of blood on a regular basis. It was Galen, writing in the third century CE, who systematised the widely used practice, prescribing how much blood should be taken for any particular ailment, and from where. For example, the vein in the right hand would be opened if you had liver problems, to which, to judge from the amount of booze that man knocked back, I am sure Thom must have been a martyr.

According to the teachings of Galen, excess of any of the humours also affected the personality. Galen's work was largely forgotten in the north and west of Europe after the fall of Rome, but not by Islamic scholars, who translated the original Greek manuscripts into Arabic; nor in the chief city of the Byzantine Empire, Constantinople, Stamboul, 'the Second Rome', where his manuscripts continued to form the basis of medicinal practice. This is not to say that bleeding people stopped being practised in the north and west of Europe; just that nobody had a clue as to why they were doing such a thing.

The Modern World got off to a start in the 1450s, with the Fall of Byzantium in 1453 and Gutenberg's first printed Bible in 1455. The conquest of Constantinople by the Ottoman Turks brought the Roman Empire to its final end, after 1,500 years of existence. Greek scholars fled the burning city, bearing away as many manuscripts as they could. They arrived in the west and north of Europe, Florence, Paris, Oxford, bringing the 'new learning' with them. Which is to say,

88　See 'Wellness' &c &c.

very old learning that had been forgotten outside Byzantium and Baghdad, in particular, the works of Plato. When Galen's work was translated into Latin and then printed, in 1490, his theories gained a new credence amongst university-trained doctors, such as those in attendance on Charles II during his final illness.

The four Galenic humours mapped onto the four elements and qualities: cold dry Earth for black bile and hot dry Fire for yellow; cold and wet Water for phlegm, and hot wet Air for blood. Too much Earth, and you were likely to be a Melancholic personality, obsessive, cautious, avoiding. A Phlegmatic, one in whom Water predominates, is schizoid, supportive, getting. One who is Choleric, which is to say, having an excess of Fire, is depressed, dominant, ruling. And they who are Sanguine, being full of Air, are hysterical, socially useful, inspiring.

There is much that I envy Thom's world, but pre-scientific medicine is not one. This traditional view of the body is done with because it is nonsense. Science chased it off. As an example of one of the most obvious problems, there are no such things as black and yellow bile, there's just bile. And phlegm was not the stuff we cough up in the morning after a night with our trusty old briars. Phlegm described such disparate gunges as sweat, semen, pus, saliva and mucus, such as you might see on an advert for biological washing powder. Galenic phlegm is a phantasm. Humourous medicine now strikes us as a joke, a joke played out over centuries.

But given how much blood Thom loses during the course of the diary, I think he suspected that he was a bit sanguine. We might think this nonsense; but Thom and his family didn't. He is bled with fair regularity throughout the diary; so are his wife and family and so are his horses and oxen. The first mention is on 9 February 1714 (OS), when he paid 'Richard Panting 1s for bleeding me'; a month later, 6 March 1714, he paid Panting another shilling for bleeding Elizabeth, when they were round Mrs. Catherine Beard's one night after church. The first record of bleeding horses comes on 7 May 1715, when Thom bled his 'old horse' and his cart horse. Thom didn't always bleed the animals himself; sometimes he called upon his good drinking pal Nick Plaw to do it for him. Mr. Plaw seems to have been the nearest thing Hurst had to a vet, though the actual doctor in Hurst, John Snashall, sometimes bled both Thom and his livestock, in addition to chopping off the odd leg around the village.

Both elite and non-elite practitioners bled their patients, for thousands of years. Between the building of the pyramids and the middle of the nineteenth century, bleeding was the most common medical procedure on earth. I wonder what insane medical procedure we undergo that will drop jaws in 300 years' time? From inside our current paradigm, it's hard to tell.

To do the actual bleeding, Richard Panting would have used a three-bladed instrument called a fleam. A fleam is a bit like a multibladed Swiss army knife, where three different-sized blades – big for horses &c, middle for grown-ups, teeny-weeny for the children – are folded into an outer case. The blades look like shark's teeth; the bloodletter would position the appropriate-sized blade over the patient's vein, and then knock it into place with a small wooden hammer. The resulting flow of blood would be caught in a bowl, the ounces of blood taken carefully measured, and then the wound bandaged. Blood-letting was so common a procedure, that it was often carried out by barbers; hence the red-and-white-striped pole. Neither the fleams nor the bandages would have been sterilised.

Travelling surgeons might offer more drastic procedures. The history of modern surgery begins at the same time as that of urology, because the first modern surgical procedure was the removal of bladder stones by 'stone-cutters' or 'lithotomists'. It involved the cutter putting their hand into the patient's anus, locating the stone through the bladder wall, manipulating it up to the bladder neck and then cutting into the patient's perineum, before reaching into the patient's bladder and hoicking the stone out with a finger. No anaesthetics, of course, or hygiene either. Many patients died from sepsis; there were no antibiotics worth the name until Ralph Foxwell was in his teens. It had been anciently mostly carried out on young boys, before their prostates became active and started to grow; it was harder to operate on men with adult prostates in the way, who, if they didn't die, were left with likely impotence, infertility and/or incontinence. Samuel Pepys got lucky when the famous stone-cutter Thomas Hollier relieved him of a stone 'the size of a real tennis ball', so much so that he kept the anniversary of the operation in 1658 as a day of rejoicing. Pepys clearly wasn't made impotent by the operation, but he seems to have been left infertile; the lack of children with his wife (or with any of his numerous intimate friends) was one of his great regrets.

The prostate gland was only identified by anatomists in 1536, though gay men may have had an inkling before that date. It took a long time to work out what it does. It's doughnut shaped and walnut sized. Piss passes through the hole in the middle, which is why prostate enlargement plays havoc with your waterworks. It does all sorts of useful and pleasant tasks – it acts as a valve to stop urine getting into your testes, it produces somewhere between a quarter and a third of your seminal fluid, and it contracts at the moment of achievement to expel semen up the urethra and out of the body. A healthy prostate feels smooth and symmetrical to the touch, I'm assured. I don't know what shape mine is, but I guess I can be proud that it has a profile unique enough that it makes proctologists say 'goodness' upon feeling it. Treatments weren't available until the late nineteenth century, so before then men with extreme or cancerous prostate enlargement died either of kidney failure due to urine retention, or from infection and scarring caused by the use of primitive non-sterile catheters.

Doctors were merely licensed quacks who could read Latin, whilst surgeons were jumped-up chancers who killed many more than they cured; though they could at least set bones. It's easy to see why Thom would resort to quackery, because he had little choice. Anyway, quackery may not have cured anybody, but it was a lot more fun than having hellebore shoved up your nose.

It was fun because quack medicine arrived in Hurst in the shape of various 'mountebanks'. A mountebank was a seller of remedies of doubtful use, who employed showmanship to sell his wares. They could perform anywhere, just by standing on a chair, or a bench, or a bank – hence 'mountebank'. Thom mentions two by name: 24 January 1717:

> A mountebank came to our Towne today, calls himself
> Dr Richard Harness. Mr Scutt and I drank tea with the
> tumbler. Of his tricks I am no judge; but he appears to me
> to play well on the fiddle.

The mountebank and the tumbler may well have been the same person, or the tumbler might have been one of Dr Harness's entourage.

Joseph Strutt, in *The Sports and Pastimes of the People of England*, published in 1801, writes of what Harness was about:

> I may here mention a stage-performer whose show is
> usually enlivened with mimicry, music and tumbling; I
> mean the mountebank. It is uncertain at what period
> this vagrant dealer in physic made his appearance in
> England; it is clear, however, that he figured away with
> much success in this country during the seventeenth
> and eighteenth centuries; he called to his assistance
> some of the performances practised by the jugglers;
> and the bourdour, or merry-andrew seems to have
> been his inseparable companion; hence it is said in
> an old ballad, entitled 'Sundry Trades and Callings'
> :- 'a mountebank without his fool is a sorrowful case'.
> The mountebanks usually preface the vending of their
> medicines with pompous orations, in which they pay
> as little regard to truth as to propriety.
> According to *The Spectator*, in the reign of James II,
> Hans Buling, a Dutchman, was well known in London

as a mountebank. He was an odd figure of a man, and extremely fantastical in his dress; he was attended by a monkey, which he had trained to act the part of a jack-pudding, a part which he had formally acted himself, and which was more natural to him than that of a professor of physic. He told his audience that he had been born and bred in Hammersmith, having a special regard for the place of his nativity he was determined to make a present of five shillings to as many as would accept it; the whole crowd stood agape, and ready to take the doctor at his word; when, putting his hand into a long bag, as everyone was expecting his crown piece he drew out a handful of packets, each of which, he informed the spectators, was constantly sold for five shillings and sixpence, but that he would bate the five shillings to every inhabitant of that place. The whole assembly closed with this generous offer, and took off all his physic, after the doctor had made them vouch that there were no foreigners among them, but that they were all Hammersmith men.

The link between charlatanry and mountebanks was well established in law; according to Edward Coke, in his *Institutes of the Lawes of England*, published between 1628 and 1644:

Here are expressed the punishments inflicted upon these imposters, mountebanks and cheating quicksalvers viz. 1. To suffer imprisonment by the space of a whole year without bail or mainprize. 2. Once every quarter of the year these mountebanks are to mount the pillory, and to stand thereupon in some market town six hours, and there to confess his or her error and afence.

This reputation for charlatanry, apparently punishable by law, doesn't seem to have bothered Thom, who appears to have enjoyed both the mountebanks' performances and their company. The longest sequence of diary entries relating to their arrival in Hurst comes in the late spring of 1721;

> The 12th May 1721. A mountebank at Towne. His name (as he says) William Luby. I agreed to keep a horse for him at 2s per week.
> The 15th May 1721. Turned the mountebank's horse to Rickman's.
> The 20th May 1721. I drank with the mountebank yesterday at the Swan.
> The 26th May 1721. The mountebanks servants were here.

What servants might they have been? Mountebanks very rarely travelled alone; as Strutt said, a fool (or a tumbler, or a musician or two) seems to have been pretty much universal, though they were often accompanied by toad-eaters, whose job was to eat live toads, very much as it says on the tin. The performer would swallow the poisonous toad, and pass out and fall into a fit, or even feign death; the mountebank would offer a sip of his potion, which would instantly revive the poor toad-eater. Imagine doing such a demeaning job for such a disreputable boss. Someone who would do anything to please their master became known as a toad-eater; or 'toadie' for short. Someone who ate live animals in American freak shows was known, not as a toad-eater, but as a 'geek'. Whatever functions Luby's servants performed, Thom seems quite happy for them to visit Little Park.

> The 2nd June 1721. The mountebank took away his little mare and sent an other.[89]

---

89 Thom always writes 'an other' rather than 'another'.

> The 16th June 1721. The mountebank at town. A smock
> race in our field.
> The 23rd June1721. A very fine day. Received 12s of Dr
> Luby for keeping his mare 6 weeks.

Dr Luby is it now? Six weeks before, Thom cast doubt even on his name. They have become pals, is what; so much so that Luby seems to have used Little Park as his headquarters while he was performing and selling his wares in other parts of Sussex. Thom enjoyed the company of these medical entertainers, but I think he may have been picking their brains out of a strong sense of curiosity. As we shall see in chapter XVI, many of Thom's descendants worked in medicine, one way or another. It seems as though Luby had gained Thom's confidence and respect, not least because he paid his bills on time.

The body was simple. It consisted of only four elements after all, and so it should be possible to find a panacea, a universal medicine, one that cured all ills. Galen was one of those who wrote about and popularised the most widespread of these panaceas, which was called 'theriac', or Venetian Treacle. Theriac had sixty-four ingredients. It took months to collect and prepare them all, which included iris, rhubarb, gentian, cinnamon, lemon grass, bay leaves, roses, lavender, rapeseed, anise, carrot, wine from the Canaries, myrrh, nutmeg oil, opium, roasted viper's flesh,[90] and castoreum, a waxy substance obtained from the anal glands of beavers. Galen said that it should be stored for six years before it was ready to use. It came to London on Venetian galleys, and was sold as the most efficacious and thus expensive remedy offered by apothecaries.

The reason for the appearance of mountebanks in the seventeenth and eighteenth centuries was because of a new potion, called orvietan, which, although just as shite as theriac, was much easier to make. The first person to promote it was a fairground performer called Gerolamo Ferranti, in early seventeenth-century Paris. He also seems to have been the first person to pretend to take

---

90   Hence 'snake oil'.

various poisons – Tonight! Live on a Bench Near You! – and then to cure himself with his newly devised orvietan. It could have as few as nine ingredients, mostly commonly found and easily cultivated herbs dissolved in wine and honey, together with a soupçon of viper meat, and the merest drop of Venetian Treacle. It was a huckster's invention which hundreds of other hucksters took to their breasts. It was sold either as a potion, or in powdered form, and it is all but certain that Drs. Harness and Luby were selling their version of orvietan, the only widely available medicine that had its origins in a fairground sideshow.

Mountebanks operated in the United States long after they had disappeared in Europe. Cher's 'Gypsies Tramps and Thieves' has her fictional father selling bottles of 'Doctor Good', whilst the band Doctor Hook and the Medicine Show also recalled a fairly recent past. The medicine shows of America were the mountebanks' last hoorah, or so you might hope. But the fascinating thing about quackery is that now we have a choice between scientific medicine that mostly works, and stuff that involves putting crystal eggs up your punani &c &c, and lots of us still go for the latter. Ours is an Age of Mountebanks, from David Icke to Gwyneth Paltrow, from Joe Rogan to Piers Corbyn. Their toad-eaters number in the millions. I'm not immune. I had peripheral nerve damage in my foot after chemo and I didn't fancy the drugs that I was prescribed, so I tried acupuncture, and it seems to have worked. And I take what you might call 'unrefined CBD oil', which I smoke in my old pipe. The internet is a mountebank who lives in our pockets.

This account of elite doctors and populist quacks, all of them men, leaves out the day-to-day healing that would have been part of a woman's work, and was certainly more effective than either the licensed physicians' or the mountebanks' concoctions. The garden at Little Park would probably have been under Elizabeth's control, and its main function would have been to provide herbal ingredients for home remedies. Elizabeth would have known how to treat common ailments, and how to care for the sick. It is highly likely that she would have kept her own household book, containing recipes for meals, but also for making remedies collected from her family and friends. We know this because hundreds of such commonplace books have been found and digitised by the Early Modern Recipes Online Collective.[91] Elizabeth, being a modern wife, might also have had a copy of Hannah Woolley's *The Accomplish'd Lady's Delight in Preserving, Physick, Beautifying, and Cookery*, regarded as the first English cookbook, which contained not just recipes for food, but for remedies and cosmetics. This women's medicine was the nearest thing to anything that worked, but it was regarded by the medical establishment as nonsensical. The Wellcome Library holds records of eighty-two midwifery manuals published between 1540 and 1699, eighty-one of them by university-trained male physicians, only one of them by a woman with actual experience of attending women in labour. This despite the fact that medical practices and herbal remedies that had been tweaked and tested by generations of women clearly worked better than anything else available. For example, the drug aspirin was derived from willow bark, which, for hundreds of years, women had used in tea to effectively reduce fever. And the greatest and most astounding success story of modern medicine had its origin in a women-only space, and it is there we must now go. I'm allowed in only because I'm a eunuch.

Five miles from the Turkish border with Greece is the ancient city of Edirne. For refugees from Syria, Iraq, Kurdistan and Afghanistan, it's the last stop before the promised land that is the European Union. A three-hour drive from Istanbul along a road thronged with refugees, Edirne has done its best to cope with the transient population desperate to cross the border with the EU. It was anciently called

---

91   Also because people still keep them. I have my grandmother's recipe book, which contains recipes and a series of the weekly menus she served to Hervey Vaughan Williams.

Adrianopolis, or Adrianople, and was named after its founder, the Roman emperor Hadrian. This gives a measure both of the extent of the Roman Empire and the closed nature of our world; once, people in Adrianopolis and people in Carlisle, hard against Hadrian's Wall, were Roman subjects together, and could move freely between the two – now, it's not so easy.

The Ottoman Turks invaded and corroded the Byzantine Empire over a century and a half, almost by stealth, until only the impoverished city of Constantinople was left to the last emperor, Constantine XI Palaeologus, who died fighting on the walls in defiance of the invaders. Adrianopolis fell under Ottoman control in 1369, and until the final fall of Byzantium in 1453 it was their capital city. The Ottomans turned it from a decaying Greek city into a thriving Turkish one. By the beginning of the eighteenth century Adrianopolis had three splendid mosques, one with minarets higher than the Hagia Sophia in Constantinople, covered bazaars, two caravanserais and extensive public baths. Handsome gardens lined the river, and large and luxurious palaces were available for the Ottoman sultan and his officials. Adrianopolis still sometimes functioned as a capital city after the fall of Byzantium, as the sultans would continue to take recourse there when Istanbul became too hot.

Women had their own spaces in the palaces, which I prefer to call zenanas, rather than harems or seraglios, which come loaded with Orientalist presumptions. The zenana was the domain of the female members of the household; it housed not just wives and concubines and their daughters but unmarried sisters and elderly widows and any amount of distant relations. They were attended by female doctors, female entertainers, female administrators, a whole phalanx of female servants, and even female guards. A zenana might contain thousands of women, leading a mostly self-contained existence. In the early eighteenth century, the most dazzlingly opulent and relaxed zenana in Adrianople was ruled over by the beautiful Fatima, wife of the lieutenant of the sultan's Grand Vizier.[92] It had its own hot baths,

---

92   His first minister.

courtyards alive with fountains, and rose-and-frankincense-scented living quarters hung with tapestries. A traveller compared it to 'the paradise of Mohammed'. And in this place was a pearl-of-great-price, a medicine which could both preserve beauty and save children's lives, held by old women in nothing bigger than a walnut shell.

In 1717, a visitor from England, Lady Mary Wortley Montagu, was admitted into this enchanted space. She came from one of the great aristocratic families: the Pierpoints. This branch of the family had thrived whilst that in Hurstpierpoint, the village that bore their name, had withered. Their seat was Thoresby Hall in Nottinghamshire. Her father was Evelyn Pierpoint, the Duke of Kingston-upon-Hull, and Mary was raised by him after the death of her mother and grandmother when she was eight. He didn't believe in education for women, but Mary did, so she educated herself in Latin and literature by hiding during the day in Thoresby Hall's extensive library. By the age of fifteen, she was corresponding with bishops and had written an epistolary novel, a romance and a great many poems, enough to impress even her father. Lady Mary Pierpoint had been toasted by the Kit-Kat Club[93] as one of the great beauties of the age, aged seven – enough to turn anybody's head then, and anybody's stomach now. She wrote in her diary, 'I am going to write a history so uncommon', which, you have to hand it to her, she certainly achieved.

Great beauty, wealth, position and, above all, her famous wit attracted high status suitors. She liked Edward Wortley Montagu, who came from a wealthy Yorkshire coal mine-owning family, whilst her father preferred Clotworthy Skeffington, a stand-up comedian on the north-east club circuit who had a minor novelty hit in 1709 called 'Who's a Clot Now?'[94] Mary got her way, eloping with Wortley Montagu in 1712 to avoid having to become Mrs. Skeffington.

---

93 A Whig drinking club whose members included John Locke, William Congreve, Joseph Addison and Charles Seymour – the Proud Duke of Somerset.

94 That's what should have happened to someone called Clotworthy Skeffington. He was, in fact, the 4th Viscount Massereene, an Irish landowner and politician.

The marriage was happy enough at first; Edward was busy as an MP, and Mary was setting London society aflame. She was friends with the new king and his circle, with old courtiers like Sarah Churchill, with aristocrats like Lord Hervey, and with writers like John Gay, Mary Astell the proto-feminist and, above all, with Alexander Pope, who fell desperately in love with her. But in 1715, Lady Mary's brother died from smallpox, and she caught it herself. The resulting pockmarks on her face marred her beauty, she felt. Her husband was pleased, thinking her pockmarked face might chase off her admirers, which it didn't. There were those, including Pope, who contended that her beauty was as great as ever.

The Austrian Empire was at war with the Ottoman Empire, and the king of England and Hanover wanted to send a peace-seeking ambassador to the Sublime Porte in Constantinople, as the Ottoman court was known. For this delicate task, he chose Edward Wortley Montagu. Lady Mary was thrilled, longing for new worlds to learn about and to conquer. Finances dictated that the Wortley Montagus could only take a small entourage of twenty, which included their son Edward, a chaplain and a surgeon, Dr. Charles Maitland. The Wortley Montagu party sailed from Gravesend on 1 August 1716. They were to take an overland route, because Edward was charged with delivering a message to the Austrian emperor in Vienna and then meeting with George I in Hanover before continuing to Constantinople. They travelled as lightly as twenty people could in 1716, as their luggage had been sent by sea.

Lady Mary was fascinated by all she saw; the orderly cities in Holland, the cultured ones in Germany and the great imperial city of Vienna. She wrote letters to her friends throughout the journey, which were collected and published after her death as *The Turkish Embassy Letters*. The Wortley Montagus departed Vienna in the depths of winter on horse-drawn sleighs, which carried them down the frozen River Danube as far as Budapest. From there, they travelled through newly reconquered territory to Peterwardein, now Petrovaradin in Serbia, the last Austrian-held fortress before entering Ottoman territory. This vast fortress had only been won from the Ottomans in a bloody battle a week after the Wortley Montagus had departed from England. This was the front line. From here on, the party would be in Ottoman territory.

The first Ottoman city they stopped at was Belgrade, from whence they made their way to Sofia, now the Bulgarian capital, where Lady Mary began wearing Turkish dress and hanging out with the girls. She wrote with delight of her first visit to a female-only bathhouse in Sofia; in a letter to one of her friends she described it by writing about herself in the third person.

> The first time she was at one of these baths the
> ladies invited her to undress and bathe with them;
> and on her not making haste, one of the prettiest
> ran to undress her. You can't imagine her surprise
> upon lifting my lady's gown and seeing her stays go
> all around her. She ran back frightened and told her
> companion that the husbands in England were much
> worse than in the East, for they tied their wives up
> in little boxes, of the shape of their bodies ... they all
> agreed that it was one of the greatest barbarities of
> the world, and pitied the poor women for being such
> slaves in Europe.

The twenty-strong party continued their journey to Adrianopolis, arriving in March 1717 after a journey across Europe of eight months. The sultan was at that time in residence. Lady Mary liked it at once, and set out to explore the city, wearing her Turkish dress of loose robes and a heavy veil, enjoying the anonymity it afforded her. She was invited into the zenana of the Grand Vizier's wife, who in turn introduced her to Fatima. A demonstration of belly dancing was laid on for Lady Mary, who was coming to relish not just the clothes, but the freedom from male interference. By the time of her second visit, she had learned enough Turkish to be able to converse with Fatima. Here it was, then, that Lady Mary first learned the secret of the walnut shell, as she witnessed the women inoculate their children against smallpox.

She described the process (which she called 'engraftement') in one of her letters to her friend Sarah Chiswell – she wrote about it in a letter to her father too, but this has been lost. Pus was collected in a walnut shell from someone with a mild smallpox infection, then shallow cuts were made to the arms of the children with a needle, before a small amount of the diseased material was introduced to the cuts. This, in turn, caused a mild infection in the inoculated patients; mild, but enough to offer lifelong immunity. Mary wrote to Sarah Chiswell that she would wage war on the medical establishment to make them take notice.

After a few months in Adrianople, the Wortley Montagus continued their journey to Constantinople. Edward was often away on diplomatic business, so Mary continued her explorations, until she was forced to take pause to give birth to her daughter, also called Mary. In addition to the embassy surgeon Charles Maitland, she was attended by a Turkish physician, a Dr. Timoni, who happened to be a member of the Royal Society, and had contributed a paper on the engraftement process to the *Philosophical Transactions of the Royal Society* in 1714. Talking to Timoni seems to have been instrumental in Mary's decision to go ahead with inoculating her six-year-old son Edward; Maitland wrote an account of the occasion, on 19 March 1718:

> The ambassador's ingenious lady, who had been at
> some pains to satisfy her curiosity in this matter, and
> had made some useful observations on the practise,
> was so thoroughly convinced of the safety of it that
> she resolved to submit her only son to it ... She first
> ordered me to find out a fit subject to take the matter
> from; and then sent for an old Greek woman who had
> practised this way a great many years. After a deal of

trouble and pains I found a proper subject, then the
good woman went to work, but so awkwardly by the
shaking of her hand and put the child to so much
torture with her blunt and rusty needle that I pitied
his cries ... and therefore inoculated the other arm
with my own instrument, and with so little pain to
him that he did not in the least complain of it.

Young Edward Wortley Montagu was the first English person to be inoculated against smallpox.[95] This was also the first inoculation carried out under Western medical supervision, and so, at least arguably, one of the first useful procedures carried out by a university-trained doctor. The lad's arms swelled, and after the third day bright spots appeared on his face. He was feverish and thirsty on the seventh day, and on the eighth day, some one hundred pustules appeared on his body, which crusted and dropped off without leaving any scars. The only scars her now protected-for-life son bore were those on his arm caused by the procedure. Mary decided not to inoculate her daughter in Constantinople, because her child's Armenian wet-nurse had not had smallpox, and she did not want to pass it on.

In May 1718, Edward Wortley Montagu was recalled from his post. Neither he nor Mary wanted to leave; Edward because he wanted to continue with his diplomatic work, Mary because she loved Turkey, and the freedom (as she saw it) that the society in the zenanas afforded women. They landed back in Dover on 30 September 1718. Four days earlier, in Hurstpierpoint, Thom noted in his diary that 'The smallpox came out on Frank Osbourne.'

On her return to England, Lady Mary didn't begin to wage her war against the medical establishment until 1721, when a severe

95   The last routine smallpox vaccinations in Britain were in 1971. I am vaccinated against it
      but my children are not, because smallpox has been eradicated. The last outbreak was in
      a Birmingham medical lab in 1978. Governments still hold stocks of the vaccine in case
      of biological warfare.

smallpox outbreak hit London. The year started with unseasonably warm weather; smallpox was spreading fast, and the mortality rate could be as high as a third. In March, Lady Mary contacted Dr. Charles Maitland, who had helped with her son's inoculation in Constantinople, and asked him to perform an engraftement on her daughter. He agreed, on condition that three other physicians witnessed the procedure and the child's subsequent progress; Lady Mary wasn't pleased, but went along with Maitland's terms, and invited friends and families to witness the event. Maitland engrafted both of the child's arms, and the three 'learned physicians' were allowed to visit 'Miss Wortley playing about her room, cheerful and well, with the smallpox raised upon her'. Miss Mary Wortley Montagu, aged three, was the first person to receive inoculation against disease under medical supervision in Britain. In 2021 it was exactly 300 years since this event; and also the year when the technology, proved and refined over three centuries, mattered more than ever.

The three physicians started to talk about what they had seen; so did Maitland, and so did Lady Mary. In the early summer, a few popular newspapers printed accounts in favour of inoculation. The success of the inoculation of Miss Wortley came to the attention of Caroline of Ansbach, the Princess of Wales, who wanted to try it on her children, but not until more engraftements had been carried out and proven successful. Six prisoners in Newgate were offered the treatment in return for a free pardon; Maitland carried out the procedure and all of the men developed mild symptoms, survived to tell the tale, and were released. A year to the day after Miss Wortley had undergone the procedure, the Princess of Wales had her two daughters inoculated. Lady Mary wrote to her sister, 'I suppose the faithful historians give you regular accounts of the growth and spreading of the inoculation of the smallpox, which is become almost a general practice, attended with great success.'

The royal imprimatur meant that elite families hurried to get their children engrafted, but there were some failures resulting in death, which sparked an intense controversy over the summer of 1722. A growing number of physicians were convinced that inoculation worked; but opposition came from a familiar source, and took aim at the usual suspects. Dr. William Wagstaffe published a pamphlet in which he called inoculation nothing but a folk-practice which put medicine into the hands of amateurs; and worse – women. 'Posterity perhaps will scarcely be brought to believe, that an Experiment practised only by a few Ignorant Women, amongst an illiterate and unthinking People, should on a sudden, and upon slender Experience, so far obtain in one of the Politist Nations in the World, as to be received into the Royal Palace.' It had been established in the seventeenth century that patients who received treatment during smallpox from medically trained physicians were much more likely to die than those lucky enough not to be able to afford a doctor; and yet physicians like Wagstaffe continued to offer Galenic treatments: bleeding, cauterisation, drinking lots of beer, dying. The person who knew best was still Lady Mary, who, while the controversy raged, travelled around aristocratic homes, personally engrafting children. From her point of view, the thing was so simple, it didn't need a doctor at all. Late in 1722, she anonymously published her own account of engraftement called 'A Plain Account of the Inoculating of the Small Pox by a Turkey Merchant':

> Out of compassion to the numbers abused and
> deluded by the knavery and ignorance of physicians I
> am determined to give a true account of the manner
> of inoculating the smallpox as it is practised in
> Constantinople with constant success, and without
> any ill consequence whatever. I shall sell no drugs, nor
> take no fees, could I persuade people of the safety and
> reasonableness of this easy operation. 'Tis no way my
> interest ... to convince the world of their errors; that
> is, I shall get nothing by it but the private satisfaction
> of having done good to mankind, and I know no body
> that reckons that satisfaction any part of their interest.

I shall leave Lady Mary[96] there, somewhat reluctantly, as, like Alexander Pope, I have fallen a little in love with her – or, at least, I can understand why so many people did. She was the bomb, she really was. She was a Great Woman, whose portrait should be on twenty-pound notes. There's an excellent recent biography by Joanna Willett called *The Pioneering Life of Mary Wortley Montagu, Scientist and Feminist*, which I recommend as a good place to go next to read about her. I haven't touched on her importance as a writer or a feminist, nor her sexuality, which has been attracting the interest of queer historians in recent years.

Great Man Theory is the idea that progress is always a consequence of the actions of 'Great Men', men ordained by God to change the world, one way or another. It might not be true, but it makes for readability, always a temptation. Historians were slow to let it go, even though it's demonstrably false. Twenty-first-century historians are less interested than previously in the doings of men, great or otherwise, though perhaps Great Women can still enjoy a moment in the sun, as they have been only lately invited to the party. Now history moves, if it can be characterised as moving at all, as tendencies; disturbances in the social, cultural, economic and political aether. Humans are pawns in the incorporeal hands of vast impersonal movements, apparently. All this strikes me as nonsense too. History is an old story told over and over until it becomes a new story. The 'Culture Wars' are waged between competing stories, not necessarily competing facts. Let's tell this story then, in this time: inoculation is women's medicine, which comes from the Middle East, and was brought to the attention of Western medical elites by a Great Woman.

---

96 Lady Mary won her war; by the end of the century inoculation was common practice. Dr. Edward Jenner, usually the first name in the history of vaccination, took the step of using cowpox pus to inoculate patients (which at least five other practitioners had tried with great success) and then deliberately infecting them with smallpox to see if they developed the disease, which they invariably didn't. He was not, therefore, the first to use 'vaccination' (i.e. derived from cows) but the first to prove it safer and more effective than using smallpox matter.

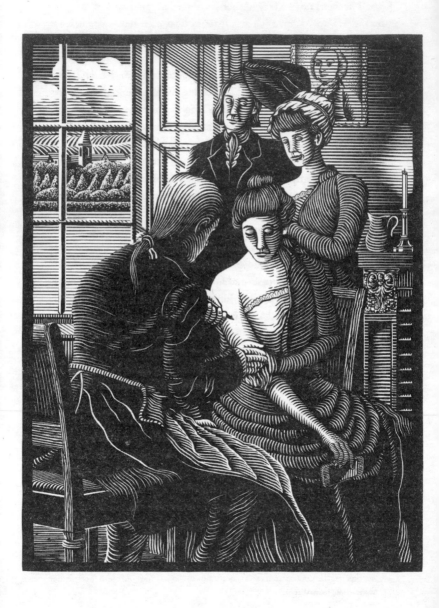

Smallpox is a persistent concern throughout the diary. The first case that Thom records is in 1714, when his brother-in-law James Ede becomes infected. The last is in 1728, somewhere very close to the end. But by late 1727, the practice of engraftement was known in Hurst. On 17 December, Thom writes in his diary, 'Mr Henry Campion went to London a Thursday I an account sent him that Mr H Civar goeing to have the smallpox.' Henry Campion was therefore travelling to London to get this new treatment. I can find no reference to 'Mr H Civar', but 'Civar' is a common Turkish name, so presumably practitioners from Constantinople had made their way into England to offer inoculation to well-heeled takers.

On 26 October 1727, having been home since July, Jacky Marchant returned to Pembroke College, Oxford, in company with one of Thom's trusted hands, Marrian Edwards,[97] who returned to Hurst on the 30th. On 16 November, Thom received a letter from Jacky; presumably Thom had written to him to tell him about the Petworth gig. Jacky didn't come home for Christmas; it was a long way after all, and Christmas was not then what it is now. So he was in Oxford the whole time that Thom was waiting on the Proud Duke. Right towards the end of the doomed Petworth experience, on 3 March 1727, Thom sent Jacky a letter with a guinea in it, either as an unexpected gift, or in the way that Mum and Ralph sent me money after I'd only been at college a month, namely, after a desperate appeal.

On the last day of 1727, 24 March, weighed down by the failure in Petworth, Thom must have received news from Oxford, as he wrote in his diary, 'Marrian Edwards set out for Oxford to fetch John Marchant home, because the smallpox is so much there.'

Lady Day 1728, 25 March, was a fine day. Less than a week

97   Marrian like John Wayne.

after Thom's ignominious retreat from Petworth, and following Elizabeth's entreaties, maybe, Thom was getting back into his stride. He went to Ditchling Fair, and dined with friends. But over the next few days, his mood slumped. He noted that William Martin, Rector of Rusper (until Jacky took his orders), was staying at Little Park because he had 'an ague'. On the 27th, he notes that he did nothing. Then the news came:

> The 19th March 1728. Marrian Edwards return'd from
> Oxford, brought word that Jack had the smallpox.

Two parties went immediately to Oxford. On the 30th, 'Thomas Elvey set out for Oxford betimes in the morning.' Thom also adds 'My cousin Bett ...' and then crosses out what he'd written about her. The next day, a gloomy Sunday, 'Mr William Martin, Mr Healy's man set out in the morning with my cousin Sarah Norton for Oxford. William Marchant and John Lindfield went as far as Leatherhead with my cousin Bett yesterday and returned today about noon.' So it looks as though the deleted entry referred to Cousin Bett setting off for Oxford, in company with Thomas Elvey; Thom 'cleard her accounts for her journey to Oxford' on 15 April. It is interesting to note that William Martin was in the second party, as he had a financial interest in Jacky's health.

On 1 April 1728, there was bad news.

> Reciev'd a letter from Oxford per post from Mr Ratcliff
> to let us know that Jack was very full of the smallpox and a
> very bad sort.

We can only imagine how Thom and Elizabeth were feeling, though the diary offers a clue: '3/4/28 Mrs Catherine Beard lay with my wife, no news from Oxford.'

On 4 April, the first of the party from Oxford returned – 'Mr Healy's man returned from Oxford, brought letters that Jack was not worse.' Two days later, Thom 'wrote to Mr William Martin per post'.

And then this:

> The 8th April 1728 Munday. Thomas Elvey and Marrian Edwards returned from Oxford and brought the dismal news that Jack Marchant died a Fryday night last about 11 aclock.'[98]

Rest in Peace, Uncle Jacky, and Rise in Glory.

Thom doesn't make mention of John or Oxford again, once he's paid Cousin Bett's accounts. Presumably, these covered funeral expenses too; Thom and Elizabeth clearly didn't feel up to the journey. I hope Cousin Bett, Mr. William Martin and Cousin Sarah Norton were able to attend before they left Oxford.

Because theirs was a society for which death was a commonplace thing, it's easy to underplay the grief that Thom and Elizabeth would have felt. They had eleven children together. The eldest died in infancy in 1701, another in 1704. Two toddlers had died in 1707, and another in 1711. Mary, aged sixteen, and Elizabeth, twenty-two, both died in 1723, in the period that Thom either didn't keep his diary or for which the volumes are lost, so we haven't got his version of what happened.

I don't think you get used to that. As parents, our biggest fear is our children dying; it seems impudent to assume that Thom and Elizabeth didn't share that fear. They lived with a burden of grief perhaps greater than our own, not less. It's not expressed in the diary, but, as I've noted, diaries were not the place where early eighteenth-century writers would have recorded their emotional states. But as John Ray wrote in his *Proverbs*, 'No day passeth without some grief.'

98   On 5 April.

We walk in a Vale of Tears, my friends. That we do so, and yet keep walking, is our daily miracle, our greatest achievement.

Mr. Thomas Marchant, Gent., of Hurstpierpoint in the County of Sussex, died aged fifty-two a little over five months after his son John, on 14 September 1728. The last diary entry was a week earlier.

> The 7th September 1728 Saturday. A fine day. Old William Brand buried here. George West carry'd 6 bushels of turnips to Samuel Hart's. Plough'd at Rickmans with 2 teems. I was at Mr John Hart's after the funeral with Mr William Martin.

And how did he die? Lung cancer and heart disease took my birth dad Alan and Grandpop Charlie. Prostate cancer might be a contender too, obviously. Apart from his regular headaches on Sundays, the main illness that Thom complained of in the diary was 'ague', by which he may have meant a cold or flu of some kind, but which could also be taken to mean malaria, not unknown in England at that time, and, if so, there might have been long-term complications arising from that. If he had a weak heart, the failure in Petworth and the death of Jacky, might both have played a part. But I can't escape the idea that he died from cirrhosis of the liver. The current recommended limit for men is fourteen units a week; very roughly, a pint of beer or a glass and a half of wine per day, whilst Thom was more of a fourteen-units-a-day man. Over twenty years, drinking only a few more units a week can increase your risk of alcoholic liver disease from 6 per cent to 45 per cent. It seems a fair bet, but nothing more; there were no death certificates, no autopsies, no coroner's reports. I cannot know.

What we can know, for sure, is our own grief, at our own loss. We can remember joy, but grief is not like that; it's not transient, something to be remembered, but a wound that is always with us. I learned this a long time ago, too young.

And here it is again. Thom is gone from the rocking chair by my fire. The beat of the clock has changed; suddenly, the seconds tick and tock once more. He was never a ghost, but alive to me.

Elizabeth and the girls had been busy all morning. After the funeral, friends and neighbours, family and servants would come back to the house for food, tea and beer. All had to be got ready, as for any social occasion. The fine elm coffin was lifted by William, John Hart, Henry Campion and Nick Plaw onto the back of the wagon, which was draped in black for the short journey to St. Lawrence's Church. Mr. William Martin took the service, and gave a fine eulogy to his friend. Then the coffin was carried to the graveside, and the pall-bearers lowered it into the ground with hempen ropes. Mary Molly and Kitty were in tears; William held Elizabeth's arm as she stood, upright and alone.

Mr. Martin threw a handful of dirt into the grave, which rattled on the coffin lid. He read from his book.

> For as much as it hath pleased Almighty God of his great mercy to take unto himself the soul of our dear brother here departed, we therefore commit his body to the ground; earth to earth, ashes to ashes, dust to dust; in sure and certain hope of the Resurrection to eternal life, through our Lord Jesus Christ ...

DISPOSAL

in which the Author learns, not for the first time, that Life is subject to Luck, and uses reason and experience to storyline a three-decker novel, which will explain why his family forgot that they were once the Marchants of Hurst.

XVI.

NONE IS A FOOL ALWAYS;
EVERYONE SOMETIMES

I first stood outside the gates of Little Park in August 2019, as I started thinking seriously about this book. I'm tall enough to look over the high gate with its combination entrance lock, if I stand on tiptoes. The house looked just as it did in pictures, but with black Land Rover Discoveries parked by the door. I didn't like to intrude further. Round the corner from the entrance to the house is Marchants Close, which leads to a track which runs over the dam at the bottom of the remaining pond. There was a sign pointing out that it was a private road, and that there was no entry. I ignored that, feeling that if anyone had a right to walk there, it was me – spuriously, of course, but, nevertheless . . .

The water in the pond was clear, and great fish, tench and carp, swam near the surface, sometimes gulping for air. Were these the descendants of Thom's turd-fattened fish? The imagination says yes.

I walked on a little way up the track, to where a public footpath started over what was once Thom's ground. In the distance, three or four fields away it seemed like, a housing estate was under construction.

My next visit was with my wife in late June 2020, as coronavirus restrictions were starting to be lifted. We had a funeral to attend in Brighton, and on the way home we drove through a locked-down Hurst to the gates of Little Park, and then to Albourne, where they caught the huge trout, and wandered around the outside of the closed church. We met a man mowing the graveyard, who, upon being told my reason for being there, took us to the Albourne brook where the great fish was caught.

My third visit was in the heat wave of July 2021. I'd at last managed to find a way to spend a few days in Newhaven; I hadn't driven but come by a slow cross-country train. It was a broiling hot Sunday, and I'd got it into my head that we could take Ralph's car for a wee drive together through some of the villages where he'd lived; Glynde, Falmer, Ditchling – ending up in Hurst. What I had forgotten was that the traffic in Sussex on a Sunday afternoon is very, very much heavier than the Monday morning rush-hour traffic in Radnorshire. We sat in a succession of traffic jams, in each of the villages. We queued for twenty minutes just getting through Hurst. So by the time I parked in Marchants Close, I was fit to burst. Unused to both heat and traffic, there was no choice. Reader, I pissed in my ancestor's pond.

We walked slowly by the side of the water. It was no longer clear, as on my first visit in 2019. Eutrophication had taken control, the ponds were thick with algae, and the fish, if they could survive at all, nowhere to be seen. At the end of the lane, newly opened to dog-walkers, the housing estate, now complete, came right up to the fence. Marchant's ground, a dog-walker told me, had been sold to the developers a few years back, for £35 million. I might have fact-checked this, but why? It was lost a long time ago, by people who valued it on a different and incommensurate scale.

I returned to Hurst once more, in October 2021. My wife and I spent the afternoon in Hurst Public Library. Afterwards, we parked in Marchants Close, and again I stood on tiptoes, and looked at the house and the cars; the gate was too high for Hilary to see over. We walked past the stagnant pond, and through the high-end new-build estate, which is very like a high-end new-build estate anywhere.

Hilary asked me, 'After all that time spent with him, do you actually like Thom?'

'Yes. I do. I love him to bits.'

And I do. He was a kind, good-humoured, hard-working extended-family man, who loved a drink and a laugh and God, who loved and wanted the best for his children, who loved and respected his wife. His friends included men and women from old gentry families, teachers, doctors, priests, tradesmen, tinkers and travelling showmen. He stunk to high heaven. Firm in his beliefs – Tory, High Church, Royalist as long as the Stuarts were on the throne – but open to new ideas about the world. Sanguine; optimistic, impulsive, funny, talkative, socially aware. An Aries. Quick-tempered, prone to depression. Worked hard on behalf of his parish, and made permanent changes for the Good. Liked to make a good deal. Didn't take any nonsense about social status. An honourable man, whose yes was yes, and his no, no, who was trusted and liked not just in Hurst, but across the county of Sussex.

How could I not love him? He's my long-lost great-great-great-great-great-great-great-great-grandpop.

Now I must tell what little I know of how Little Park Farm was lost; lost and then forgotten utterly. Thom and his diary, Little Park Farm and our life in Hurstpierpoint were unknown to our family, unknown to anybody since my great-grandfather, and he wasn't talking. It's not unusual for people not to know much about their ancestors, but they can usually pick up the odd story about their immediate antecedents. My mum, for example, liked to tell a story about watching her paternal grandmother pissing into a bucket whilst smoking her clay pipe. My grandpop Charles Jesse and his sister Madge didn't know so much as the names of their grandparents. Their father, my great-grandfather, Thomas the Baker, simply refused to tell them anything about his family and their origins. And I think I know why he didn't want to talk about his origins. I feel a duty to tell them at last where they are from, and why he couldn't talk, even though they are not here to listen.

At Thom's death in 1728, Elizabeth inherited Little Park, which was presumably managed in conjunction with Will. He married Cousin Sarah Norton at Wivelsfield in 1730. She was one of the parties who had hurried to Oxford on hearing of Jacky's smallpox; had this brought her closer to Will? Were they engaged already when Jacky died? Whatever, it's clear the family thought a lot of her. I think Will and Sarah thought a lot of one another too, since they had ten children before her death in 1756.

Mary Molly married the son of the sometime vicar of Hurst, Jeremiah Dodson, whose name was Christopher, the vicar in his turn of New Shoreham. She died in 1745. Elizabeth left Mary's four children £50 each in her will.

In 1736, Thom and Elizabeth's youngest daughter, Kitty, married Philip Cheale, the son of one of Thom's good pals. They had no children who survived, but very close readers may remember that my grandpop Charlie's building firm was called Marchant and Cheale; one way or another, our families have travelled through centuries together. There's a memorial to them both in Henfield church:

> In a Vault near this pillar Lies interred the body of
> PHILLIP CHEALE Esq late of Shiprods deceased.
> He was the youngest son of John and Mary Cheale
> who departed this life the 8th of December 1746 in
> the 29th year. In the same vault also Lyeth the body
> of Catherine Cheale his widow who died of the
> smallpox, the 28th of February 1747 in the 33rd year
> of her age.

So even after Jacky's death, Thom and Elizabeth lacked the wherewithal to have their children inoculated, despite knowing of its efficacy through Henry Campion. Perhaps it was still a largely aristocratic practice; or perhaps they were anti-vax. I hope the former, of course, but I have no way of telling.

Elizabeth died in 1757, having outlived all her children bar William. In her will, along with modest bequests to her Dodson grandchildren, she left her grandson Thomas Marchant, son of William, 'the sum of One Hundred Pounds of Lawfull money of Great Britain', and, what's more, 'I likewise give to my said Grandson all my household goods linnen plate and books.' Will got the rest, including Little Park.

Thomas Marchant was William and Cousin Sarah's eldest son, born in 1731. His grandmother clearly thought a great deal of him, since she appointed him co-executor of her will with his father, even though he was sixteen at the time it was written in 1747. When William died in 1776, Thomas inherited Little Park, along with everything else that Elizabeth had already left him.

Thomas became a surgeon; perhaps that's why his grandmother wanted to provide for him before he came into his estate, because by sixteen he may already have been in training. An eighteenth-century surgeon usually served a seven-year apprenticeship in a hospital before they were licensed. The wars of the eighteenth century meant that surgeons had become skilled in repairing wounds from military combat, especially those arising from explosive or gunshot wounds. By 1790, surgeons were performing amputations, Caesarean sections, could remove gallstones and cataracts, and were beginning to develop antiseptics.

Thomas seems to have done well for himself. He was known in Hurst as Dr. Marchant. He married a woman called Elizabeth Morton. They had three sons: William the Surgeon, Naughty Thomas and Foolish Uncle John.[99]

This latest William, our Thom's great-grandson, was born in Hurst in 1759, and, as you might have guessed, he became a surgeon, like his father. He also married an Elizabeth, née Graham. They had three children, two of whom survived: Thomas ('the Sailor') and John ('the Orphan'). He did very well for himself, did William the Surgeon, my four-times-great great-grandfather, and was appointed Surgeon to His Majesty's Powder Mills at Waltham Abbey in Essex

---

99 I've had to give the different Williams, Thomases and Johns nicknames, in the hope it helps the reader keep track.

in 1787. Although there had been gunpowder manufacturing on the site since the Restoration, His Majesty's Government only nationalised the mills in 1787. So William was almost certainly the first surgeon appointed to the gunpowder mills. He owned property in Cheshunt. He was on the up.

It was a position of some peril. There were at least five explosions reported in the three years that William was there, some of them fatal. Presumably a surgeon at a gunpowder factory spent a lot of time dealing with burns. He might well have wanted to make sure everything was in order, in case of accident. So William made a will.

> This is the last Will and Testament of me WILLIAM MARCHANT of the parish of Cheshunt in the county of Hertford Surgeon for the disposal of my Estate and Effects after my decease viz I give and bequeath unto my loving wife ELIZABETH MARCHANT one third of my personal Estate and Effects of what nature or kind soever and that I may die possessed of and the other two thirds thereof I give and bequeath unto all and every my children (if more than one) that shall be living at the time of my decease and I do hereby appoint my dear and honoured father THOMAS MARCHANT of Hurstpierpoint in the county of Sussex Surgeon sole guardian of my infant children until they shall arrive at the age of twenty-one years.

His death came suddenly, and was noticed in the *Gentleman's Magazine*: 'Mr. William Marchant. Surgeon to His Majesty's Powder Mills at Waltham Cross. b1759, killed Waltham Cross 13/12/1790.'

It wasn't a gunpowder explosion that killed him. Or, at least, the powder mills' accident reports of the period don't think so. For the longest time, I was sure he died in a coaching accident. When the railways arrived, one of the considerations of nervous early passengers was the alarming frequency of coaching accidents. Since coaching accidents were so common, they argued, often resulting in injury and death, how much more dangerous would trains be going at three times the speed? But trains run on tracks, whilst coaches fell into pits, capsized into rivers, became stuck in snow drifts and collided with one another. They hit low bridges. Their wheels fell off, their harness rotted, their axles broke, their reins snapped, their iron tyres warped, and I wouldn't have fancied it one bit. The outside passengers were susceptible to serious injuries and death, but from that point of view the inside was not much better. The point of inside (apart from it being dry) was that it was reassuringly expensive, affordable only by passengers with wealth and status. They derided those who were forced to ride on top of the coach, calling them 'outsiders', which is where the term comes from. Many accidents were caused by drivers falling asleep at the reins, and, literally, 'dropping off' the coach. That's where that comes from, too.

So it would have been not uncommon for men like William the Surgeon to be killed in a stagecoach accident. And I can't rule it out, though I also can't find a for-sure reference. But I have found several contemporary references which suggest that his father, Dr. Marchant, died from 'head injuries after chaise overturned', returning from Lewes races. A 'chaise' was most likely a two-wheeled chair-backed carriage with seating for one or two, pulled by a single horse. Was it a dark night? Was he going too fast on unlit roads? Was the state of the roads to blame? Ralph Foxwell told me the story of riding a cart behind a cob on the road from Ditchling to Glynde, and the horse losing its footing and throwing Ralph into the roadway, with resultant serious bruising. Horses are horses, when all is said and done, and things can go wrong.

It's possible, of course, that William the Surgeon was killed in a coaching accident, and that a decade later, his father, Dr. Marchant, was killed in his chaise. It's also possible that references have got mixed up. William the Surgeon was somehow killed, and his father died in a road accident. More than that, I don't know.

What I do know is that the killing of William the Surgeon in

1790, however it happened, is the moment when the family fortunes took a turn for the worse.

Since William the Surgeon was the eldest son, he would have hoped to come into possession of Little Park at the death of his father. As he predeceased his father, it was not Little Park that he was passing on to his sons, but only whatever property he had in Cheshunt. This was placed in trust, presided over by Dr. Marchant. When he was killed after a day at the races in 1801, William the Surgeon's two sons, Thomas the Sailor and Orphan John, were sixteen and fourteen respectively. At the time of their grandfather Dr. Marchant's death, they were both living in Hurst with their mother.

If I was an experimental writer, I would at this point write a pastiche of a melodramatic 100,000-word Victorian triple-decker novel called *At The Turn Of A Card*. Don't worry, I shall save you the whole thing, but this is the plot – which is based on a true story, I think, or as close to the truth as I can make it out to be.

Rather than leave Little Park to his teenage grandsons following the death of his eldest son, which strict primogeniture might have entailed, Dr. Marchant left it to his youngest son, Foolish Uncle John. Naughty Thomas, Dr. Marchant's second son, seems to have been excluded because of an inability to keep his breeches buttoned up. In 1780, Dr. Marchant was forced to sign a bastardy document on behalf of Naughty Thomas, accepting responsibility for the offspring of one Jane Norris, who was 'Great with Child', thanks to Naughty Thomas's profligacy. Dr. Marchant signed a bond for £300 with the Overseers of the Poor in Hurstpierpoint parish, guaranteeing that he, and not they, would be responsible for the maintenance, education and upbringing of the child. Clearly, from Dr. Marchant's point of view, with William dead and Naughty Thomas in disgrace, it would be best for everyone if Little Park passed to Foolish Uncle John.

Dr. Marchant left more than Little Park itself, if the Land Tax return of 1799 is anything to go by. He paid a total of £35 12s on five properties; two areas of farmland, and three houses in

Hurstpierpoint: Little Park itself, one called 'Chandler House', and one called merely 'house.' To give an idea of how well off Dr. Marchant was, Henry Campion III at Danny paid £44 in Land Tax the same year. We know that Sailor Thomas and Orphan John lived with their mother in Hurstpierpoint after William the Surgeon was killed, but we don't know where for sure. Is it too far-fetched to speculate that they lived in one of Dr. Marchant's other houses? In the novel, they do – distressed gentlefolk to whom Dr. Marchant has an obligation, because he is holding his grandsons' property in trust.

After Dr. Marchant's untimely death driving home after a day at Lewes races, this obligation, with its attendant trusts, passed to Foolish Uncle John. I think Sailor Thomas was hardest hit in the short term, because it's highly likely that he had been training with Dr. Marchant. After his grandfather's death, his training must have continued elsewhere, because Sailor Thomas was registered as a surgeon with the Royal College of Surgeons, and then joined the Royal Navy, aged twenty-one. He was assistant surgeon on HMS *Sybille* from September 1805 until May 1808. He was then promoted to surgeon from 1808 until June 1812. Under the command of Captain Clotworthy Upton,[100] HMS *Sybille* participated in the Second Battle of Copenhagen in 1807. In the summer of 1809, HMS *Sybille* patrolled the edge of the Greenland ice sheet, to protect whalers from pirates. Sailor Thomas then joined HMS *Zenobia* as surgeon in September 1812, where he served until the end of the Napoleonic Wars in 1814. When Ex-Sailor Thomas left the Navy he ran a small surgical practice in Cornwall until 1831, when he declared himself to be unfit, as he was going deaf and had shaky hands due to rheumatism. No obstacle to writing books, I find, but not great for a surgeon.

This left Orphan John and his mother Elizabeth at the tender mercies of Foolish Uncle John, who held the trust until Orphan John reached twenty-one in 1807. Was Foolish Uncle John trustworthy?

100   It's a rare book that has two people called Clotworthy in it, I think you will admit.

His (slightly unfair[101]) nickname suggests not. By 1820, he was in big trouble, because he had run out of cash. And why had he run out of cash? In Hurstpierpoint, I've been told twice, at different times, by different people, that Little Park was 'lost on the turn of a card'. This may be a village myth, but it explains a lot. He was a punter; probably in Brighton, the Las Vegas of Georgian England.

Short of cash to pay his gambling debts, he did what any self-respecting wannabe high roller would do; he put his house on the line. He approached his old friend and neighbour William Borrer for a mortgage; and Borrer was more than pleased to be able to help. He lent Foolish Uncle John £1,500 for a year at 5 per cent, with the lands at Edgerley (where the new-build estate now is) as security. Foolish Uncle John assured him that his financial issues were of a fleeting nature – punter talk for 'I'll win it back'.

He hadn't got lucky by 1833 when a local landowner, Sir John Dodson, heard stories about the state of Little Park. It was old and run-down, with outbuildings in urgent want of repair. The land was badly managed, and in need of improvement. He offered £8,000 for the whole estate (somewhere in the region of £900,000 today). Foolish Uncle John, so far from paying off his fleeting financial problems had compounded them; he didn't take Dodson's offer, but he did start selling parcels of land, which he advertised in the *Brighton Gazette*.

> To be sold by private contract, several plots of freehold
> building ground, in the preferable part of the beautiful
> village of Hurstpierpoint, eight miles from Brighton.
> Terms and particulars may be ascertained of Mr
> Marchant, Little Park, Hurst, and of Mr Ridley
> Auctioneer, Brighton.

---

101 People in the village thought a lot of him. He was 'the people's churchwarden', who had
championed the interests of small farmers, and was remembered as a fine batsman for
the village team.

It was a popular offer, which must have raised decent money, but it wasn't enough to pay off the mortgage, which Foolish Uncle John seems to have kept secret from his family, and certainly from the wider community of Hurst. The last year that the Marchants spent Christmas at Little Park was 1843; in February 1844, Foolish Uncle John died, leaving a will of Byzantine complexity, as you'd expect in a Victorian triple-decker novel. It was his desire that the estate be liquidated as quickly as possible, which presumably meant that the mortgage was at last paid off. He still had enough money to leave his children, but Little Park was left to 'Edward Duke of Brighton', who sold it a few years later to the Smith Hannington family, who ran a department store in Brighton.

Orphan John's fate is less clear than that of either his brother Sailor Thomas or his Foolish Uncle John. This is awkward, because it is from him that I'm descended, which took some working out, in a field full of Johns, Thomases and Williams. When I first saw the family tree, I made the lazy assumption that I was the 'eldest son of the eldest son' in the direct line, but this is not quite true, it turns out. Had William the Surgeon survived his father, one third of the Little Park estate would have passed to Orphan John, and then I might well have been in for some of that £35 million. But William was killed, and Orphan John did his best to fade from history.

Orphan John married young, before he came into his inheritance in 1807, whatever that amounted to. His wife's name was Sarah Pratt. They had three children, Sister Sarah (1805–68), Thomas the Beloved of Genealogists &c (1807–72) and William the Luckily Not Mentioned Again (1808–79). Much more than that, we don't know, not for sure, but the novel form gives extra scope for speculation. Orphan John's wife Sarah died in 1838; but we have been unable to find him in the 1841 census. Had he fallen out with his children? Was he homeless? We know (or think we know) that he died in Brighton Workhouse in 1848 of kidney failure, but the workhouse at the time was in a state of chaos, so the records don't exist. It's possible that he was there as a patient rather than as a pauper. It's now Brighton General Hospital, hard by the racetrack, and in 1848 it seemed to have been operating as a hospital as well as a poorhouse, but, again, records are flimsy at best. The novel demands that he die as a pauper, and an intriguing note that we found on Ancestry seems to confirm this: 'Money: Apparently, before gambling his fortune away his lawyer persuaded him to settle £2000 on each of his children.'

It's possible that this actually referred to Foolish Uncle John; but it could also be right. Orphan John might well have been a reckless punter like his uncle. Perhaps after the death of his wife, he pocketed whatever fortune he had come into, and did it in up the Race Hill, or at the numerous card tables which were still at the heart of social life in early Victorian Brighton. If this is true, I'm not sure he followed his lawyer's advice, because this is pretty much the last trace of family money that we've been able to find; his son Thomas the &c doesn't seem to have had any.

Thomas the Beloved of Genealogists &c was born in 1807, in Hurstpierpoint. By 1841, Thomas the &c was living with his wife Jane at 'Little Danard' in Hurst. They shared the house with Sister Sarah and her husband John Pratt, a relative of some kind of their mother. Both Thomas the &c and John Pratt are recorded as 'agricultural labourers'. Also living in the house was Thomas the &c and Jane's four-month-old son, Elkanah. God bless them forever! They went on to have six other children: Eugenia, Adonis, Uriah, Demetria, Drusilla and Parker, and, after them, all doubts evaporate, and no one has to have a stupid name made up by me, because they already have stupid real ones. This is why Thomas the &c is beloved of his genealogically inclined descendants; because his children are so easy to trace. Younger readers can bestow this favour on historians; although if you call your children Z'Kaybeez or Princess Nutnut they will have a terrible childhood, your descendants will bless you.

In 1849, rather than working as an agricultural labourer, he was farming thirty acres in Woodmancote; and by 1852 the family were living at Bridge Farm in Cuckfield, where Thomas the &c was farming 130 acres. He didn't own the farm; he was a tenant so far as I can see, but I'm not sure who he rented his ground from. He did

OK, because by 1861 he employed a house servant and two farm hands. OK, but not spectacularly well, because when Thomas the &c died in 1872, he died intestate, leaving effects of less than £2,000, the administration of which fell to his eldest son, Elkanah. This, I think, is where the novel ends, with Thomas the &c on his deathbed, poor, but happy, surrounded by a large clan of children with ridiculous names.

After this, I can say things for sure. For example, Elkanah is the first person in this whole story to have a definite physical characteristic of which I'm aware; he had a terrible scar on his face.

According to the 24 January 1852 edition of *Sussex Agricultural Express*:

> A shocking accident happened on Saturday last to
> the eldest son of Mr Thomas Marchant, of the Bridge
> Farm, near St John's Common. Mr Marchant was
> foddering his stock and not having quite enough hay
> to finish with, sent his son, a lad about twelve years
> of age, to the stack for a little more hay which was
> already cut, there being two cants began. The lad, in
> jumping up slipped and caught hold of the handle of
> the knife; he fell to the ground and the knife inflicted
> a severe wound under the ear, extending along the
> jaw bone for four or five inches. The poor youth
> nearly bled to death; two minutes more would have
> terminated his existence. Mr Byass and his son from
> Cuckfield were in attendance and also Mr Holman
> jun. of Hurstpierpoint, who deemed it necessary to
> send for Dr Laurence from Brighton. The lad still
> remains in a very dangerous state.

It occurs to me that my own existence hung on those two minutes.

Elkanah was a publican by vocation. In 1868, he moved seven miles from Bridge Farm to become the landlord of the Windmill Inn in Keymer with his wife Anne, whom he had married in 1865. They had seven children together, two of them boys who survived into adulthood, Thomas 'the Baker' Marchant, born 1871, and George Morton Marchant, clearly named as a tribute to Dr. Marchant's wife Elizabeth Morton – perhaps even as a reminder to Foolish Uncle John's descendants that Orphan John's family still existed. The family moved around a bit. In 1874 they took over the Nutley Inn in the Ashdown Forest, a little way south of East Grinstead. Elkanah also tenanted a small farm of ninety acres, a few miles away in Maresfield. Between 1883 and 1887 there's a reference that has them living in Rusper, thrillingly, and where, if this were still a novel, Elkanah would have been landlord at the newly opened Plough. There is no evidence for this that I've been able to find, but landlording seems still to have been his trade, because the family returned to Keymer in 1888 to take over the Windmill again, which they ran for another year, until the death of Elkanah's wife in 1889.

In the 1891 census, only his seventeen-year-old daughter Anne was living with Elkanah. All the children who were included as living with Elkanah and Anne in 1881 were working as servants or apprentices. In August 1891, aged fifty, Elkanah married Eliza Tucker, aged twenty-nine, who was a servant at Holmesdale House in Keymer. They married in St. Anne's, Soho, where Eliza gave her address as 5 Bateman Street, Soho, the family address of Annie Matthias, another servant in Holmesdale, but whose mother lived in Bateman Street. So it looks as though they pretty much eloped. Elkanah and Eliza then had a further two sons, William and Leonard, born in 1893 and 1894 respectively. Leonard didn't die until 1968, so it would have been possible for me to meet my great-great-(half)-uncle, had anyone known that he existed. The new family moved to Burgess Hill, where Elkanah worked as a jobbing carpenter, butcher and gardener; he died in 1931, a few weeks after the birth of his great-grandson, my birth dad Alan.

If the death of William the Surgeon in 1790 was the moment when Little Park began to slip through our fingers, Elkanah's marriage to Eliza in 1891 is the moment where we started to forget that it, or Hurst, ever existed. Thomas the Baker was twenty, and his new stepmother had been taken up into his father's bed in his mother's place, and was only nine years older than him. At the census of 1891, he was living at the Jolly Farmer in Bramley and was working as a baker's assistant. Elkanah's marriage seems to have prompted him to stay there.

It is hard to see someone in your mother's place, especially if she died before her time. Divorce doesn't seem to have quite the same effect, presumably because you haven't lost your mum, but just gained a fun new person (if you're lucky). Elkanah had remarried within only two years of the death of Anne. So Thomas the Baker had no home, because his mother was dead and there was a usurper in her place. What's more, there were now two babies, his half-brothers, apparently, in place of his own beloved brothers and sisters. It was this that he didn't want to talk about with his children. So far as Grandpop Charlie and his brothers and sisters were concerned, Bramley had always been home.

I feel so sad for him. Of all the people in this story, Thomas the Baker is the one I'd most like to hold, if I had that time machine. 'You have to try and forgive your father,' I would tell him. Easily said, I guess; we have this in common, after all, the Baker and I – that we never forgave our fathers. As I write this I feel my own mortality very strongly. The pain is rising, my mobility is lessening, week by week. I would like, before the end, to cry for my father.

In 1895, Thomas the Baker married Emma Baker. In 1901, they were living on Shalford Green, and Thomas was working as a journeyman baker. By 1911, they had their own premises in Bramley, and had six children together, one of whom was my grandpop, Charles Jesse, born in 1904. And then, in 1913, Emma died. And there's another secret here, I think; Birth Dad Alan told me that he suspected she'd died by suicide. No one ever said it to him, as such, but his Aunty Madge had dropped dark hints. There was a lot of not talking in the Marchant family, it seems.

So what did Thomas the Baker do, after all the hurt that Elkanah had caused by remarrying? He got remarried, of course, to Rosie

Louisa Truelove, in 1914. He was forty-three; she was twenty-one. He may have seen his case as a different one – his eldest child, Frederick, was fifteen, and his youngest, Winifred, was only six. Thomas the Baker and Rosie had a child of their own, John, who was born in 1916. I certainly never so much as heard of him, though he died in 1971. So Rosie Truelove became de facto mother to six stepchildren, as well as having a child of her own.

Thomas the Baker died in 1928 – Alan wondered if he'd died by suicide too. He didn't die rich – he left effects valued at £390 to his widow. Rosie Truelove is such a lovely name that she can only be something of a villainess. Her stepchildren seem to have disliked her intensely, though they never excluded her from the family. She was known to Alan and his brothers and sisters as 'Bramley Gran', who they were forced to visit as children. Alan felt that she disliked him in particular, and he carried a lifelong grudge against her.[102] In fairness, she had brought up another woman's children, and that's never easy. My grandpop was only nine when Emma died; Rosie raised him, and he was a good man, and that must mean something. She died in 1964.

My dear old grandpop, Charles Jesse, was born in Bramley in 1904. He married Annie Ekins in 1929, and they had four children, Pam, Alan, Tony and Eileen. He was deaf as a post and bald as a coot. His figure was Burgundian. He wore tweed suits with a weskit, and, in its pocket, an old-fashioned hearing aid. He smelled of tobacco; he smoked Player's untipped. My mum adored him; in her early married life with Alan, Charlie would sometimes take the afternoon off work and whisk my mum off to the races at Lingfield or Sandown. He was funny, and laughed a lot. He gave me half-crowns for Christmas, and five shillings for my birthday, which he called a dollar. Family Christmases were joyous round Grandpop and Nanny Marchant's – they were well off, and lived in a big old thirties house on the edge of Shalford, not far from his yard. All my cousins would be there, all my uncles and aunts, laughing and

102   In which she was not alone.

joking and getting pished. After lunch, we watched the queen;
Grandpop was one of the first people in Shalford to get a set, in
time for the queen's coronation in 1953, when the whole of Station
Road crammed into their front room to watch. After that, we played
games into the evening, and the cousins were allowed to stay up and
sip sherry. But when my parents divorced in 1968, I spent less time
there, though I watched the moon landings in Grandpop's company
in 1969. After that, I only really got to see him if my dad deigned
to take me on one of his access weekends, no more than two or
three times a year, or sometimes, access Christmases, held by then
at Uncle Tony and Aunty Jean's house in nearby Witley. I worried
old Charlie; the divorce worried him; he never understood it, and
never quite knew what to say to me after that. We were marked by
the same sadness, I think. He felt I should become a bricklayer, and
go to work for him, aged sixteen, promising me £100 a week once I'd
served my apprenticeship. In 1979, when I left St. David's University
College in Lampeter without a degree, but with a pregnant wife, I
found a job with Mecca Bookmakers in Brighton. Grandpop called
me up. 'So, you've got a job in a bookies and a girl in the family way.
I told you you should come and work with me instead of going to
that ruddy university.' We took the baby to see him a few times
before he died of heart disease in 1984, aged eighty. She was his first
great-grandchild.

He had three older brothers, including Fred, who died in
1918, flying for the RAF in the Italian campaign. He also had two
sisters, Ellen Marjorie, known as 'Madge', and Win. Aunty Madge
was the uber-Marchant, the one who had all the finest traits that
Marchanthood can confer. She had been a cook-housekeeper for a
gentleman in Merrow, who she married after his wife died, and who
himself died shortly after, which made her both comfortably off and
a great cook. She was big and buxom, jolly, laugh-aloud funny, kind
and generous. It was Aunt Madge who told us cousins that her father
would never say where he was from. After Nanny Marchant died in
1970, Madge went to live with her brother, which greatly increased
the family laughter quotient, because going to Grandpop's house also

meant getting to spend time with Madge. To my delight, Hilary still uses Aunty Madge's Bible.

At Grandpop's funeral in 1984, I met Aunt Win, I think for the first time. She lived in Bristol. I asked her what she knew of the family, which was very slightly more than Charlie and Madge. She told me that we were a Huguenot family, who had come over from France, but more than that, she couldn't say. She said that there's supposed to be a family Bible somewhere, but where, she didn't know. This threw me off the scent for many years. A lot of people called Marchant did come over with the Huguenots in the early seventeenth century, but they mainly made their homes in London. I became convinced that the name meant 'Walker', that is to say, homeless refugees. Meeting Thom and Elizabeth meant I could put that right.

And then we get to my birth father, Alan Raymond Marchant. He was born in Farncombe, just across the River Wey from Shalford, 13 November 1931, a few weeks before his great-grandfather Elkanah died forgotten in Burgess Hill. He did his National Service in the Royal Artillery, where he was made lance-bombardier. His commanding officer told him that if he wanted to stay in the army he'd recommend him for officer training. Alan always claimed that this was the spark that lit his ambition. He married my mum in 1954; I was their only child, born in 1958. He got a job as a technical draughtsman with Calor Gas, who sent him to night-school to get an HNC in engineering, and with whom he became a production engineer, then a production manager and finally production director of Calor Gas UK, until he was ousted in a boardroom coup when he was sixty. He always told me that 'work came first', which, fair enough. Having a bet came second, shagging third, and nothing else seemed to come even close to fourth.

He betrayed everyone who ever loved him; we stopped trying to have any kind of relationship in 2007, after I got back from visiting him in Florida, where he lived with Wife Five, Martha, an American lady he'd met in Mexico. She thought it was sad that we had such a bad relationship, and invited me out for a hellish fortnight. In Orlando airport on the way home, I wrote her a letter, telling her that I wanted nothing more to do with Alan, and that I wanted writing out of his will. All he cares about is money, I wrote, so he can keep it. When I landed at Gatwick, I called Ralph, and told him that he had always been my Real Dad, anyway.

In 2009, Alan called me from Waterford in Ireland. He had left Martha. He now had no family and no friends, but he didn't care, because all he wanted to do was go singing in pubs in Ireland, to which he had a fanatical devotion, despite the fact, that as I hope I've made clear, the Marchants are not even the tiniest bit Irish.

In 2010, I got a call from a nurse at Waterford General Hospital, telling me that Alan was dying, and had named me as his next of kin. We spoke on the phone; even in death, he attempted to manipulate me. He told me to tell him I loved him, which I did, even though I didn't. Love is a verb, Daddy.

I couldn't get over until a few days after his cremation. My job was to sort out his flat, and bring back his ashes to the Tillingbourne Valley. Sorting out his papers was easy: a bundle of napkins on which he'd written his system for winning the Florida Lottery; eight pornographic cartoons; all his divorce papers; a tattered blue vinyl wallet containing 'Britain's First Decimal Coins'; 500 euros and half a krugerrands, which I pocketed; and two meticulously kept account books, in which he recorded every penny he'd spent since 1976. Thom did something similar, you might argue, except he also gave account of the people and places he loved and cared for. Alan had no photos of his children, grandchildren, five wives. Nothing. My favourite stepmother, his second wife, told me at the interment of his ashes that there had been other account books, going back to the fifties.

All that said, I am blessed that Ralph Foxwell has been, not just my ascendant second cousin once removed, or my mum's husband, but my Father in Truth. Families are too complicated just to be expressed in a tree.

And then there's me. Pisces, and my name is Ian. I have been married three times. First to Rowan Manby (1956–87) with whom I had one daughter, Esme, who has two daughters, Cordelia and

Aurelia – and then to Jillian Stuteley, with whom I had another daughter, Eleanor. My third wife is Hilary Wallace, who gave me two stepdaughters, Victoria, who has a son, Rafael, and Steph, who is still at home.

And so on, if the cards fall right ...

Right at the beginning of the process of making this book, an old friend asked me if discovering my Marchant roots, and the place where my ancestors were from, and the place where their ancestors were from in turn, had changed my view of myself.

I thought I might have come up with an answer of some kind at the end of my lockdown sojourn with my long-ago family, but I'm not sure I have, because a change has been forced upon me by circumstance, one which trumps all other changes. Every three months I go for a Zoladex implant. These implants have kept me alive at least this long, but they have changed me completely. Throughout my life, I was driven by various ambitions, fuelled, as it now seems to me, by testosterone. I know this, because the point of the Zoladex implants is to stop the production of testosterone, which feeds cancer as much as it does desire. I have come to see them as analogous. They bear a family resemblance.

At the age of fourteen, I decided that I wanted to be a rock and roll star, because music was my all. I fancied making loads of cash from poncing about on stage and sitting about in recording studios. I liked the idea of taking drugs, and I looked forward to meeting hundreds and hundreds of girls, who would all be greatly impressed by me. At the age of twenty-eight, it became clear that things weren't running to plan. For one thing, I found that I couldn't say everything I wanted to say within the confines of a three-minute pop song. So I decided I needed to write prose instead. I bought a word processor, and went back to school. I fancied making enough cash from sitting in front of a computer and poncing about at literary festivals to live off comfortably. I liked the idea of moderate ingestion of various high-class intoxicants, and, when I got published, I would surely meet dozens and dozens of impressionable ladies. This, to some extent, came off. I've made a living of sorts from books and poncing about talking to interesting people, I am able to keep my old pipe stocked, and I'm quite content trying to impress just one woman. I have become, rather than a hyped-up young gun, a placid old beast, like an amiable seal with a pipeweed habit. It's not that the ambition has gone, just that it has folded into memory, sometimes sad, occasionally nightmarish, but pleasant as often as not.

The cancer has been a blessing, albeit one that comes at a high price. I mean this, with all my heart. I love the people I love with a new intensity, which I never imagined possible. Family, friends, neighbours, home, all seem beyond precious. And to my wife, my children, my grandchildren, my beloved brother, my ex-lovers, pals – from childhood, from college, from Lancaster and Hay and Devon, from all the places I've lived – my colleagues, my fellow habitues of Elda's Colombian Coffee House, High Street, Presteigne, the guys in the band, line-bashers, rivet-counters, pub-crawlers, creatures of the night, beats, hippies, heads, freaks, punks, ravers, new-age fellow travellers, dog-on-a-rope brew crew crusties, I just want to say thank you, and I love you. It has been a blast.

Writing this book has been a blessing. I wanted to finish it more than anything.

But the greatest blessing has been the chance to meet Thom and Elizabeth and get to know them, and remember how close to us they are. Elkanah's youngest son died in 1968, when I was ten, though I never knew of his existence. When Elkanah was born, Orphan John, his grandfather, still had seven years to live. His grandfather was Dr. Thomas Marchant the Surgeon, whose grandfather was Thom the Diarist. That's only five steps to cover 300 years. I hope that my daughters, my grandchildren, my great-great however many times great-grandchildren don't forget, like we forgot, the world of Thom and Elizabeth. Or me, and mine.

One recurring image keeps coming back to me, that of the smock race in the field behind Little Park, of laughing girls running barefoot through a sunlit meadow. That feels like life, then, now and forever.

> Then shall the maidens laugh in the dance, both young
> and old together; I will turn their mourning into joy,
> and will comfort them, and make them rejoice from
> their sorrow.

ENVOI &C

in which the Author takes a slow train home.

XVII

LIFE IS HALF-SPENT BEFORE WE KNOW WHAT IT IS

The last time I saw my mum was just before Christmas 2019. She was not well, and had been getting worse since her eightieth birthday, six years before. She was blind, doubly incontinent, and was becoming highly emotional and easily distressed. She was very frail, curled up double when she walked. Ralph had had a fall the previous October, and, as Mum's principal carer, he'd struggled. I got down as often as I could, which amounted to about once a month. But somehow they managed, just barely. I fixed up for a carer to come in twice a week, but they soon saw her off, to their great amusement, claiming that there was nothing much for her to do.

I didn't get to Newhaven in the January or February of 2020, because I was too ill, and too involved with being tested; but I didn't tell them that was the reason I couldn't get down. After I had my final confirmed diagnosis, I summoned up the courage to tell them, just a few days before lockdown began.

They were deeply upset about my diagnosis, but they were managing OK, and felt ready for the lockdown. My mum couldn't get out anyway, and neighbours were delivering supplies. They were under siege, but they imagined themselves back to their childhoods in the war, and drew on deep reserves. They almost liked it, or so it seemed. It gave them something to do that was outside themselves. I called them most nights; at the end of the call, I would never let my mum say 'Goodbye'.

'Not goodbye, Mum. Just cheerio,' I'd say. 'I'll get down as soon as I can.'

'Don't you come down!' she'd say. 'We're fine, we're safe, we're shielding.'

'Still just cheerio, though,' I'd say.

She would laugh.

'Cheerio!'

On 30 April 2020, I got a call from Ralph. Mum had had a fall, and had been admitted to the Royal Sussex County Hospital in Brighton. She had a bad wound on her hip where she had fallen. They had suspected a fracture, but an X-ray showed this wasn't the case. On 1 April she was discharged; and on the 2nd, she was readmitted. She was in great pain, and the wound on her hip wasn't healing. They kept her in for the next fortnight, in an attempt to get the wound to heal, and all we could do was try to get through on the telephone. It's always hard to get through to a hospital when you want news about those you love. If you're lucky, you get through to the ward. If your luck holds, a nurse who knows something about the case picks up. If you are very fortunate, and the stars shine on you, the nurses are not wildly busy and can talk. The wound was bad, but they were trying everything. Once or twice, I got through to speak to my mum. She and Ralph shared a mobile phone for emergencies, but it hadn't occurred to them that she should have it in hospital. So I was reliant on the kindness of the nurses, who would sometimes take the phone over to her. Because of Covid, Ralph wasn't allowed to visit.

She was scared. She wanted to go home. She said, over and over, that she was afraid to die. I told her that she'd be home soon, that the doctors and nurses felt sure they would be able to get her wound to begin to heal, so that the district nurses would be able to look after her at home. This was achieved by 15 May, when she was sent home, her wound on the turn, helped by a dressing soaked in manuka honey. On 20 May, the prime minister of the United Kingdom of Great Britain and Northern Ireland was enjoying a smashing cheese and wine work event in his garden with his toad-eaters, for which he subsequently apologised when caught, while I was not allowed to get down to Newhaven to visit my parents. Apology not accepted.

The nurses came every day to change the dressing. The wound was healing, but my mum was shaken and in pain. She felt dreadful, and had another fall. Ralph called the ambulance again. On 25 May, she was rushed back into the hospital, with suspected Covid-19. That evening, Dominic Cummings made his statement in the rose garden at Number 10 about his eye-testing jaunt to Barnard Castle, whilst all around him were bringing in suitcases of booze, ready for that evening's work gatherings.

The next day, the 26th, Covid was confirmed. Mum was moved to a Covid ward. Days passed. She was deteriorating, they told us. She was stable. Her heart was fibrillating. Her potassium was non-existent. She was on an oxygen mask. She was deteriorating. She was stable. Ralph spent most of his days trying to get through; he wasn't allowed to visit, of course. I contacted the chaplains, who were wonderful. They visited her every day, and sat by her bed in the Covid ward for hours, telling her Bible stories, helping her to pray. They gave her an olive wood holding cross, which she liked, because it gave her something to turn over in her hands. This matters when you are blind.

I spoke a couple of times to the consultant, who told me she was very distressed. They put her on the 'Recovery' programme. They gave the participants drugs (or didn't), not to help the patients, as such, but to see if they could find something/anything that might help future patients. The consultant told me that my mum's stools were black, that he'd never seen anything like it. We are flying in the dark, he said.

On 3 June, she was diagnosed with pneumonia.

On 4 June, the nurse called, and said, 'I've got someone here who wants to speak to you.'

'Hello Mum ...'

'Hello Ian ...' Her voice was faint, her breath came in gasps between bouts of coughing. As John Ray noted in his collection of country sayings, 'A dry cough is the trumpeter of death.'

'How are you doing?'
'I'm afraid.'
'What are you afraid of?'
'Dying.'
'Don't be afraid, Mum. It's just a step.'
She gasped for air.
'I love you,' she said.
'I love you too, Mum.'
'Goodbye, Ian.'
'Goodbye, Mummy. Goodbye.'

On the 6th, she passed into a coma, and Ralph was finally allowed into the hospital, where he sat in a hazmat suit holding her hand, until she died the following afternoon. He was left alone with her body for three hours while the hospital tried to arrange transport. In the end, he left my mum, peeled off the hazmat suit, walked out of the Covid ward unnoticed and hailed a taxi to take him the nine miles home. He had no contact from Test and Trace, or his GP. At no point was he offered a test. He was wildly in love with Jean for seventy years, even when she was someone else's wife. He still is.

> *Oh say don't you see that little turtle dove,*
> *sitting under the mulberry tree?*
> *Hear him making a mourn for his own true love*
> *as I shall mourn for thee, my dear,*
> *as I shall mourn for thee.*
>
> *Fair thee well my love, I must be gone,*
> *and leave you for a while.*
> *If I roam away, I'll come back again,*
> *though I roam ten thousand miles, my love,*
> *though I roam ten thousand miles.*

It's eight o'clock in the morning, and I am going home after a visit to Newhaven. I wish I could get down more, but travelling is becoming harder. Soon, I suspect, it will become all but impossible. Already traffic is backed up along the A259 outside Ralph's house. I reach to shake his hand, think better of it, and take him in my arms. I don't let him say 'goodbye', just 'see you soon', though we're neither of us sure when that might be. I pull my suitcase behind me to the end of the close, and turn to see him, white-haired and bent by grief, a hand raised in farewell.

Dragging my suitcase alongside the fuming immobile traffic trying to get along the coast road to Brighton, past McDonald's and Sainsbury's, past KFC and Lidl, I say aloud, 'I remember when all this was factories.' Ralph remembers it before the factories, when he and his brother farmed the long-gone fields. Now litter chokes the verges, and plastic bags hang from half-dead bramble bushes. At Newhaven Town, I catch the train for Lewes, a trip I've taken more than any other. Newhaven still calls itself 'the Gateway to Europe', a gateway framed by a flyover, scrapyards, piles of gravel, a huge rubbish incinerator. But then the valley opens up, and the familiar lowlands flicker past, where Ralph farmed, where Mrs. Woolf drowned. The grey tide in the river is at its highest, and almost tops its raised banks.

Cancer gives you cause (and long railway journeys give you both time and space) to think and to remember. They put things into some kind of frame; one might almost say perspective. Your life is bounded. It always was, of course, but now the boundaries are clear. Your future is not what you thought it was, and your memories, the long time of your past, take on greater significance. The clock still ticks at 0.5 hertz, but the ticking has got louder, and each tock takes you closer to something inevitable; just a step, but unwelcome. You want to make things right for those you love, and you need to start now, but you don't know what to do.

In the months when I was taken down by chemo and couldn't write, I read every morning an essay by the great American writer Wendell Berry from his collection *The World-Ending Fire*. When I finished reading it, in March 2021, I wrote him a letter in longhand telling him that he had given me hope. That afternoon, I got back into my chair and reopened the manuscript of this book, for the first time since chemo started, six months before.

In May, I got his reply. He queried what he saw as an easy idea of hope. He wrote:

> I seem to be putting less trust in hope and more trust in our human sense of 'the right thing to do'. … When I look from the little I know of the Western tradition of the Middle Ages to the little I know of the sages of ancient China to the little I know of the wisdom of the American Indians, it seems to me that they are all saying very close to the same thing; that we humans are not smart enough to be gods, that we are too smart to allow ourselves to become brutes, that we need desperately to be careful, that there is such a reality as loving care for the world and for one another. And so I guess I could say that I am relying more and more upon the old instructions and grounding my hope in them. And I am relying almost not at all on our 'big brain' and the possibility that it will come up with a really clever global solution.

These 'global solutions' are being chased by the untouchable billionaires who own and control the world. They don't think they are bad people; they really think that all the problems that industrialisation has caused can be made subject to an industrial fix, that this is worth pursuing at all costs and that their wealth (and their self-declared 'big brains') entitles them to try. The people in power who owe them everything agree, as you would, if you want to stay in power. Think what a handful of multibillionaires own and control; not just untellable wealth, but, through their political toad-eaters, unthinkable military power. They don't need a conspiracy to take control — they have it already.

And if you think I've had to dig deep to find this stuff out; I haven't. Clicking a few links on Dominic Cummings's blog took me to some dark places. It's quite clear, because some of them admit it with relish, that many current Tory MPs read and reread Ayn Rand. William Rees-Mogg, father of uber-fucknut Jacob, wrote *The Sovereign Individual*, the handbook of billionaire survivalists everywhere. The group of thinkers and activists advocating untrammelled freedom in the pursuit of personal advantage, who served their apprenticeship in the Revolutionary Communist Party[103] founded in the 1970s by Kent University academic Frank Furedi, such as Brendan O'Neill, the editor of *Spiked*; Munira Mirza, until recently the Number 10 policy head; and the foul Baroness Claire Fox, have the hearts and minds of the Conservative Right and thus the ear of government.

The problem, they argue, is politics itself. Politics prevents things from getting done. Do away with politics, and let efficient corporations run the show. This is good, because the only measure of value is money. Everyone can just get on, enjoying their untrammelled freedom as consumers of goods and services. Then the corporations and the billionaires who control them can get on with finding the technological fixes that will save us all, guided by the so-called 'California ideology' – which states that Technology is a White Knight. This will enable them to achieve the ultimate goal of humanity, which is to expand the industrialised free market across the Galaxy; first stop, Mars, which they take to be their property already. The Earth can die, because our Manifest Destiny lies in the stars. If this sounds mad, look up. Witness the satellites that Elon Musk is launching, which are the first step, as he sees it, towards a Mars colony.

The idea of colonising the stars has an in-built fault, which should ring alarm bells in the twenty-first century. Colonisation? Really? That went well? If our descendants somehow found an inhabitable planet, capable of supporting creatures who had evolved

---

103 A very different beast from the Revolutionary Communist Party of Great Britain (Marxist-Leninist), I should make clear.

to live on Earth, and worked out a feasible way to get there, they would be, at best, like rats disembarking from ships in New Zealand, and, at worst, like Cortés landing in the Aztec Empire. There is no hope in this. Over the last few years, scientists have begun to argue that this planet is the only planet in this galaxy with any kind of life. We might find a way to travel to the stars, but when we get there, we will find only dead planets, places where there is no life, and never has been. We were born into life, and life is here.

Other billionaires are sceptical of space being the answer, and are, instead, putting vast sums into life-extension research. They wish to live forever. This philosophy is called 'Prometheanism'. It has two strands. One is to find anti-ageing drugs – a favourite idea of Jeff Bezos. It's taken a knock recently with research that shows an absolute upper human age limit of 120 years. Some Prometheans think there's a way round this by genetic manipulation, or 'eugenics' for short. But the most credible route to immortality, as they see it, is the Promethean hope that somehow they will be able to upload their consciousness onto 'the Cloud', instead of dying. So far as I can see, lots of people spend their conscious attention on the Cloud anyway, which strikes me as a kind of death. Who wants Jeff Bezos, Mark Zuckerberg or Elon Musk to live forever? But absolute power corrupts absolutely, and they have it.

No one seems to have noticed the fact that 'the Cloud' is not deathless, because nothing is, except *tat tvam asi*. They do not care that death, our deaths, make way for life, new life. They refuse to notice that the human brain is not a computer, or anything like one. If you really need to compare brains to gadgets, it's much more like a transducer, which translates one kind of energy into another. Better still might be to compare it to a window, or a door. It lets in light and air. Technology is not our White Knight. We need more politics, not less, because politics is the working out of democracy. And we need to base our politics on the fact that, as Mr. Berry says, 'There is such a reality as loving care for the world and for one another.'

I shall follow in the footsteps of my ancestors, and die in my place and time, and, also like them, in faith. At that point, hope will prove itself.

I change at Lewes. From here the line curves through Plumpton and Wivelsfield to meet the main London–Brighton line just before Haywards Heath, a railway town, with a Waitrose next to the station, and a place that didn't really exist when Thom was keeping his diary. Just north of Haywards Heath, the line crosses the Ouse Valley on a viaduct which was at one time the largest brick-built structure in the world. I have always felt this crossing to be the point where I leave Sussex behind, even though it isn't really. Really, that's just the other side of Gatwick, before the train passes through South London, crosses the Thames, and worms into Victoria.

In August 2021, for the first time in eighteen months, I went to an actual concert of actual live music, in St. Andrew's Church. It was a warm night, so I'd left my studio/study window open, and I must have rushed out, because I'd left the daylight lamp on – sorry. When I got back, there were no moths in my room. There have been fewer and fewer over the years, that night, there were none.

At the time, I was reading Isabella Tree's *Wilding*. She is married to Charlie Burrell, and together they own Knepp Castle, ten miles north-west of Hurst. The Burrells were friends of John Ray's, and Thom did business with them sometimes. Knepp is the best-known rewilding scheme in Britain, and it seems like the tide is turning in their favour. One of the wonders of the Knepp Estate is the turtle dove population. The British Pilgrimage Trust has sometimes run a three-day walk from Rusper to Knepp, starting by singing 'The Turtledove' outside the Plough, and ending by hearing the sound of turtle doves. This bit struck me as particularly apt on my moth-free evening:

> We are blind to the fact that in our grandparents'
> day there would have been species-rich wildflower
> meadows in every parish and coppice woods teeming
> with butterflies. They would have heard corncrakes

and bitterns, seen clouds of turtledoves, thousands of lapwings and hundreds more skylarks. A mere four generations ago they knew rivers swimming with burbot – now extinct in Britain – and eels, and their summer nights were peppered with bats and moths and glow worms. Their grandparents in turn, saw nightjars settling on dusty country lanes and even hawking for moths around the streetlights in towns, and spotted flycatchers in every orchard, and meadow pipits everywhere from salt-flats to the crowns of mountains. They saw banks of cod and migrating tuna in British waters. They saw our muddy North Sea clear as gin, filtered by oyster beds as large as Wales. And their grandparents in turn, living at the time of the last beaver in Britain, would have known great bustards, and watched shoals of herring five miles long and three miles broad migrating within sight of the shore, chased by schools of dolphins and sperm whales and the occasional great white shark. We don't have to look too deeply into the history books, into contemporary accounts, for scenes dramatically different to our own to be normal. Yet we live in denial of these catastrophic losses.

The first thing we learn as children is not to shit the bed, but we are quite happy to shit the water, the soil, the air, life. But Isabella Tree's work is hopeful; she can both lament what is lost and imagine a different future. It made me think again about Ideal England, how all of its iterations seem to me bogus; Oi Oi Ingerland, Grim Oop North, Bloomsbury Country – and how we need a new dream of what England might be; better still, an old dream revisited.

Perhaps we need to dream again of Albion. Albion is openly and proudly a thing of the Imagination. For William Blake, the Jerusalem that he hoped to build in England's green & pleasant Land would be a place where English folk would be at liberty to 'live truthfully'.

Blake felt that in order to live truthfully, we need to be true to our imaginations. My mentor John Moat, the poet, novelist and founder of the Arvon creative writing foundation, felt that the soul and the imagination were identical, that Creation is an act of imagination in the mind of God; and that only through the exercise of Creative Imagination can we approach the Divine. We need to imagine a better way to live, not be in thrall to those who can't imagine change.

In the Albion I wish to imagine, Robin Hood is our patron saint, not St. George. Its well-ordered fields are full of fair folk, growing their own food and their own pants. Grass grows up the middle of the roads, because the trains are so good. In Albion, people shop in co-ops and farmers' markets for food from market gardens and local producers. We enjoy sewage-fed fish and, on high days and holidays, very expensive meat whose history we know. Energy comes from sun, wind, waves and human endeavour, or it doesn't come at all, and we learn to live well without. There are friendly societies, and credit unions; the roofs of the banks have fallen in. Ivy climbs the walls, and rooks nest in the old chimney stacks. Ramblers ramble at will, cycle clubs annoy nobody because everybody belongs. There's a dance in the community hall, a band in the pub, a concert in the church. The pantomime is rehearsing for Christmas, and, when they're through, the pan yard is warming up for Mardi Gras, even though it always rains. Albion echoes with song; there are gospel choirs, pop choirs and choral societies. Nobody works on Monday, but everyone lives well, because wealth is communal, neighbourly, invested in parks and gardens and schools and reading rooms and colleges, where people learn to understand science, practise the arts, feel history. In the towns, there are beloved cottage hospitals that serve the sick and the well, the newborn and the dying. We are free to speak, but not to hurt our neighbours with our words. In Albion, we look forward to the Notting Hill Carnival and Brighton Pride and Glastonbury, but in every community there are local festivals and fairs, and in the spring and summer people ride over on electric bikes to the next-door places, to go to their festivals and fairs in turn. Fireworks light up the sky at Diwali and Eid, at New Year and on Bonfire Night. In

Albion, honour and fairness matter more than power and greed. In Albion, the imaginative ability to put ourselves in our neighbour's place reminds us of Wendell Berry's 'human sense of the right thing to do'. And so we do it.

Albion! Arouse thyself!

Unlike Billy Bragg, I am looking for a New England; but for now, I'm just looking for a way through Victoria, and into the Tube. My heart fibrillates as I carry my suitcase down the stairs. Now I'm up against it. I've not been through London for three years. No one seems to be wearing a mask on the Victoria Line up to Euston. I feel unsafe, unwanted, unwelcome, and far from home. The carriage is silent. All the other passengers have headphones in, and are glaring at their devices, fearful that they might look up and catch someone's eye, and be forced to recognise that they are not alone.

We know that the way we live is all wrong, and that it can't continue for much longer. We are not here on this unique planet, in this unique state of consciousness, simply to work in a fulfilment centre and shop at Boohoo. We are here, I think, to pay attention.

Somewhere in the eighteenth century, starting around the time that Thom was writing, the long-held values in Britain began to undergo a sea-change. Values are at the heart of Thom's economy – values like neighbourliness, sharing and honour. Values like let your yeah be yeah, and your no be no. Thom and Elizabeth lived in a network of co-dependency, and accepted it as natural. They helped their neighbours and were helped in their turn. They paid high taxes, because they thought it was right that their community look after its elderly, unfortunate and infirm members. Property was a trust, not a sole possession.

One hundred years later, Foolish Uncle John could spunk the lot off at the gaming table, because it was his to do what he liked with. Adam Smith and David Ricardo had begun to equate 'value' with price, because capitalism, industrialisation, colonialism, enslavement, the suppression of women and the exploitation of children had all come into bloom, from buds that were only just starting to appear in

1720. Now we are at the rotten end of it, and it needs deadheading. To Ayn Rand, beloved prophetess of the new Right, there is no value except the dollar sign. And we know from inside our bowels that that is not true.

We are forgetting our value, and our values. All the economic metrics to which we are subject assume continued 'growth'. I know all about unrestricted growth, because that's what cancer is. We have to change our idea of what progress means. We are in danger of forgetting how to live, other than by destroying life.

The Tory Party to which Thom belonged bears no relation to the current Conservative Party, except, perhaps, that they both saw themselves as parties of 'the country', rather than the towns and cities. I am a countryman, and I want a New Country Party.

The countryside faces many problems; top of the list, falling and ageing populations and escalating housing costs. We need immigration. We need new blood. We need people with families, whether they come from Syria, or Lebanon, or Afghanistan, or Ukraine, or Birmingham. They need somewhere to live; second homes should be a badge of shame, not a source of pride. We need to build sustainably designed new housing, to open up the flats above the shops in our high streets, to encourage self-build schemes and work/live units. We need to teach the arts of renovation and maintenance. We need tools and skills in our libraries as much as books and free internet access.

Food producers need fair prices. I'm sorry, but they do. The New Country Party's least popular policy is higher food prices, mitigated by a new allotment movement. The more local we can make our food economies, the better we will be able to keep prices under our control, anyway. Parks, leisure centres, sports facilities, community spaces, village halls get priority funding, road schemes and car parks less so. We need community owned and controlled public transport and car clubs, really urgently.

We need conviviality. This is an idea from a Jesuit worker priest called Ivan Illich. Largely forgotten now, his ideas were vital to the self-sufficiency movements of the 1970s. According to Illich, economic development has not promoted human flourishing, but has only brought about what he called 'modernised poverty'. He saw speed as the enemy of a good society. In opposition to this, Illich wanted to make access to tools a human right, a state of being that Illich calls 'conviviality'. We can take it to mean that our streets, our shared spaces, our institutions, need to be more convivial in the old-fashioned sense too: open, operating at the speed of a bicycle, friendly, lively, enjoyable, welcoming, keen to help.

I am coming to suspect that the New Country Party, of which I am currently the sole member, is a William 'Not Just a Wallpaper Designer' Morris socialist party. Morris's version of socialism involved a globe-spanning co-operative society based on freely undertaken, creative, ecologically sustainable work, which Morris took to mean craft work, either by hand, or by machines that save labour rather than producing profit for our chums the billionaire kleptocrats who behave as if they own the place just because they do.

I am also coming to suspect that we here at the New Country Party are advocating that we all live on one of those utopian planets in *Star Trek*, where Kirk and Spock beam down, and Spock reveals his human side by falling in love with a beautiful alien in a toga, but decides that he must, in the end, choose duty to Starfleet rather than living somewhere lovely with a proper lass.

Perhaps I am advocating just that. Spock blew it. Living somewhere lovely with a proper lass has much to recommend it. This book is about coming home, coming back to what we always had. Don't it always seem to go? But what if, this time, we do notice what we've got, before it's gone?

Euston is enough to knock utopian dreams out of anyone. I catch a train bound for Glasgow. The carriage stinks of shit. When it was built in the 1840s the London to Birmingham railway was the largest engineering project undertaken on Earth since the building of the pyramids, but it's hard to see that now. I seem to be the only passenger looking out of the window. It's a semi-fast train; Watford, Milton Keynes, Stafford, Crewe. Fulfilment centres flicker past.

Only by imagining something better can we hope to bring it about. But if people are not given the chance to imagine the past, how can they imagine the future? The most important school subject is history, and that's why its teaching is being degraded and controlled by Conservative politicians. There is no profit to be had from young people learning the truth of how they came to be. The point is, the system works well for those who own it, and so those who might change it mustn't be taught that change is possible, unless it be helping Elon Musk colonise Mars. Only the status quo is allowable. Without a history, young people become compliant victims of the present.

I like this quote from Nora Waln's *The House of Exile*, written during her time in China in the 1920s:

> 'Events that happen,' so a rickshaw runner explained
> as he pulled me to market one morning, 'are not put
> away in books. That would not be fair. Only a few folk
> have leisure to read, and history belongs to everyone.
> It flows in every mother's milk and is digested by every
> babe. Thus it becomes a part of everyone's experience
> to use when needed. That which happens is not past.
> It's all a part of our now.'

What might happen if history was a part of our experience, to be called upon at need? Not nostalgia for a mythical past, but actual history. Thom's diary is one of the last accounts of how a pre-industrial society functioned; you could argue that it represents pre-industrial society in England at its highest point. Was Thom's life less rich than ours? He didn't travel abroad, but he travelled a good deal in Sussex; we visit places, but he knew them. He never ate an avocado, but he knew where his every mouthful came from. We now have medicine that can actually cure people, but when it's unobtainable by most of the world, what's the point of it? Half a million children under five die every year from diarrhoea, but you can get an MRI scan for your cat. We need to see that everyone, all our brothers and sisters who share this planet, have sewerage, refuse disposal, clean water, sterile bandages, soap. That doesn't take technological innovation; it takes the kindness of which we hear so much and see so little.

Until everyone is free, no one is free. Until everyone can be fed, we are always hungry.

My birth dad Alan used to assert that, although socialism was a good idea, it couldn't work because of the immutable state of 'human nature', and that he would, therefore, be voting Conservative. In order for Albion to work, it needs human nature to change, and we're told that is impossible. But I now know it isn't. Thom was not like us. He was not a self-interested individual out to maximise his personal well-being by means of the invisible hand of the market. He was, above all, a member of a community to which he did honour.

We could be that. We can change. We just need to remember what we were, to pay attention to what we are and to imagine what we could be.

At Crewe there's time to get a coffee-flavoured drink and a doughy cheese salad baguette before the train from Manchester to Cardiff arrives. It's a Transport for Wales train; the signs are bilingual, mask wearing is mandatory, and I'm beginning to unbend. I alight at Shrewsbury, piss out the coffee-flavoured drink, and get on the slow, old train for Swansea that takes five hours to traverse the single-track Heart of Wales Line. There's only one carriage on today, but the toilet seems to be working, which is all I ask. There's a neighbour on the train, who commutes three days a week from Presteigne to Shrewsbury, where she runs a charity that promotes breastfeeding. I'm pleased to see her and we wave hello. As the line leaves Shrewsbury, the hills start to rise on the horizon; Caer Caradoc, the Long Mynd. Nearly there, they say. At Craven Arms, the driver stops to collect the wooden token which allows him to take his single carriage onto the Heart of Wales, which peels away to the right from the Manchester to Cardiff mainline. The track runs alongside the infant River Teme, whose bed is almost dry.

At Knighton station the Number 41 bus is waiting, and I flash my bus pass. Twenty-eight seats, and no one on but me. Six miles from Presteigne. The bus labours up the great hill that separates the two towns. From the summit, as the road crosses Offa's Dyke, the view is of the Radnor Valley; the Whimble is in sunshine, but cloud is lowered over the Black Mixen. Then down the long slope to Presteigne, and I'm smiling. I get off by the police station, remove my mask and drag my suitcase down through the town, down Broad Street, past the Assembly Rooms, past the library, past the pub, past Lisa's 24 Hour Honesty Shop, past the Judge's Lodging, past Louisa's house, past St. Andrew's Church.

The air is clean. That's what I always notice first.

My wife is waiting for me at the door.

'Well, you're home,' she says.

The Old Grammarye, Broad Street, Presteigne,
Radnorshire. Sunday, May the First 2022. A fine day—

KEEP GOOD MEN COMPANY, AND YOU SHALL BE OF THE NUMBER

My thanks to:

Authors' Contingency Fund, the Royal Literary Fund, Arvon at the Hurst, Presteigne Festival of Music, my editors at September, Hannah MacDonald and Charlotte Cole, who have made this a much better book, as has the eagle-eyed copy-editor, Liz Marvin; my agents, Annette Green and David Smith, Dr. Ruza Ivanovic (and her mother, Sara, truest and dearest of friends), Prof. John Milsom, Prof. Phil Gibbard, Prof. Daniel Szechi, Prof. Matthew Hilton, Prof. Gregory Leadbetter, Mrs. Sue Corcoran, Mr. Peter White, Prof. Peter Harman, Prof. David Craig, Prof. Craig Muldrew, Prof. Pete Smith of the Bluefoot Institute of Neolithic Technology, Kevin Jackson, a.k.a. the Moose, John Moat, Wendell Berry, W.R. 'Bill' Bruce, S.M. 'Sandie' Sanders, Mr. Lyn Jenner of Nut Knowle Farm, Fr. Nick Flint, last Rector of Rusper and many times removed cousin, Richard Beard, Lois Pryce, Richard 'Bugman' Jones, Patrick Grant, Andrew Taylor of Bridge Farm, Paul Williams, Lady Louisa Collings, Victoria Cañas-Mason, Sharon Hall Shipp, Mary Ward-Lowery, Sarah Swadling, Heather Simons, Caroline Chartres, Elda and Estevan and Inga (for keeping both my caffeine levels and my spirits high😊), Stuart Anthony, Paul Walmsley, Peter Salmon, who saved the day, Karen Welch, whose work on Ancestry proved highly valuable, and Dominic Marchant, who paved the way.

I also wish to thank the librarians at the University of Wales, Trinity St. David, Lampeter; at the Sussex Archaeological Society in Lewes; and at Hurstpierpoint Library, all places where staff went beyond to help me, in spite of lockdown restrictions.

And I also offer heartfelt thanks to the staff at Presteigne Health Centre, at Knighton Community Hospital, and at the Macmillan Renton Unit at Hereford County Hospital.

Mr. Julian Dicken would like to thank his friends and family for tolerating his long preoccupation with this project, and his wee mammy for encouraging him to draw in the first place, whenst he were but just a nipper. But most importantly of all, he would like to thank Mr. Ian Marchant himself, for kindly asking him along on this incredible journey and importantly, for occupying the role of a perspicacious spiritual uncle.

But, y'know, a 'punk rock' uncle. A punkle.

In gratiam, old bean.

Think much, speak little and write less

Odd to be thanked in your own book, but nice too. I want to thank Jules in return, for his unique collaboration with me. I've known Julian Dicken since he was seven, i.e. about twenty-five years, because he's the son of two of my pals from Morecambe, and so I really am his uncle, in the old-fashioned way that, when I was a lad, I called my parents friends and neighbours Uncle and Aunty.

A few years back, I saw some gig poster designs that he had done for legendary Lancaster band the Lovely Eggs, which I loved at first sight. When Vintage asked me for ideas for the paperback cover of my book *A Hero for High Times*, I suggested Jules, and it became my favourite of all my book covers, until now. When the idea came to illustrate this book, I wanted no one else to do the job. He followed his own idiosyncratic path; we consulted, but I wanted to give him space to do his own thing. I'm really glad I did.

I wept when I was born, and everyday shows why

'Discoverie' was written between the start of the first lockdown in March 2020, and the start of my chemotherapy in September 2020.

Chemo lost me about six months, so 'Discernment' and 'Disposal' were written between March 2021 and May the First 2022.

ONE STORY IS GOOD UNTIL ANOTHER'S TOLD, OR: A NOTE ON THE DIARY

The diary seems to have stayed at Little Park until the house was sold after Foolish Uncle John's death, when it passed to John's surviving daughter, Mrs. Mercy Skinner. The Rev. Turner borrowed it from her to make his partial transcription, published in 1873. After that, the text pretty much disappeared from history.

In the 1990s Anthony Bower, a Hurst resident and a descendant of Thom's, determined to track it down. He was told that it was held in Yale Library, which turned out not to be the case. He writes in the (all-too-brief) forward to the full transcription that he 'almost gave up the quest', until he was given the address of Mr. R.H.M. Kelsey who was the 'present owner'. Bower arranged for a copy to be made available in the West Sussex Record Office, and he in turn took a copy of that. Bower and three friends worked for 'many months' to make the transcription, and then his wife typed it up. They published it privately in 2005. Without Anthony Bower and his dedication, and that of his team, I would not have been able to write this book.

Pardon all men, but never thyself

With regard to the veracity of the family tree, Hilary and I worked on it together during lockdown. We split the tasks in two; Hilary did all the work, and I take all the responsibility. We have used Ancestry. com as our main genealogical tool, which has made us aware of its limitations. It's a friend, but a sometimes unreliable one, best taken with a large sack of organic artisanal-cropped-by-hand sea salt. As far as possible, we've cross-checked all of the entries. Where there seemed to be contradictions or lacunae, we have dug as deep as possible, under the circumstances, into parish records, records of wills, registers of births, deaths and marriages, census records, newspapers &c. We are as sure as we can be that we have got it right, but that's not quite the same as 100 per cent for sure right. Much of the work on the Marchants was done by my cousin Dominic in record offices before the advent of the internet. After I die, he and his son will be the ones to carry the name forward.

Think of ease, but work on

The bibliography is long, and so I've put it on the *One Fine Day* pages on my website. You'll also find contact details both for me and for Julian. Merch is available through Julian's Moonshake Design pages; the link is on my website. There are also links both to mine and Stuart Anthony's version of the 'The Turtledove', and to the original Ralph Vaughan Williams recording. You can also find links via BBC Sounds to all the *Open Country* shows I mention. www.ianmarchant.com

The wife is the key of the house

Mrs. Hilary Marchant and I were driving into Hereford one day and I said, 'I'm a bit concerned about what I might say about you in the acknowledgements. I thought of writing, 'This book would not exist without Hilary. Researcher, librarian, proofreader, codebreaker, one woman style guide, speed typist, book-keeper, conscience, carer, best of wives, dearly beloved, that sort of thing. But I'm worried that I might sound like the usual White Male Middle-Class Middle-Aged Privileged Non-Fiction Writer Wife Thanked Last In Acknowledgements Geezer.'

She said, 'But that's what you are.'

And so I am. But that's what she did.